ho

Unmasking the magistrates

Unmasking the magistrates

The 'custody or not' decision in sentencing young offenders

Howard Parker
Maggie Sumner
Graham Jarvis

Open University Press
Milton Keynes · Philadelphia

Open University Press
12 Cofferidge Close
Stony Stratford
Milton Keynes MK11 1BY

and

1900 Frost Road, Suite 101
Bristol, PA 19007, USA

First published 1989

British Library Cataloguing in Publication Data
Parker, Howard, *1948–*
    Unmasking the magistrates: the 'custody or not'
    decision in sentencing young offenders.
    1. Great Britain. Young offenders. Justice.
    Administration
    I. Title   II. Sumner, Maggie   III. Jarvis, Graham
    344.1105′8
    ISBN 0–335–09936–X (cased)
          0–335–09935–1 (paper)

Library of Congress catalog number is available

Typeset by Scarborough Typesetting Services
Printed in Great Britain by
Bookcraft (Bath) Limited

Contents

Acknowledgements

The authors would like to thank the many hundreds of court officials, social workers, probation officers and magistrates whose co-operation made this study possible. Thanks also to Andrew Rutherford, Chris Green, Ken Pease and Andrew Ashworth for help on the way. Thanks to young James Parker for Yellowtown's pseudonym – because it uses too much 'custardy'. Special thanks to Tina Benson for all the word-processing and administrative help.

This book stems from an investigation commissioned by the Home Office Research and Planning Unit. We should like to thank the staff of that Unit for their help. The responsibility for the final contents is however ours and not theirs.

Abbreviations

CJA	Criminal Justice Act
CS	Community Service Orders
CYPA	Children and Young Persons Act
DC	Detention Centre
IT	Intermediate Treatment
JP	Justice of the Peace
NAPO	National Association of Probation Officers
NACRO	National Association for the Care and Resettlement of Offenders
PSDs	Petty Sessional Divisions
SA	Specified Activities Requirement
SER	social enquiry report
YC	Youth Custody Centre

Introduction

The United Kingdom alone hosts three separate approaches to the doing of criminal justice: one in Northern Ireland, one in Scotland and one in England and Wales. The British example of divergent practice is repeated in the rest of Europe and North America. It is clear that there are very disparate views about how to deal with issues of law and order, justice and punishment.

This book is about how criminal justice is done, and not done, in England. While the English approach is parochial the issues raised in this study should be of much wider interest, particularly for those concerned with penal policy in western societies as it affects the rate of incarceration. Our research highlights how a system relying on lay or amateur sentencers operates – and gets into difficulty. We look at the everyday work of magistrates through their own and other court workers' eyes and set this on a back-cloth created by tracing the fate of some 240 young offenders found guilty of either a serious offence or repeated crime. In short we are looking at how English courts deal with offenders 'at risk of custody'.

For England and Wales at the beginning of the 1990s the sentencing practices of its 27,000 magistrates is a crucial matter. While the judges sitting in higher courts do process much serious crime and pass longer prison sentences, over 90 per cent of all criminal cases are dealt with by the magistrates. This gives them immense powers. We will show how they individually and collectively use this power as we analyse and describe what is a fascinating decision-making system bound together by a potent ideological framework. One way or another the magistrates are involved in a system, one of the most punitive in Europe, which leads to over 70,000 offenders being sentenced to custody each year in England and Wales; 24,000 of these are young offenders. In sorting out who does and does not go to prison the magistrates also largely control the workloads of the probation service and juvenile justice social workers.

In theory, the judiciary, the magistrates and judges, stand back from the politics of law and order and merely administer legislation. A key principle of the English 'constitution', enshrined in official discourse, demands the separation of the legislative and the executive, the political and judicial processes. In short, so it is said, the magistrates and judges in England and Wales do not interfere with the making of law by Members of Parliament, who in turn are restrained from interfering with court decisions. The official guardians of this separation are the civil servants whose presence, in this case in the Home Office, the Departments of Health and Social Security and, more obscurely, the Lord Chancellor's office, acts as both buffer and official conduit. The integrity of the two institutions of law and order are thus somehow preserved.

Such a clear distinction is of course not easy to find on the ground. It is diluted by 'consultation' both between the two constituencies and with other 'interested parties' such as the police, lawyers, probation service, and so on. At one level it is hard to find fault in such an open exchange and free debate. Why shouldn't magistrates as both servants and members of the community make it known to government, through the Magistrates' Association, what instruments they need to sentence properly? Why shouldn't senior police officers hold forth about the state of morality in contemporary Britain or government ministers let slip their personal concerns about the lenient sentencing of certain judges into public speeches?

The purist's answer is that these things should not occur because they threaten the separation between legislative and executive and so potentially compromise the quality of justice. Our reply is somewhat different. We believe that such exchanges are merely the spillage into the public arena of negotiations which take place routinely in the private world of state agencies and indeed the professional classes. Having said this the exchange is not equally balanced. A well-observed characteristic of the relationship in Britain is that the judiciary is very well protected, by continuity and secrecy and institutional power, from interference by the politicians of the day. Moreover as we shall demonstrate the nature and wording of English criminal law, to date, passes enormous discretion on to the courts. Any attempts to break this tradition are fiercely resisted, as are all interventions which appear to be at odds with the judiciary's own perceptions or vision of its responsibilities. These perceptions, this vision, are part of a highly functional ideology. To know the nature and workings of this ideology is to know why magistrates sentence as they do. By understanding these matters we can also begin to see why Britain locks up so many of its citizens.

In Chapter 1 we trace the socio-political roots of the legislation which presently frames sentencing policy and practice in England and Wales. Such histories are not hard to come by. Our main concern is to note how the political and judicial processes interact. Certainly over the past twenty years the Magistrates' Association has had no difficulty in applying effective pressure on the politicians of the day in order to encourage certain sentencing powers to be enacted: powers which are then used in the local magistrates' courts.

Chapter 2 introduces the four English courts where our fieldwork took place. It describes these areas, outlining their socio-economic profile and crime rate and in particular the features of the courts themselves. It shows how each court has sentenced young offenders over the years. In Chapter 3 we describe our research methods and also attempt to measure the 'seriousness' of the 240 cases we followed through the prosecution process. 'Seriousness' is looked at via criminal records of both previous offences and sentences as well as at the current offence.

The 1982 Criminal Justice Act has been the most significant sentencing statute of the 1980s in England and Wales. It reconstructed the nature of both custodial and community-based disposals and laid out criteria to define when custody should be used. Chapter 4 describes what magistrates have made of this Act. It illustrates both how they reinterpret and reshape different aspects of sentencing law to fit their own agendas and how they search for and utilize discretion. These processes, magistrates believe, must be undertaken to allow them to balance competing demands about protecting the community and having concern for the offender.

Chapter 5 looks at the reasons magistrates gave for their sentencing of the sample cases. It begins to uncover the 'sentencing mystery' by showing how magistrates sort and sift through various verbal and written reports and apply what they regard as very special skills in reaching the correct decision for every case.

In Chapter 6 we look specifically at the way sentencers negotiate the 'custody or not' decision. We isolate the factors which are most influential in pushing a case towards or away from the prison. We also evaluate whether those cases which receive custody are measurably more serious than those that do not, and try to explain the substantial differences in practices between our four courts.

In Chapter 7 we look briefly at the contents of school reports. These reports provide sentencers with a vital source of social information. We demonstrate how the magistrates' insistence on making moral assessments about young offenders is fed so effectively by the rich imagery and anecdotal style of these reports from the school.

Chapter 8 takes a detailed look at the content and style of social enquiry reports. In it we compare and contrast the strategies of report writers with the actual impact of their interventions on magistrates' decisions. There is not always a good fit and this chapter highlights several major problems which social work agencies must confront.

In the final chapter we consider where English penal policy is likely to go and consider briefly the unfortunate consequences. There are alternative scenarios available, but for reasons which the reader will surely discover in this book these are unlikely to thrive. The magistrates, because they really are true believers in what they do and who they are, will see to it.

1 The right to punish

Introduction

For much of this century two distinct strands have been discernible in the criminal justice system in relation to young adult and juvenile offenders. The notion of punishment, incorporating retribution, deterrence and rehabilitation, provides one and 'welfare' the other. While being consistent with rehabilitation, 'welfare' has tended to emphasize the need to see young people as different from adults, less culpable, more in need of care and protection or supervision and to be, in part at least, the products of their environment. Magistrates' powers to punish young offenders co-exist side by side with the juvenile courts' responsibility to have regard for the welfare of children who are 'in trouble'. The relationship between these conflicting strands has been continually renegotiated through successive pieces of legislation: at certain times the social and political climate has brought one to the fore, then the other, and so on. Welfarism has tended to be associated with a diminution of magistrates' powers, since welfare-based disposals have usually involved handing over discretionary powers to the social work agencies. The determination of punishment rests primarily with the magistrates and, in a decreasing number of cases involving juveniles, the judges. Not surprisingly therefore, the Magistrates' Association, with its scepticism about welfarism, has fought to retain, and indeed to enhance, the magistrates' right to punish young offenders.

The politics of punishment

Notions of deterrence and retribution run very deep through English society. Punishment has therefore played an influential role in criminal justice legislation and has always been at the very core of the courts' work. If, as we will argue later, welfare has existed primarily in the discourse surrounding juvenile justice then punishment has existed at the level of everyday sentencing practice (see Harris and Webb 1987). Throughout this century punishment has provided the main way of dealing with offenders.

Borstals were introduced in 1908 as part of an attempt to prevent the contamination of young offenders by adult prisoners. During the 1920s steps were taken to detach Borstals from the prison system whereby Borstal officers came out of uniform and regimes were steered towards the principles of treatment and rehabilitation. This period of idealism regarding Borstals' rehabilitative potential had lapsed by the 1950s when steps were taken to reintegrate Borstals into the prison system. A special 'punishment' Borstal was introduced and, in 1952, a Home Office committee recommended harsher regimes throughout the Borstal system.

For over fifty years the Magistrates' Association had pressed for a short custodial sentence to complement the Borstal-type sentencing. The Maloney Committee, which was set up in 1925 to examine the treatment and protection of offenders under the age of 21, rejected the idea of such a sentence on the grounds that it would interfere with school attendance. The 1938 Criminal Justice Bill, piloted through its second reading by the Conservative Home Secretary Sir Samuel Hoare, again rejected all demands for a short-term custodial sentence for under-21-year-olds, preferring the approach put forward by Maloney which included setting-up community-based hostels (to be called 'Howard Houses') rather than punishment-orientated institutions (see Rutherford 1986).

The Second World War meant that the Bill had to be abandoned, and when the matter re-emerged in 1947, the Magistrates' Association had a further opportunity to press home its demands for a sentence to bridge the gap in the tariff between probation and Borstal. A leading juvenile court chairman used a style of rhetoric that has since become closely associated with the detention centre when he called for a 'short sharp punishment to bring the offender to his senses and act as a deterrent in the future' (Watson 1942).

Indeed the post-war period saw a new enthusiasm for the punishment approach and, somewhat surprisingly, the magistrates' demands were eventually taken up by the Labour administration in 1948. The contrast between the Conservative government of 1938 and the post-war Labour administration was quite marked: Labour's Home Secretary, Chuter Ede, clearly accepted the need for a residential regime operating a particular style of punishment:

> There is a type of offender whom it is necessary to give a short, sharp reminder that he is getting into ways that will inevitably lead him to disaster. . . . Their regime will consist of brisk discipline and hard work.
> (quoted in Rutherford 1986)

In retrospect much of the foundation of the present juvenile justice system was laid by the 1948 CJA (Criminal Justice Act), which dealt primarily with measures designed to punish young offenders. Detention centres were introduced for male offenders to replace whipping and attendance centres were established to provide a non-residential punishment. The first detention centre was opened in 1952 and not unexpectedly the Magistrates' Association kept up the pressure for the extension of this provision across the country.

Punishment does, therefore, exist as a fairly continuous strand through the history of juvenile justice. However, for a short period during the 1960s it looked briefly as though there might be a profound shift in the balance between punishment and welfare, this time with welfare coming to the fore. We will, in the next section, describe the short-lived ascent of welfarism under the Labour administration of 1964—9 which introduced what was potentially one of the most radical items of legislation ever to emerge in this field, namely the 1969 CYPA (Children and Young Persons Act). In practice, however, welfare triumphed only in terms of the political discourse about juvenile justice; the actual conduct of the courts, thanks to a change in government, remained largely unaltered (Harris and Webb 1987). In a number of significant ways the authors of the 1969 CYPA intended to wrest discretion away from the magistracy, and relocate it with the welfare agencies. The social work profession was to have greater influence in the decision-making about who should go to court and under what jurisdiction. Social workers were also to be responsible for the practice-treatment plan for juveniles made the subject of supervision and care orders. Had the Act come to fruition, civil care would have been preferred to criminal proceedings, attendance centres and detention centres would have been replaced by community assessment and supervision, and Borstal for offenders under the age of 17 would have been abolished.

Little of this was to come about for, at a crucial point in 1970, a Tory government, which had in opposition argued against many aspects of the Bill, was returned to power. Well-established groups in the penal system breathed a sigh of relief. Magistrates who had sat in the juvenile courts for many years felt sure that their demands would now be met. The probation service had also opposed their traditional responsibilities in juvenile courts being re-allocated out to social workers in the relatively new child care service or even to an as yet unestablished 'family service'. Not surprisingly the new government had little enthusiasm to implement the 1969 CYPA and key sections were never brought into effect. Mark Carlisle, Under-Secretary of State for the new government, announced the intentions of the new administration:

> The age for prosecution will not be changed; children from ten upwards will remain liable to criminal proceedings. The courts will retain their present powers to order borstal training, to commit to junior detention centres and to order attendance at junior attendance centres. Probation orders will be replaced by supervision orders for those under 17; but courts will retain complete discretion to select probation officers as supervisors for children of 10 upwards in both care proceedings and criminal proceedings.
>
> (quoted in Packman 1975)

It is impossible to say whether the full implementation of the Act would have fundamentally altered the way juvenile offenders were dealt with although the experience in Scotland suggests it might. What is now clear is that throughout the 1970s the number of young people entering the 'official system' and being sent into custody rose dramatically. Between 1971 and 1977 there was a 200 per cent increase in the number of boys sent to detention centres. The only partial implementation of the 1969 Act meant that magistrates continued to determine patterns of sentencing. As an examination of post-war sentencing shows, the period after 1969 merely demonstrates a continuation of pre-war sentencing trends. The use of detention centres, attendance centres and committals for Borstal had increased fairly steadily since 1964. The 1969 CYPA was in the end merely the vehicle for continuing the escalating use of custody.

The first of three successive Tory governments saw no reason for this tendency to be checked when it came to power in 1979. An early move was to announce an experimental regime imposing a yet brisker tempo into two detention centres. These new-style detention centres were evaluated by prison department psychologists (Prison Department 1984), and despite their conclusion that the new regimes had no discernible difference on reconviction rates, some aspects of the tougher regimes were extended to all detention centres in 1984. Thus a sustained parliamentary lobby had eventually paid off for the Magistrates' Association.

Perhaps even more importantly the rhetoric of the 'short sharp shock', which has pervaded the political discourse around the subject, had forged a closer link between retribution and deterrence, rather than training and rehabilitation as was originally envisaged with Borstal training. The introduction of the sentence of youth custody in 1982 marked the demise of the notion of custody as a form of treatment for young offenders, for the new emphasis upon 'justice' means that these new determinate sentences are to be fixed according to the seriousness of the offence and the culpability of the offender, and not by the needs of the individual. Moreover, despite the threat posed by a resurgence of welfarism in the 1960s, punishment had retained a firm grip on the criminal justice system that has persisted into the 1980s.

Talk about welfare

Concern about the welfare of children who are 'in trouble' can be traced back from the nineteenth century, although this concern has remained subservient to punishment except for the 1960s period described above.

The 1908 Children Act established juvenile courts. In the same year the Prevention of Crime Act created the legal category of young adult offender. The upper age limit for juvenile court was initially set at 16, being raised to 17 in 1933. These juvenile courts were very similar to adult courts; the child was held to be fully culpable for her/his actions, and sentence (discharge, fine, probation and removal from home) was decided in terms of the seriousness of the offence and the general interests of the public. The welfare function of the juvenile court is largely derived from the tradition of Children and Young Persons Acts. The phrase 'to have special regard to the welfare of the child or young person' first appeared in juvenile justice legislation in the 1933 CYPA and created 'fit person orders' and Approved Schools for those deemed to be in need of 'care and protection'. The tradition of welfare has a somewhat broken history in English legislation, and its uneasy partnership with punishment continued through the post-war period with the simultaneous introduction of a Children Act and a Criminal Justice Act in 1948, reflecting the duality of purpose. This uneasy balance continued into the 1960s when the potential contradictions between the two sets of objectives re-emerged with force with two Labour-initiated White Papers: *The Child, The Family and the Young Offender* (Home Office 1965) and *Children in Trouble* (Home Office 1968). The first White Paper was the more radical and proposed nothing less than the abolition of the juvenile court, which was to be replaced by a system of family councils and family courts. All this met with considerable hostility, not least from the Magistrates' Association and the Probation Service. Consequently the second White Paper attempted to adopt a stance that was politically more acceptable. The controversial family council concept was abandoned and the juvenile court was to be retained, but the Labour government hung on to the proposal to raise the age of criminal responsibility to 14. The 1969 CYPA was to have been a far-reaching piece of legislation in which 'essential need replaced essential guilt as the condition for state intervention' (Collison 1980). The fact that similar proposals for the setting up of Children's Hearings succeeded in Scotland where the vested interests of magistrates did not exist is, if it is needed, further proof that the politics of law and order, in relation to young offenders, is profoundly influenced by the Magistrates' Association and the more so when a Conservative government is in power.

However, events did not work out quite as the liberal reformers of the early 1960s had hoped, for, as we have shown, the intentions behind the 1969 CYPA were lost in a series of compromises:

> The reform movement, therefore, was embroiled in a battle which was fought on the fields of ideology and of self-interest. The result was compromise: the second White Paper compromised the first; the legislation compromised the second; and the implemented legislation further compromised the Act in its pristine form.
>
> (Harris and Webb 1987)

Even after ten years of operation, the 1969 CYPA could find no friends. It was a débâcle for those emphasizing diversion and decarceration; indeed the theoretical and ideological underpinnings of the new alternatives to custody movement were formed through a critique of the Act. The Act also received a 'thumbs down' response from those preferring a 'justice' approach. In political terms, however, the Act was most effectively routed by the 'law and order lobby', which campaigned to shift the emphasis even further away from welfare and treatment approaches.

Welfare in disrepute

The law and order lobby

As we have already implied, the Magistrates' Association is, amongst other things, a highly effective pressure group (e.g. Tutt 1981). Its desire for change during the 1970s, fanned by a growing moral panic about the rise in juvenile crime, rested, publicly at least, on two beliefs. First, it believed that strong punishment was necessary to deal with young offenders committing serious crime, and second, it believed that the social work discretion which had been retained by the revised 1969 Act was being misused.

> It is an unhappy fact that criminals are getting younger and younger, and that offences commited by juveniles are becoming more and more serious. The police, and most magistrates, believe that the existing law, the Children and Young Persons Act 1969, is proving itself to be incapable of dealing with rising juvenile criminality. The Act has, it is argued, allowed young offenders to commit crimes with virtual impunity: and by placing the emphasis on the treatment and care of delinquents, rather than on the deterrence or punishment, freed persistent child criminals to carry on their nefarious activities.
>
> (*The Times* 10.7.78, quoted in Morris *et al.* 1980)

As early as 1972 the Magistrates' Association's annual meeting called for a review of the Act, and throughout the 1970s voiced grave concern that young people were 'getting away with crime' and that the Act was bringing the law into disrepute.

> The youngsters were learning to laugh at and to flaunt authority and to treat the law with contempt.
>
> (Hertfordshire magistrate, quoted in Rutherford 1986)

For some magistrates the increase in the number of young people in custody did not point to a failure of sentencing policies, but rather to a growing number of incorrigible 'hard core' offenders. The success of the magistrates' campaign of criticism against the 1969 CYPA is borne out by the setting up of an enquiry by the subcommittee of the House of Commons Expenditure Committee (1975) which closely reflected the magistrates' desire to 'satisfy society's wish to punish an offender'. However, by suggesting that the cause of crime lay in social deprivation and that some offenders therefore needed welfare intervention, while also advocating the containment and punishment of some 'hard core' offenders, the subcommittee neatly embraced the conflicting perspectives – or fudged the issue!

The law and order lobby were also concerned that social workers were taking inappropriate decisions following the making of a supervision or care order. This belief, held by many magistrates, rested on the mistaken assumption that former Approved Schools had succeeded in preventing further offending, and that children were now almost invariably sent home where they quickly reoffended. Research findings that such fears were largely unfounded (Cawson 1976; Zander 1975) did little to quell the Tory party's or the Magistrates' Association's opposition to the 1969 CYPA. A House of Commons Committee (Home Office 1976) recommended substantial new powers for the sentencers, whereby magistrates and social workers should agree in court what should happen to a child. The Committee also proposed a new secure care order.

An interdepartmental White Paper (Home Office 1976) offered a compromise solution. It affirmed the separate functions of social workers and magistrates, whereby social workers decide what is to be done within the framework of an order imposed by the court. The Magistrates' Association, the Society of Conservative lawyers, and the Conservative Parliamentary Home Affairs Committee (all quoted in Rutherford 1986) were unappeased and pressure for a residential care order continued.

The 1977 Criminal Law Act further readdressed the relationship between welfare and punishment by making fines and the attendance centre available to the courts for breach of a supervision order. The law and order lobby thus continued to make incremental progress in dismantling welfarism.

There is an irony behind the law and order lobby's vitriolic condemnation of social work 'solutions'; for supervision and care orders, at that time, accounted for only 17 per cent and 6 per cent of disposals for indictable offences for 14–16-year-old males. The Magistrates' Association's criticism of welfare was not well founded. They were, in fact, attacking a straw man.

Justice for children

During the late 1970s a group of academic liberal lawyers were no less critical of welfare 'solutions'. Influenced by a general trend in academic criminology favouring the 'just deserts' model of sentencing (Von Hirsch 1976; Morris *et al.* 1980) they focused on the incompatible welfare–punishment roles of the juvenile court, and the injustices thereby produced. They were critical of the discretionary powers invested in social workers. They offered impressive examples of how unilateral decisions about the future of a young person were routinely taken in private and without legal safeguards. Morris *et al.* (1980) suggested that, in their struggle to convince the courts that welfare treatment is as capable of effectively controlling delinquents as detention centres or Borstals, social workers pushed for 'earlier intervention over more children for longer periods'. To rectify this situation they proposed a set of principles to ensure that justice is done in the juvenile court. These principles related to the commission of the offence, the proportionality of sanctions, determinate sentences, least restrictive alternative sentences, a juvenile's right to counsel, limitations on intervention prior to adjudication and deposition, visibility and accountability of decision-making. As we shall see elements of this strategy did find their way into the 1982 CJA.

Social work alternatives to custody and care

A series of research studies, led by Lancaster University, produced a critique of the practice of welfare since the 1969 CYPA. According to this critique, welfare had failed to divert young people from custody, while simultaneously heavy-handed or inappropriate social work intervention had produced unintended consequences. Institutional care came to be regarded as a considerable curtailment of liberty for many young people who, often for minor offences, were effectively being punished by social work treatment. D. Thorpe *et al.* (1980) studied 427 children subject to Section 7(7) care orders in five local authorities and found that 80 per cent 'failed the "care or control" test on all three criteria'. All the departments studied ran intermediate treatment schemes but

> None of them used intermediate treatment exclusively as a device to keep children out of care or custody. In fact, they all preferred personal need as a criterion and so most of the children on their intermediate treatment programmes were non-offenders.
>
> (Thorpe 1983)

D. Thorpe *et al.* (1980) also indicated that social work intervention was poorly targeted, with up to one-third of care orders having been made on first offenders and one-third on second-time offenders in some local authorities.

Thus during the 1970s liberals in the criminal justice system were deeply disenchanted, not only with penal establishments, but also with residential care, as a response to juvenile crime. Clearly there was scope for an improvement in social work practice, and in the prevailing climate of opinion the pendulum swung away from welfare and towards justice.

This academic critique of juvenile justice since the 1969 CYPA produced the conditions for the emergence of a progessive form of social work practice, based on a radical commitment to alternatives to custody and care, and which involved a practical blend of justice and welfare principles. The monitoring of local juvenile justice systems, the creation of a 'practice theory' for establishing intermediate treatment (IT) as a genuine alternative to care and custody and the option of manipulating the sentencing scale (Parker *et al.* 1981; Jones 1983) emerged in the early 1980s. Identifying tariff sentencing allowed social enquiry report writers the opportunity to 'manage' the role of supervision and IT recommendations to ensure proportionality between the offence and sentence, and, ideally, to prevent the early use of care or custody.

Three 'schools' of criticism – the law and order lobby, the justice for children lawyers and the social work revisionists – thus emerged during the 1970s and early 1980s. Although they spoke from rather different viewpoints all three were highly critical of the present juvenile justice system and by implication the 1969 Act.

New powers for magistrates

The Conservatives came to power in 1979, having fought the election on a law and order ticket which echoed many of the concerns voiced by the Magistrates' Association. Their firm line on law and order specifically stated an intention to strengthen the sentencing options for juveniles and young adults. It made particularly welcome reading for many magistrates.

The new government's White Paper *Young Offenders* (Home Office 1980) met most of the demands made by the Magistrates' Association since the advent of the 1969 CYPA. It set out to increase the punishment options available to the courts and was more concerned with changing the pattern of custodial sentencing than with developing alternatives to custody.

The White Paper's most far-reaching proposals concerned the structure, nature and purpose of custodial sentences. Shorter custodial sentences, long argued for by the Magistrates' Association, finally found favour with a proposed new minimum three-week detention centre order. A new sentence of youth custody, proposed to replace Borstal training for 15–20-year-olds and prison for 17–20-year-olds, amounted to a significant enhancement of magistrates' powers. With an effective maximum of twelve months this sentence was to relieve magistrates of the necessity of committing an offender to Crown Court for Borstal training. The 'lenient' sentences passed by some judges had been the source of considerable disquiet among magistrates. In 1982 only 65 per cent of persons committed in this way actually received Borstal: 14 per cent were given detention centre orders and a further 20 per cent given a non-custodial sentence (Home Office 1982).

Young Offenders did make important proposals for supervision and care orders. It addressed the issue of social workers' and probation officers' discretionary powers, a matter that had been a bone of contention with the sentencers. It proposed to redistribute discretion in supervision and care orders in favour of magistrates by making it possible for the court to decide what would happen on an order. *Young Offenders* also criticized the existing arrangement whereby 'magistrates do not necessarily know what, if anything, will happen under the order' and consequently the court may 'hesitate to make a supervision order, particularly in the case of a serious or difficult offender'. The increase in custody noted earlier in the White Paper was thought to have

> no single clear explanation, though it is hard to resist the inference that many courts do not have sufficient confidence in some of the existing non-custodial disposals to make use of them instead of custodial sentences.

To rectify this, it was proposed to give the magistrates the power to order an offender under supervision to undertake certain specific activities. It was hoped that the magistrates' ability to specify programmes would give the courts greater confidence in the supervision order and in the use of 'intermediate treatment' type schemes.

The White Paper formed the basis of the 1982 Criminal Justice Bill, which was welcomed by Ivan Lawrence, QC, MP, as 'the reflection of public opinion which says we are fed up with letting sentences be decided by social workers rather than the courts . . . encouraged by wet socialist intellectuals from all over the place' (quoted in Rutherford 1986). The Act was, however, fractured by its passage through Parliament; it went in with 50 clauses and came out with 85, and there were 135 amendments in the Lords (Thomas 1987). The Act thus contained some new sections not covered by *Young Offenders*: some emerged from government policy while others resulted from back-bench amendments. With one exception – the Section 1(4) criteria for the use of custody – the additional clauses further enhanced magistrates' discretionary powers.

The Bill dealt with requirements on probation orders and Schedule 11 4B redressed the decision in *Cullen* v. *Rodgers* (1982) and cleared the way for day centre requirements. Other restrictive requirements were appended to supervision orders, whereby an offender could be required to refrain from certain activities or to attend a specified place. There was a good deal of debate about the feasibility of enforcing negative requirements, and the obvious example of an order banning attendance at a football match was mentioned several times, and was generally thought to be unenforceable. However, the government thought there were circumstances where negative requirements could be both practical and desirable. The most restrictive requirement of all, the curfew or night restriction order, was introduced by a Tory MP at the behest of the Hertfordshire Magistrates' Association. Home Office ministers were not keen on curfew requirements, but eventually it was carried through by back-bench Tory support.

In its eventual form the 1982 Act was the end product of pressure from several different sources. The Parliamentary All Party Penal Affairs Committee was responsible for most of the 'progressive' amendments, the most significant of which was restrictions on the imposition of custody. Initially these criteria were two legged, but following a long debate in the Commons a third criterion was added largely because it was felt there were some serious offences which were unlikely to be repeated, but nevertheless merited custody. The government were uneasy about the criteria; they accepted them as a reasonable limitation on the use of custody, but would have preferred them to be laid down judicially by the Court of Appeal rather than by statute. These criteria are, however, potentially quite wide and initially there was little guidance about exactly what constituted serious offending or from what the community must be protected. It was also unclear whether an offender must have failed to complete a previous order before a court could decide if she/he is unwilling or unable to respond to an alternative to custody. It was open to courts to interpret questions of this kind and there is some evidence that the courts were doing so on an individualistic basis (Reynolds 1985; Burney 1985b). Indeed some courts seemed to be failing to interpret the criteria at all.

More recently the situation regarding the use of the Section 1(4) criteria appears to have improved. There is some evidence that the effective use of the appeal system has ensured that the intentions of the criteria have been followed (Stanley 1988).

Clearly the criteria need to be specific if they are to be effective as a means of preventing 'unnecessary' custodial sentences. Again largely in response to the proposals of the Parliamentary All Party Penal Affairs Group, the 1988 CJA adds a greater degree of specificity to the Section 1(4) criteria. Under the new Act the offender must now have a 'history of failing to respond to non-custodial penalties'. Presumably the term 'history' means that re-offending after a single fine or conditional discharge will no longer constitute a failure to respond and, therefore, will be an insufficient reason for custody. Similarly the revised criteria lay down that custody may be used only where it is necessary to protect the public from 'serious harm'. Moreover the court must also give reasons in open court, using ordinary language, explaining why it is imposing a custodial sentence. It now remains to be seen how effective the revised criteria will be in 'toning down' the courts' use of custody.

The use of these criteria is also extended to some supervision orders with a specified activity requirement, which may now be made explicitly as a direct alternative to custody. Should such an order be breached any sentence may now be imposed, including six months' detention. Clearly, therefore, there are inherent dangers in this new provision, for, if badly used, it could provide another route into custody.

The 1988 CJA has granted magistrates one further new power in criminal proceedings by allowing them to impose regular school attendance as a condition of supervision.

Taken overall, the two CJAs of the 1980s represent something of a triumph for magistrates and may be taken as evidence of just how effective the Magistrates' Association is at parliamentary lobby. For juveniles in particular, the Acts have provided magistrates with a vast range of sentencing options. The new custodial powers together with compensation orders as a principal disposal, community service for 16-year-olds and 36-hour attendance centre orders, add up to an impressive array of punishment options. Indeed if the greater structure given by requirements in supervision and care orders is also seen as an extension of control, we have two key features in relation to juveniles: a much wider array of sentencing options and the potential for harsher punishments both custodial and non custodial.

Moreover it is not insignificant that the government has chosen to deal with the revision of the law relating to juvenile offenders within the framework of CJAs rather than a Children Act. While those under 14 are defined as children who are not appropriately dealt with by penal establishments, 14–16-year-olds, though still differentiated from adults over 20, are regarded as fully culpable and to be treated in ways largely commensurate with the penalties available for young adults. The loss of the suspended sentence for 17–20-year-olds, the introduction of youth custody for 15–20-year-olds of both sexes, the intro-duction of CSO for 16-year-olds and the development of packages of require-

ments with probation orders which mimic intermediate treatment requirements, all mean that there is now scarcely any difference between the sentencing
options available for a 15-year-old and a 20-year-old. There is then a move
away from the special welfare considerations which have normally
accompanied legislation affecting young offenders.

The situation for young adults is, however, somewhat different in that while
there is the same potential for more custody, the range of non-custodial options
is not yet as great. Although the availability of day-centre-type 'packages'
through probation orders is increasing, provision is still patchy (Parker *et al.*
1987; Walker 1987). Furthermore, the loss of the suspended prison sentence
and the growing possibility that community service will already have been
'tried' for 16- and 17-year-olds actually reduces community-based options
available for young adults. The extension of community-based supervision and
control for young adults is, as we will see in Chapter 9, the next stage in the
government's agenda.

Finally, it would, of course, be quite wrong to attribute these shifts in penal
policy solely to the campaigning activity of the Magistrates' Association. The
covert but nevertheless far-reaching shifts in penal policy contained within the
1980s legislation have been possible because the whole political mood of the
times has applauded punishment and 'just deserts' while condemning welfare as
a 'soft option'. In this sense, the well-rehearsed debate about 'justice and
welfare' or 'care versus control' needs revision. A recent book by Harris and
Webb (1987) does succeed in shifting the now rather moribund debate by using
the notions of power developed by Foucault (1977) and subsequently by
Donzelot (1979). Foucault's concept of power as exercised through, rather than
by, the various juvenile justice agencies, collapses the distinctions that have
often been drawn between welfare and punishment. To rather oversimplify their
argument, Harris and Webb point to a 'blurring of the assistancial and the penal'
by the creation of steps between them. This intermediary discretionary area is, of
course, the space occupied by the social welfare agencies and the decarceration
movement. While this book is primarily concerned with the dynamics of sentencing, in Chapters 5 and 8 we will look at how magistrates and social work
agencies negotiate at the threshold between the penal and assistancial before
returning to the political fray and Britain's penal crisis in Chapter 9.

Every court is different

Having attempted to set out the legal, academic and political context within
which criminal justice is done it is now time to move into the everyday reality of
sentencing at the local level.

The increase in magistrates' powers described in the previous section raises a
number of important penological issues. The questions that concern us here
relate to the effect these changes have had upon sentencing both in terms of the
national statistics, and equally importantly, of consistency between local Petty
Sessional Divisions (PSDs) as well as within individual courts. Existing

research, much of which is now rather dated, points to a worrying degree of disparity in sentencing by the lower courts in Britain and North America. In the USA and Canada, where all cases appearing before a court are dealt with by a single 'magistrate' who is a full-time employee of the court, it has been comparatively easy for researchers to examine sentencing by individual members of the judiciary. In England and Wales, where most courts are served by Benches of two or three lay magistrates who attend court somewhat infrequently and often irregularly, researchers have tended to take the court or the PSD as the unit of study. Despite these differences most of the studies that have offered explanations for discrepancies in sentencing have tended to stress the 'human factor'. That is to say they have attributed uneven patterns of sentencing either to the proclivities of sentencers or to the sentencing traditions generated within local jurisdictions.

Two early North American studies by Gaudet (1949) and Green (1961) indicated that county court and quarter session judges exercised their sentencing discretion in individual ways. A more recent and influential study by Hogarth (1971) discovered considerable variation between seventy-eight magistrates in the Canadian courts. The disparities in sentencing were said to be strongly related to individual magistrates' beliefs about the aims of sentencing and the effectiveness of measures. These opinions and prejudices were in turn related to more general differences in personality, temperament and background. In particular magistrates' attitudes towards crime and criminals were said to reflect their social origins and the types of communities in which they lived.

Early English studies tended to regard differences in the official sentencing statistics as an indication of sentencing disparities. Grunhut (1956) and Patchett and Maclean (1965) found markedly different patterns of sentencing, sometimes even when the courts were near geographical neighbours.

Hood's better-known and more substantial studies (1962) went much further towards explaining the disparities in sentencing, or perhaps it would be more accurate to say that Hood's analyses identify factors that did *not* account for the discrepancies. Unlike many of the earlier studies, which had tended to assume that because different patterns of sentencing were found to exist it automatically followed that injustices had been revealed, Hood developed the notion of 'equality of consideration' to see if roughly similar considerations were applied in each case, and examined whether courts imprisoned the same types of offenders. He did find evidence of unequal treatment of equals whereby men who were imprisoned by some courts would probably have received a different sentence elsewhere.

Tarling's (1979) statistical study of sentencing disparities in thirty English courts found that 'objective' factors accounted only partially for disparities between the courts' sentencing patterns. In attempting to explain these differences both Tarling (1979) and Hood (1962) laid stress on the organization of local courts as more or less self-contained organizations, each with their own traditions and restraints, the overall effect of which was more pervasive than personal psychology in its effects on sentencing.

A more recent investigation by Parker *et al.* (1981) confirmed these earlier findings but, in studying the impact two radically different versions of local juvenile justice operating in Merseyside had on the perceptions of young offenders themselves, showed how this inconsistency badly marred the moral authority of the courts in the eyes of its customers.

These investigations are not popular with the courts and not surprisingly a study of Crown Court sentencing by Ashworth *et al.* (1984) was not permitted by the Lord Chief Justice, Lord Lane, to go beyond a pilot study. Ashworth interviewed twenty-five judges, analysed ninety-six cases and conducted sentencing vignettes in order to gauge the

> philosophy, attitudes, beliefs and the knowledge of judges about crime, criminals, punishment and the various agencies of criminal justice. Our intention is not merely to examine attitudes and opinions but to look in detail at sentencing practices and at the wider legal, social and practical setting within which the sentencing is carried out.

Many of Ashworth's findings parallel the results from this study. This was especially true of the judges' own description of their basic approach to sentencing, for like many magistrates they laid stress on the idea that 'every case is unique'. 'No two cases are the same' was an often-repeated maxim and judges made repeated reference to the notion that sentencing can be understood only 'through access to the full facts'.

Nor in general did judges have consistent views about responding to crime, preferring instead to bring issues down to individual cases. In view of this tendency it is not surprising that judges rejected the notion of tariff sentencing, and described it in such derisory terms as 'slot machine justice'. Judges were found to devote little thought to the principles on which they act and demonstrated scant awareness even of their own accumulated practice, let alone the practice of their colleagues. Not surprisingly therefore, they sometimes believed that they had passed a relatively lenient sentence when in fact they had not actually done so. Indeed some sentences thought of as 'light' by the judges were found to be quite punitive when compared with other cases they had themselves dealt with in the past.

These sentencing disparities, noted throughout the literature, call into question whether such wide discretionary powers can ever be justified. In a sense the courts cannot be blamed for the disparities in sentencing since there are few effective mechanisms in the criminal justice system to promote consistency. Structures hardly exist, for example, to facilitate communication between clerks from different areas, a matter which, in Tarling's view, requires urgent attention if equitable sentencing is to be achieved. Similarly Parker *et al.* (1981) advocate a tightening of control over the courts; 'sentencing brackets' or restrictions should be introduced to reduce magistrates' idiosyncrasies and clerks, it was suggested, should be subject to stricter rules to prevent 'official deviation', or rule bending, becoming an everyday occurrence.

Unfortunately the new powers granted to magistrates by the 1982 CJA have not been accompanied by a commensurate growth in the system of checks and balances limiting their discretion. Clearly there is a danger here that the differences between the sentencing patterns of some courts will become even greater.

How have the courts used their new powers?

The short answer to the question of how magistrates are using their new powers is that the 1982 CJA does not seem to have brought about a serious disruption of long-term sentencing trends. Concern about sentencing has tended to focus on the use of custodial penalties and in this respect there are important differences between juveniles and young adults. The initial fear voiced from some quarters, particularly those from the decarceration lobby, that the Act would bring about a sharp increase in the use of custody has not been realized for 14–16-year-olds. After a rapid escalation in the use of Borstal and detention centre orders in the 1970s the custody rate appears to be levelling off for 14–16-year-olds. The proportionate use fell slightly from about 12 per cent in 1979–85 to just below 11 per cent in 1986–7.

Given the Magistrates' Association's enthusiasm for the 'short sharp shock' it is perhaps surprising to find that beneath the overall picture of a fairly stable custody rate for juveniles, there has been a discernible shift away from the shorter detention centre orders. In 1982 8.6 per cent of juvenile offenders received this sentence compared with only 7.7 per cent in 1984 and 7.0 per cent in 1986. On the other hand 3.7 per cent and 3.6 per cent of all 15–16-year-olds received youth custody orders in 1984 and 1986 respectively, whereas only 2.2 per cent were sentenced to Borstal in 1982. This suggests that the longer sentence of youth custody has replaced not only Borstal training but also some detention centre orders for offenders aged 15–16.

There are, however, some grounds for believing that the 1980s alternatives to custody movement may, in some areas, have succeeded in turning the tide as far as custody for juveniles is concerned. NACRO has monitored the impact of the 1983 DHSS Intermediate Treatment Initiative which has contributed to the funding of 110 projects providing alternatives to custody and care in 62 local authority areas in England. NACRO (1987a) found that the custody rate for 14–16-year-old males in these areas was down to 7.7 per cent for the second half of 1986 compared with the national annual figure of 11 per cent. The report concludes:

> The right young people in greater numbers are being placed on schemes; care and custody for juveniles are being effectively eroded: programmes are being successfully completed, and all without any apparent 'net widening' effect.

In some parts of the country (e.g. Basingstoke and Northampton: Bowden and Stevens 1986) where well-established 'alternative' schemes have exerted a 'bottom end up' pressure on the local criminal justice system, some fairly profound changes have occurred. In these areas the growth of police cautioning has developed alongside intermediate-treatment-style provision to make substantial inroads into the custody rate for juveniles.

Although part of developing trends, these are, of course, isolated examples. Other areas of the country, often with long histories of punitive justice, have remained largely untouched by these developments.

Yet even these 'progressive' developments have not occurred for 17–20-year-olds, where the picture is rather different. Here the number of persons sentenced to custody increased to its highest level ever in 1985, despite a fall in the number of those found guilty in this age range. In 1985 25,300 received custody compared with 22,700 in 1982. The proportion of males sentenced to immediate custody has also risen from 18 per cent in 1982 to 21 per cent in 1985, 1986 and 1987.

It is evident, therefore, that in respect to the courts' use of custody, rather different circumstances now pertain for juveniles than for young adults. For while the national custody rate for juveniles has fallen slightly over the 1985–7 period, the figure for young adults continues to rise and is now 3 per cent higher than it was ten years ago.

While the statistics provide a macro view of custodial sentencing in England and Wales they mask the very real differences in sentencing behaviours between local courts in the wake of the 1982 Act. Burney (1985a) conducted research in nine courts in the south-east of England and found that overall custody rates were down. A very different picture emerges from some other parts of the country. For example a study in three juvenile courts in Cleveland carried out by Teesside Polytechnic (Macmillan and Whitehead 1984) reveals a quite alarming 51 per cent increase in the number of boys going into custody in the first half of 1984 compared with 1982.

This book concentrates not just on *what* happened in four PSDs but also on *how* and *why* such idiosyncratic forms of justice emerge from our local courts. Much of what follows in Chapters 2 and 3 is geared towards establishing whether or not these differences in the courts' output can be justified by differences in their input. That is to say we investigate whether the individual sentencing traditions of the courts can be related to genuine differences between the courts' caseloads in terms of different levels of crime or kinds of offenders. In general our findings indicate that the divergent patterns of sentencing cannot be so justified and we thus attempt in Chapters 4 and 5 to ascertain how sentencing takes place and why certain decisions are made, while Chapter 6 looks for the factors that lead English courts to use custody more frequently than almost anywhere else in Europe (NACRO 1987b).

Recent legislative changes have handed down greatly enhanced powers to magistrates and judges and, along with this, further opportunity for yet more divergent sentencing. This means that it is more important than ever before that a closer understanding of the dynamics of the sentencing process is developed for inconsistent sentencing is, by definition, unjust and must call into question the moral authority of the law and the state.

2 Four just courts?

Introduction: The four areas

The discrepancies in sentencing between local areas and between age groups, discussed in the last chapter, characterize English justice. There is no national bench-mark which courts refer to but instead a montage of local sentencing traditions which collectively produce a national picture (see also Burney 1985a). While our sample courts were chosen to illustrate this local differentiation we also had to select court areas with certain basic similarities in order to make comparisons between them valid. We thus tried to gain access to courts with similar 'inputs' but traditionally distinctive 'outputs', that is sentencing patterns.

First, our four courts were located in different parts of the country so that there is coverage of different regions. This is important given regional variation in sentencing. Second, all were located in metropolitan areas and processed average or above average numbers of cases. As well as having certain practical advantages from the research point of view (e.g. a sufficiently high volume of work to enable the collection of sample cases within the time limits set, while small enough to provide an appropriate arena for the detailed nature of the fieldwork), they were probably also more typical of the types of courts in which the majority of criminal matters are dealt with nationally than either the very busy central city courts or the smaller more rural courts. As we shall show, the sample courts are in fact close to the national average on a number of measures.

It is important for this study that the courts chosen should be comparable with each other in such important respects as the volume and nature of court business, and the availability of new 'alternatives to custody', for example. This was a third criterion.

The significance of existing sentencing 'traditions' might well be expected to have implications for the way in which a major piece of legislation like a CJA is implemented. Thus it was essential that one criterion for the selection of the sample courts should be the patterns of sentencing existing prior to the relevant Act. By selecting courts which appeared to have rather different sentencing histories, it is possible to examine how far the assimilation of legislative change is mediated by these existing patterns. On the basis of these criteria, the PSDs of Yellowtown on Merseyside, Redtown in South Yorkshire, Greytown in Greater Manchester and Bluetown in the West Midlands were selected. We begin with a description of each court and community where our fieldwork was conducted before looking at the nature of crime in these areas and the ways these courts have traditionally dealt with offenders.

Yellowtown

The present PSD was formed by the amalgamation of three smaller PSDs. As well as riverside dockland areas, it included a number of large areas of council housing which extended into dormitory towns and villages and well-heeled, semi-rural areas. Two of these council estates in particular were said to be the source of most of the area's crime and also to be the centre of its drugs problem. While Yellowtown was generally a depressed community with high levels of unemployment, it also had pockets of considerable affluence. There were, as one magistrate put it, 'millionaires as well as the unemployed'. Although spatial boundaries between rich and poor were clearly demarcated by motorways and trunk roads, Yellowtown was still an area where the middle classes feel threatened by the close proximity of poverty and unemployment.

The main courthouse was a typical Victorian municipal building which dominated a once elegant square near to the river. The building stood as a monument to a former prosperity based on the nearby docks. It was here that the bulk of adult criminal work was dealt with although, because of inadequate space, some trials were held in another building a few miles away, where the juvenile court also sat twice a week. The separation of the two sites seemed to cause a number of problems, with defendants, solicitors, magistrates and court papers (the last often spoken of as if they had a perverse independence) all on occasion arriving at the wrong place. The main courthouse at Yellowtown was extensively refurbished during the fieldwork, a fact which may have led to our impression of the courts as being somewhat less than smooth running. Court business was dealt with in five traditional, formal courtrooms, each of which had a specialist function. Most of our observation of young adult cases took place in a special sentencing court.

Yellowtown's main courtrooms were ranged around two waiting areas, from which defendants were called into the court by the clerk over a tannoy system. One area served three courtrooms and had interviewing rooms for solicitors and probation officers leading from it, as well as a stall selling tea and coffee. It was therefore much noisier and busier than the second waiting area. Both were carpeted, and housed wooden benches. Although not exactly comfortable they were, however, quite palatial in comparison with the waiting-room facilities at the juvenile court. Facilities for defendants here were very poor: bare walls and floors, inadequate heating, little natural light, and not enough chairs. Refreshments were available from a stall upstairs in the waiting area used for adult hearings. The only advantage to this building was that the layout of the courtrooms downstairs was somewhat less formal than those of the other courtrooms.

Facilities for magistrates were not a great deal better than those for defendants: certainly nothing that would nurture delusions of grandeur! The retiring rooms were bare and not particularly comfortable, having no more than basic, shabby furniture. Although coffee was provided for magistrates, there was otherwise little to encourage them to stay for conversation and discussion with colleagues.

Yellowtown had 225 magistrates, of whom 59 were also members of the juvenile panel, which seemed to be regarded as a distinct specialism. It was a large Bench (too large according to some of its members) in comparison to the other three courts, but the impression gained from the fieldwork was that a much smaller number of magistrates sat very frequently and that the Bench was, in this sense, dominated by middle-aged and middle-class women. In general, although there were exceptions, the middle-class members of the Bench seemed to carry with them a sense of Yellowtown as a divided community, of 'us' under attack from 'them': their fears perhaps being most strongly articulated in their comments about burglaries of dwelling-houses. Although the JPs believed the Bench to be a fairly representative cross-section of the population, criticisms voiced by a local Member of Parliament about the lack of working-class representation were supported by the Chief Clerk, who had experienced difficulty in finding a broader range of people who would allow their names to be put forward.

The Bench was served by an establishment of twelve clerks, but there were several vacancies, including one Deputy Clerkship. The authority was apparently willing to appoint only at the bottom of the pay scale, and there was little hope of promotion. There was, in consequence, difficulty in attracting and keeping experienced staff. Morale amongst court staff generally appeared low and the efforts of a then newly appointed Deputy Clerk to act as a new broom were ill-received and treated with fairly open ridicule by some staff. The Yellowtown courts seemed caught in a cycle of low resources, low morale amongst staff and poor levels of administration which meant that over-listing of cases, cancellation of courts, missing papers and so forth had come to be regarded as routine. Clerking in Yellowtown was by no means an easy straightforward task, some unfortunate individuals seemed particularly accident prone, and we witnessed some memorable clerking 'howlers' during the fieldwork.

Redtown

Despite its incorporation into a large metropolitan area, Redtown retained its discrete identity which was largely derived from its roots in coal-mining. In contrast to Yellowtown, there was a cohesive sense of community in Redtown, and generally speaking its inhabitants were proud to be associated with the town. Apart from the town itself, the PSD included a number of surrounding mining villages, some of which had a bad reputation locally for the aggressive and anti-social behaviour of their inhabitants even before the notoriety brought by the disputes in the mining industry in 1984–5. The disputes brought some bitter conflicts, involving almost everyone in the community, with the result that clerks often had difficulty in finding 'disinterested' magistrates to deal with these cases. Consequently the time taken to sort out a panel of magistrates for a particular court was a source of delays in court business. Despite the recent decline in the mining industry and a concomitant increase in unemployment, Redtown had not experienced the prolonged poverty associated with economic recession in some areas. On the other hand, there was little ostentatious display of wealth, Redtown's small middle class being over-shadowed by its larger skilled working class. As one of the magistrates described it, 'Redtown is an old-fashioned sort of place'.

Redtown's court buildings and facilities were very different from Yellow-town's. Built during the 1970s to Home Office specification, the building was shared with the probation service. Standing in a slightly elevated position, with its own underground car park complete with attendant, the building contained six courtrooms. Four branched off from a spacious and well-lit waiting area, with two further courts, away from the main area, providing a measure of privacy for juvenile and civil court proceedings. With its colourful, modern decor, the building was impressive but not intimidating. Magistrates seemed proud of it as a civic amenity.

Most groups using the building were well provided for. The waiting area for defendants was bright and comfortable. The court employed staff to provide refreshments, which were of a sufficiently good standard to attract local people en route to the Fines Office. Solicitors, social workers and police officers had private interviewing rooms at their disposal. Facilities for magistrates were also good: each court had its own retiring room and there was a separate common-room, which was used by magistrates as a social gathering place and which had an atmosphere of camaraderie. This facility for magistrates to meet together was perhaps encouraged and fostered by Redtown's social character as a small town with a network of interlocking interests.

Redtown had one hundred Justices, of whom fifty-four, a high proportion, sat in juvenile court. Redtown's economic and social characteristics revealed themselves in the composition of the Bench. The Chief Clerk said that the Lord Chancellor's Inspector had thought the social mix of magistrates to be 'pretty good'. More of the non-professional classes had been drawn into the magistracy than in our other sample courts, perhaps reflecting the strong

Labour and Trades Union influence in the political history of the area. Magistrates from this background generally appeared to adopt a paternalistic approach to sentencing and a consensualist approach to court proceedings. There were, of course, magistrates who did not fit this pattern at all.

The Bench was served by eight clerks, who were usually courteous and helpful to defendants. Again there were some notable exceptions. One 'old school' clerk, for example, who was something of a maverick, adopted a rather high-handed and authoritarian attitude towards both defendants and other court officials.

Greytown

Unlike the other courts, this PSD was not conterminous with the administrative unit of the borough, having chosen not to amalgamate with its neighbouring PSD at the time of local government reorganization. As in Redtown, magistrates were conscious of their separateness from the other towns comprising the metropolitan borough. Greytown's economic decline was long standing: poverty was very apparent in the older council housing around the court, compared with the more prosperous metropolitan centre nearby. This area, with its broken and boarded-up windows and unswept streets, was regarded as a major source of crime by court staff; a reputation stoked, perhaps, by the legend 'Fuck the Law' sprayed on to a wall just opposite the rear of the court. Beyond this area, straddling one of the major roads, were more council estates, but this time of the 1960s high-rise development type. From this road, the pleasanter and more affluent suburbs were not visible: even for the magistrates who lived in these areas, the face of Greytown was largely one of poverty and hardship.

This was also reflected in the facilities of the court buildings. Like Yellowtown's main courts, those in Greytown were upstairs at the back of a Victorian town hall, facing a small square off a busy main road and backing on to glass-littered streets which were its parking facilities (and which, according to court regulars, carried a significant risk of car theft). Despite the imposing entrance hall of the building, the courtrooms had an air of dilapidation with paint peeling from grimy walls. Office space for court staff was cramped and looked as if it had changed very little from when first built. Of the three main courtrooms, only two had direct access to the police cells. One of these, where most of our adult sample cases appeared, was used for the daily round of criminal matters, including short trials, and was known as the 'Prisoners' court'. The others were used for juvenile court on one day a week and otherwise for trials, committals, fines courts, and so forth. The two subsidiary courts, one little more than a small retiring-room and the other a former council chamber, which was a masterpiece of Victorian decor but quite unsuitable as a court, were not used for criminal matters.

Pressure on courtroom space meant a great deal of switching of cases between courts, which often caused a certain amount of confusion. The research was accompanied here, as in Yellowtown, by the noise of building work being carried out. The upgraded courts were designed to provide more courtroom space, but some of the problems of physical layout seemed likely to remain: the distance between the courts and the lack of communication between them, other than the ushers' journeys to and fro with the court diary (no computerization or appropriate internal phones here) and to attempt to locate lawyers whose presence was required.

Facilities for everyone were poor. The probation officers had a very small office which they allowed the social services court officer to use and there was a room available for solicitors to interview their clients. Provisions for defendants were particularly poor. The waiting area for Prisoners' court was simply a couple of wooden benches in a corridor outside. This was important since Greytown defendants seemed to bring friends and family with them to court: the public benches at the back of the court were often quite full. For the courts used for juvenile matters, the waiting area was a dark recess in a busy corridor, with rows of pew-like benches, the Dickensian atmosphere relieved only by a piece of graffiti: 'I got done for burglary and got away with it'. On the day on which the two juvenile courts ran, this area was crowded with defendants (some of them handcuffed to police officers because the main juvenile court had no access to the cells and there was difficulty in knowing exactly when a particular case would be scheduled), their families, social workers and solicitors all milling around while the ushers attempted to assemble together all those involved in a particular case. The ushers spent more time doing this than they did in court, so that they would sometimes shepherd people into court at the wrong times (including during the hearing of another case), thus interrupting court proceedings. Ushers were also repeatedly requesting that the buzz of conversation from the waiting area be quietened. The only refreshments available were from the dungeons of the town hall canteen, two floors below. This was where magistrates also had lunch when court sessions carried over into the afternoon, as they often did. Several magistrates expressed concern about queueing up for lunch with defendants and suggested that incidents of verbal abuse, at least, had not been unknown. Magistrates did have their own common room with a kettle, but this was situated on a different floor and at the other end of the building from the court accommodation and was not very much used. When retiring to consider cases, they used a large, cold, formal 'boardroom' leading off the main juvenile court, or the Stipendiary Magistrate's office, between the 'Prisoners' court' and the other main court-room. It was quite possible to have two separate Benches discussing cases in this room while its usual occupant was also working there. The cramped and incon-venient facilities, though magistrates frequently complained, were accepted with a kind of stoic humour: Greytown, although it deserved better, was used to hardship and lack of funding from government. This attitude of 'making the best of things' is one that was also found amongst the clerks, despite the variations in their styles.

Greytown was the only one of our courts to have a Stipendiary Magistrate.

His approach to court procedure and to sentencing seemed quite distinct from that of the lay magistrates, many of whom felt that he was too lenient. The seventy-eight lay magistrates, of whom thirty-three were members of the juvenile panel, were thought by the Chief Clerk to be representative of the political spectrum of the community overall, although because of the way in which the magistrates were organized for court sessions, he felt that this would not necessarily be true of any individual panel. Magistrates in Greytown were organized into rota groups which each cover all the courts held on particular days. A similar rota system operated for the juvenile court work, which was not popular, according to the clerk. He also said that rota groups tended to draw together people of like mind, rather than a mixture. This was significant because magistrates appeared to identify very much with their rota group, rather than with the Bench as a whole, and often said that they knew very little about the sentencing practices of other rota groups. Despite its smaller size, therefore, Greytown was a fragmented Bench.

Bluetown

'A strange borough' according to some of its magistrates, Bluetown was very much a creation of local government reorganization, being an amalgamation of a quiet country town and an 'overspill' estate created by urban redevelopment. It was this estate which was seen by magistrates as being the source of the area's crime. The amalgamation was not well received by some of the residents of 'old' Bluetown, from whose ranks the magistrates were largely drawn, who identified themselves much more with the nearby rural 'shires' than with the region's principal city and resented the appendage of the 'overspill' estates. This social division within the borough was revealed in the sharp contrast between the affluence of the old town, with its large detached houses with private drives, and the bland modern housing of the council estates, where some boarded-up windows and abandoned cars were to be seen. Although there are parallels here with Yellowtown, the difference was that in Bluetown the sharp social divisions were also more clearly reflected in spatial divisions: the rich at one end of the borough and the poorer at the other.

The basic layout of Bluetown's modern court complex was very similar to Redtown's, though adapted to meet the particular requirements of the site. As in Redtown, there was an underground car park, with a uniformed attendant. Defendants were not quite as well catered for as in Redtown although the physical environment was similar in that Bluetown relied on a local voluntary agency to provide basic refreshments for a few hours each morning. Facilities for magistrates, however, confirmed their high status as a group and could hardly have been more different from those in Greytown. Home-baked biscuits were served with morning coffee and a three-course lunch, cooked on the premises, was served by uniformed waitresses. Magistrates here were an indulged group in comparison with their colleagues in other areas.

Thirty of Bluetown's one hundred magistrates were members of the juvenile panel. As in Yellowtown, some difficulty had been experienced in finding magistrates from the more working-class areas of the borough. The majority of the magistrates were drawn from the Conservative heartland of 'old' Bluetown, with a smaller group which is perhaps best described as the 'county set' within that. It was a confident middle-class Bench.

Bluetown Courts were served by a young and efficient group of clerks (whose level of job satisfaction was no doubt enhanced by the use of a squash court in the building!). Their confident efficiency was aided by what are, by Greytown standards at any rate, 'hi-tech' innovations such as checking the court diary by picking up a desk top telephone. Given an effective computerized administration and much less pressure in terms of the volume of work, the general impression was of a relaxed and smoothly running court.

Demographic and socio-economic features of the four areas

The above descriptions show very clearly that each of the sample areas and courts had its own distinctive features. Nevertheless, the four areas were in some important respects quite similar. It is evident that Bluetown served a considerably larger population than the other courts (about 339,000), and that Redtown and Greytown were of similar size (225,000 and 245,000 respectively), while Bluetown, with a population of just under 200,000, was the smallest. Despite the differences in size, the demographic structure of the four areas was very similar in terms of the proportions of the population in the 14—16 and 17—20 age bands, that is the age groups with which this research is concerned. The relative size of these age groups in the sample areas was virtually identical with the national average.

Although Yellowtown and Bluetown were at the extremes in terms of their size, they were most similar in terms of their socio-economic characteristics. Over a quarter of Yellowtown's population and nearly a third of Bluetown's were within the Registrar General's social classes I and II, compared with 13—14 per cent of the population in the other two PSDs. Redtown and Greytown had a correspondingly higher proportion of manual labourers compared with Yellowtown and Bluetown.

In these senses Yellowtown and Bluetown appeared to be 'better off' areas. But Yellowtown, in common with Redtown and Greytown, had a much higher proportion of its household heads registered as 'economically inactive' in the 1981 census. This does not of course equate with the numbers of unemployed, particularly for the age groups with which the research is concerned. When the overall number of unemployed is considered, Yellowtown appeared to have a higher level than the other three. What this might suggest is that Yellowtown showed more 'extremes' in terms of its socio-economic characteristics than the other three, sharing some features with relatively affluent Bluetown and others with Redtown and Greytown.

Levels of crime in the sample PSDs

The crime rates for the sample PSDs were not available, but a comparison of the figures for the police areas serving the sample courts suggested that Yellowtown, Greytown and Bluetown were in areas with about average levels of recorded crime, with Redtown having a crime rate slightly below the national average. Nevertheless Redtown was in an area where recorded crime was increasing more rapidly than in the other areas: a particularly steep increase in burglary, for example, was evident.

It is perhaps questionable what influence officially recorded crime rates have on magistrates' decision-making. Certainly Tarling (1979) observed that the crime rate was not related to courts' use of custodial penalties, but our interviews with magistrates would suggest that their assessments of the levels of crime and of particular types of crimes are based to a large degree on less formal sources of information (see Chapter 4) and that these perceptions may have a stronger influence on sentencing practice than the number and types of cases appearing in court.

Table 2.1 shows the average numbers of offenders in the relevant age groups dealt with in the four courts over the period 1979–86. Clearly Yellowtown dealt with a higher number of cases overall and Bluetown with rather fewer than the other courts. Although this is broadly what might be expected from the relative population sizes, in line with national demographic trends there had been a substantial drop in the numbers of juveniles dealt with in recent years, particularly in Yellowtown, and also to a lesser extent in Greytown. The number of 14–16-year-olds began to fall rather later in Bluetown and Redtown.

The practice of cautioning juveniles has reached record levels in recent years and this clearly affects the number of young people appearing before the courts. Cautioning had increased in all the four areas during the period 1979–86. Yellowtown and Bluetown were in police areas with cautioning rates for juveniles close to the national average, with the other two courts falling a little below the average. The rates for young adults were also close to the national average, with the notable exception of the Redtown's police area which had a cautioning rate twice that of England and Wales as a whole.

Type of offender appearing before each court area

A key factor influencing sentencing is obviously the previous record of the defendant. We could not, of course, make this comparison between the courts for all defendants, although obviously it is an important element in comparing sample cases. It is, however, important to note at this stage that the extension of cautioning might seem likely to have a qualitative impact on the nature of business in the courts as well as having an impact on the volume. One possible effect is a decrease in the use of 'low tariff' disposals, such as the discharge, as increasing numbers of young offenders appear in court with one or two formal cautions behind them. A concomitant rise in the proportionate use of custody

Table 2.1

Number of 14−16 and 17−20-year-olds dealt with in each of the four PSDs 1979−86

14−16-year-olds

Year	Yellowtown	Redtown	Greytown	Bluetown
1979	410	381	421	242
1980	430	481	405	239
1981	414	416	389	251
1982	417	447	472	245
1983	353	408	372	245
1984	287	401	345	260
1985	237	370	340	148
1986	206	307	232	115

17−20-year-olds

Year	Yellowtown	Redtown	Greytown	Bluetown
1979	586	439	363	248
1980	653	430	408	304
1981	674	487	469	363
1982	702	495	524	396
1983	751	470	456	338
1984	843	565	433	295
1985	711	490	426	335
1986	566	392	351	326

could follow. The inverse relation between cautioning rates and the use of discharges by the courts, shown in previous research (Ditchfield 1976), is evident in some of our sample areas but, more generally, the relation between cautioning rates and discharges no longer follows this pattern. Nationally the use of the discharge has been slowly but steadily increasing, despite the massive increase in cautioning, suggesting that the relationship is not a simple one.

Tables 2.2A and 2.2B show the average number of defendants dealt with in each court for the various categories of indictable offences. In general terms the patterns in the four courts were quite similar. However, there were some differences to be noted. Perhaps the most striking of these was the high percentage of 'other indictable' offences dealt with in Yellowtown both for juveniles and, more particularly, for young adults. It seems likely that this was because of prosecutions for drugs offences: misuse of drugs being a significant issue in this community. Magistrates in Yellowtown commonly expressed the view that drug users were responsible for a high rate of burglary in the area.

Table 2.2A

Average numbers and proportions of offenders aged 14–16 sentenced for various categories of indictable offences 1979–84, in each of the four PSDs

	Yellowtown	Redtown	Greytown	Bluetown
Violence against the	40	36	27	17
person	10.4%	8.4%	6.7%	7.1%
Sexual offences	1	3	1	2
	0.3%	0.7%	0.2%	0.8%
Burglary	113	129	144	66
	29.4%	30.1%	35.9%	27.5%
Robbery	2	2	3	1
	0.5%	0.5%	0.7%	0.4%
Theft and handling	199	233	201	135
	51.7%	54.4%	50.1%	56.3%
Fraud and forgery	5	3	3	2
	1.3%	0.7%	0.7%	0.8%
Criminal damage	7	14	9	7
	1.8%	3.3%	2.2%	2.9%
Other indictable	7	1	1	1
(excluding motoring)	1.8%	0.2%	0.2%	0.4%
Indictable: motoring	11	8	12	9
	2.9%	1.9%	3.0%	3.8%
Total	385	428	401	240
	100%	100%	100%	100%

Greytown dealt with a substantially higher proportion of burglaries in its courts and had done so over several years. Nevertheless, the proportions of 14–16-year-olds dealt with for this category of offence rose in Yellowtown and to a lesser extent in Bluetown over the period under consideration.

There were, of course, other minor differences in the kinds of cases dealt with by the courts. Redtown, for example, had, for a number of years, dealt with a slightly higher percentage of offences against the person than the other courts. Such differences were, however, fairly insubstantial and no individual PSD could be said to suffer from more serious crime than the other court areas.

Availability and use of resources

Legal aid

Very few juvenile cases were refused legal aid in Greytown and Yellowtown (2.1 per cent and 0.7 per cent respectively in 1984). Bluetown had a higher refusal rate, 11.7 per cent in 1984, with Redtown fluctuating between 0.6 per cent in 1982 and 13.2 per cent in 1984.

Table 2.2B

Average numbers and proportions of offenders aged 17–20 sentenced for various categories of indictable offences 1979–84, in each of the four PSDs

	Yellow-town	Redtown	Greytown	Bluetown	England and Wales (1,000)[b]
Violence against the person	58	69	36	39	50.45
	8.3%	14.3%	8.1%	12.0%	11.12%
Sexual offences	3	5	4	2	6.81
	0.4%	1.0%	0.9%	0.6%	1.5%
Burglary	131	91	116	56	70.40
	18.7%	18.9%	26.2%	17.3%	15.5%
Robbery	0	a	0	0	3.91
	—	—	—	—	0.9%
Theft and handling	368	248	238	173	228.68
	52.5%	51.6%	53.8%	53.4%	50.4%
Fraud and forgery	29	12	17	10	24.63
	4.1%	2.5%	3.8%	3.1%	5.4%
Criminal damage	12	16	10	11	11.16
	1.7%	3.3%	2.3%	3.4%	2.5%
Other indictable (excluding motoring)	66	6	7	5	29.88
	9.4%	1.2%	1.6%	1.5%	6.5%
Indictable: motoring	34	34	16	29	27.68
	4.9%	7.1%	3.6%	9.0%	6.1%
Total	701	481	442	324	453.6
	100%	100%	100%	100%	100%

Notes: [a] < 0.5
[b] Offenders of all ages: the criminal statistics do not provide a breakdown by age

The refusal rate for young adults was rather higher, ranging from 12.9 per cent in Bluetown to 2.8 per cent in Redtown. In all courts the refusal rates for young adults increased in 1983 and 1984, probably because the number of Crown Court committals, a type of case with a particularly low refusal rate for legal aid, declined following the Criminal Justice Act.

Social work and probation services
Tarling (1979) noted a significant relationship between the amount of probation resources available to the court and the use of probation. The same point applies to the resources provided by Social Services Departments to the courts. At the time of the research, Bluetown was the only one of the sample courts which did not have Schedule 11 'packages' available at all. Redtown did technically have access to such provision but it was located in the principal city

some fifteen miles away. Yellowtown had provisions locally (although requirements for this were technically made under Section 4(a) rather than 4(b)) and also had access to a scheme in the nearby city. The schemes available here and in Greytown seemed typical of the kind of facilities which our national survey of the Probation service has shown to be offered in other parts of the country (Parker *et al*. 1987). That is they offered structured and intensive, skills based, group work programmes, lasting for thirty or sixty days, aimed primarily at the unemployed and not being strictly limited to those attending under statutory requirements.

In respect of juveniles the situation and the impact of the 1982 Act upon it is rather more complicated. The distinction between intermediate treatment requirements in general and specified activities in particular remained unclear in a number of areas. Which clause was used seems to depend on how much confidence magistrates had in the existing schemes as much as on the provision of new schemes. All four courts were offered intermediate treatment schemes, which were seen as alternatives to custody or care by the agencies providing them prior to the Act, although the quality of these schemes and their credibility in the courts varied. Existing provision in some cases remained alongside new provision financed under the DHSS initiative: thus Greytown had an 'alternative to care' scheme run in conjunction with the education committee and a group run by the probation service as well as its DHSS-funded 'intensive' scheme. At the time of the research, three of the sample areas had provision under the DHSS initiative, and the fourth area, Yellowtown, subsequently obtained this.

Despite their strong individual identities the four courts did appear to be roughly comparable on a number of important counts. First they served areas with broadly similar demographies and social constitutions. Second they dealt with about the same size of caseloads, comprising of roughly similar kinds of offenders. Third they were all resourced by the social service and probation departments in a fairly 'standard' way. In the next section we examine the courts' sentencing histories in order to see if the similarities in their 'input' is reflected in their 'output' in terms of the penalties they imposed.

Sentencing patterns in the sample courts

There were quite marked differences in sentencing patterns, particularly in the use of custodial penalties. Redtown and Greytown showed similar patterns in their use of custody for both juveniles and young adults, with Redtown rather below the national average and Greytown slightly above. But Bluetown and Yellowtown showed quite opposite tendencies in their general use of custody. For Yellowtown, there had been a much higher rate of custodial sentences for juveniles, while for the 17–20-year age group, the level was close to that for England and Wales as a whole. Bluetown, by contrast, had shown a much higher custody rate for young adults. This characteristic of the Midlands court is even more pronounced if suspended sentences are included in the custody figures. The loss of this disposal following the 1982 CJA affected Bluetown far more than the other three courts.

The patterns in the use of custody did not appear to be directly attributable to objective features of the type of case dealt with in the four courts. The levels of crime were quite similar in the four areas, and they were also broadly similar in terms of the types of offences dealt with; nor were the courts dealing with very different levels of offence severity. Burglary is a type of offence which is particularly likely to attract a custodial sentence. The use of custody for this offence in all the sample courts was significantly higher than the overall rate. But there were marked differences between the courts in respect of this offence between 1979 and 1984. They were less similar to each other in this respect than they were in their overall custody rate: Greytown, for example, which dealt with a higher proportion of burglaries, did not have the highest custody rate, either for this particular offence or more generally.

Interestingly when the use of the different forms of custodial penalties are compared it was the courts with the lowest overall custody rates (i.e. Redtown and Bluetown) which made relatively more use of detention centres than either committals to Crown Court or of youth custody. This is in striking contrast to Yellowtown, where only half of the custodial penalties given in juvenile court in 1984 were for detention centres, considerably less than the national average. The image of Yellowtown as a generally punitive court also applies to its sentencing of young adults. The Yellowtown magistrates made extensive use of their new powers to impose longer sentences in preference to detention centre orders.

Penalties involving the use of social work supervision in the community

Juveniles

Nationally during the mid-1980s the use of supervision order had held fairly constant for the 14–16 age band, although the strengthening of this order by the CJA has done little to alter things. Indeed all four sample courts tended to use supervision less than the national average which stood at about 17 per cent of all disposals in 1984 (Home Office 1984). Within this picture of a comparatively low usage there were, however, important differences between the courts. In Yellowtown, the only court without an available high intensity 'Package', the use of the supervision order increased quite sharply in 1983 but fell even more sharply in 1984. A similar sharp drop in 1984 occurred in Bluetown which had previously been in line with the national average. This might be explained by the realization by magistrates of their limited powers in respect of breach although in Redtown 1984 saw a reversal of the previous decline of this disposal, and in Greytown a continued growth of its use.

Young Adults

Nationally the introduction of new additional requirements in probation orders has led to a slight increase in their use (about 10 per cent of all disposals in 1984:

Home Office 1984). This has also been true of three of the sample courts, the exception not being Bluetown as might be expected, since it is the only one of the courts without access to a 'package' scheme, but Yellowtown, where the use of probation had in fact been increasing up to 1983. Yellowtown's use of this disposal was, however, higher than the national average, and it may be that this was related to the decreasing use of fines in a context of high unemployment (Crow and Simon 1987). Greytown's use of probation, however, was slightly below the national average, although increasing both prior to and after the 1982 CJA. Redtown's use of probation had levelled off from the decline prior to the Act and Bluetown's had continued to increase, so that both of these courts were very close to the national pattern, although Bluetown did not have a 'package'. One explanation for the growing use of probation here might be that it had to some extent replaced the suspended sentence, which was used more extensively than in the other courts.

Care orders
As for England and Wales as a whole, the proportionate use of this disposal for juveniles was low and decreasing, falling to below 3 per cent of disposals in 1984. This was true of all our sample courts, with a particularly sharp, though uneven, drop for Yellowtown which had at times been well above average. Redtown's use of the care order remained stable but its use of this disposal was in any case very low.

Attendance centre orders
All the courts used this sentence more than the national average and this was particularly true of Bluetown, which had a consistently high level. Redtown had also increased its use of attendance centre orders quite dramatically since 1979. Three of the courts made little use of attendance centre orders for 17–20-year-olds, in keeping with national figures (about 2 per cent of disposals in 1984). It was, however, a very popular disposal in Bluetown (11 per cent of disposals in 1984).

Community service orders
Apart from Yellowtown our sample courts show trends in the use of community service orders for young adults which were very similar to the steady increase of the national average (11 per cent in 1984). Redtown's enthusiasm for CS relative to the other sample courts was very apparent in its reception of the extension of availability to 16-year-olds. Its rate for use of this disposal was 7 per cent, more than twice the national average.

Fines
The decline of the fine as a penalty in recent years at national level is generally thought to be related to high unemployment which clearly affects the defendant's ability to pay. The proportionate use of the fine in the sample courts was not, however, explicable in terms of unemployment levels in the four

PSDs. Bluetown, with the lowest level of unemployment, did not use financial penalties more than the other courts.

Three of our four courts imposed a lower proportion of fines on juveniles than the national average (about 25 per cent in 1984), but the exception, Redtown, though showing the same downward trend, was well above the national average. In Bluetown's juvenile court, the decline in the use of the fine had been reversed since the Act. This may be related to the changes in liability for fines between parents and juveniles, but the effect was not very marked in the other courts.

As far as the 17–20 age group is concerned, Redtown showed a very similar pattern to its juvenile court: a steady decline to about 50 per cent in 1984, but proportionately well above the national average. Greytown and Bluetown fined at about the average level for England and Wales (44 per cent in 1984) and in both cases the decline in usage had levelled off since the Act. It is possible that the fine has to some extent replaced the suspended sentence in these courts. Yellowtown, in contrast to its juvenile court, imposed a much higher proportion of fines on its young adults, but here the decline in the use of this penalty has continued.

Discharges
Nationally, and despite the massive increase in cautioning in the last few years, the use of discharges has steadily increased to around 21 per cent in 1984. In three of the sample PSDs an increase in cautioning had occurred, but for juveniles in Bluetown this had been accompanied by a decline in the use of discharges in 1983 and 1984. Greytown, where the level of cautioning was lowest, had shown less of an increase for juveniles (around 34 per cent in 1984), but its use of discharges was considerably above the national average, the other three courts being slightly below.

For 17–20-year-olds, Greytown discharged 17 per cent of its defendants compared with a national average of around 10 per cent, but generally followed the curve of national trends. Contrary to national trends, Redtown's use of this penalty had been declining, so that it was around the national average, although this decline showed some signs of levelling off in the period following the Act. Yellowtown and Bluetown made less proportionate use of discharges than the national average, with quite a sharp downward trend for the Midlands court in evidence.

Summary

The criteria for the selection of our sample courts were that they were of similar size, within metropolitan locations, representative of different parts of the country and of the kind of court within which most criminal matters are dealt with.

The selection of courts with similar 'inputs' is of crucial importance to this study. While there is some difference in the population size of the four PSDs, their demographic structure, as far as the 14–20 age group is concerned, is very similar and almost identical with the national average. A comparison of socio-economic characteristics of the four areas again revealed some variation, for example in social composition, but the PSDs were comparable on these measures. All had average or above-average levels of recorded crime and all showed increases comparable with or above the national average.

The number of cases dealt with in the courts varied, but this is not a major difference when considered in the context of demographic factors. The impact of police practice in relation to cautioning on the numbers appearing in court was also considered. Cautioning had increased in all four police areas for juveniles in recent years, as is the case nationally. For adults, two of the areas were close to the national average cautioning rate, with Greytown and Redtown having above average rates. The courts were also similar in the types of offences with which they dealt.

All the courts had access to some form of intermediate treatment scheme which was said to be an alternative to custody, though the extent of this provision and the role of DHSS-funded schemes varied between the courts. Bluetown was the only court to have no access to Schedule 11 'packages' for young adults.

Despite their similarities, the courts had different sentencing patterns. An analysis of these patterns over the period 1979–84 revealed that Yellowtown had a very high custody rate for juveniles, while being quite close to the national average for young adults. In Bluetown, the reverse was the case, with young adults receiving a high proportion of custodial sentences, even when Bluetown's more extensive use of the suspended sentence is taken into account. Greytown and Redtown had steadier custody rates for their juveniles and young adults, with Greytown being above and Redtown below the national average. For non-custodial penalties, the courts showed some similarities; for example all had used supervision orders in a lower proportion of cases than the average for England and Wales. In relation to other disposals local preferences are also apparent. Bluetown had made extensive use of the suspended sentence and of senior attendance centres, whereas Redtown imposed a high proportion of fines and community service orders and Greytown had a high rate of discharges.

Having thus selected four courts with fairly similar 'inputs' but with quite distinctive 'outputs', we were then able to commence the fieldwork.

3 Methods and measurements

In this chapter we begin by describing our research methods and offer some insights into the 'art' of gathering data in the semi-private world of the court. We then go on to discuss how we attempted to measure the 'seriousness' of the sample cases in each court.

Data collection in and around the courts

A diverse range of methods and techniques was required to secure the data for this project. Semi-structured interviews with magistrates, direct court observation, a postal survey of social workers and probation officers, case file analysis and statistical analysis were all employed. This chapter begins by describing the various methods and techniques used and highlights some of the difficulties which were encountered.

At least partly as a consequence of the status, influence and good offices of the Home Office, we gained access to all four 'first choice' courts. As a research team we took full advantage of our 'Home Office' credentials which felt more appropriate than 'sociologist' or 'criminologist' labels in terms of putting court officials at ease.

The most sensitive area of the fieldwork concerned interviewing magistrates after they had sentenced a particular case, which would often have involved the use of custody. At the time of setting up the fieldwork we were pessimistic, partly about obtaining such permission from senior staff, but mainly about individual magistrates' being willing to discuss specific cases. However, as this request was positively welcomed by the clerk to the first court we visited, we were able to successfully 'snowball' our request to the other courts, pointing out that their colleagues elsewhere had agreed to such a request. In the event all four courts readily agreed to such interviews taking place. Only 6 out of 240 cases are without interviews due to the unavailability of magistrates: only one magistrate refused to be interviewed as a matter of principle. Our success in getting magistrates to recall, often in quite intimate detail, how they had decided the sentence, in the retiring-room, was again due in large measure to our status as 'Home Office Researchers', which meant that we were 'bona fide' in the courts' own terms.

Having spent several weeks negotiating access to school reports from the education departments, social enquiry reports from the probation service and the social service departments, and antecedents from the police we commenced what turned out to be twelve months' fieldwork in the four court systems. This took place during 1985.

Given that we were to be in each court complex for several months, sitting in different courts on different days, it was essential that we paid particular attention to getting our role and behaviour absolutely right. Essentially we were guided by the politics of diplomacy. As outsiders we had to become acceptable quasi-insiders by making sure that we were introduced appropriately, had a legitimate and comprehensible role, fitted in in terms of appearance and manner, and were helpful, courteous and non-judgemental.

The fieldwork involved tracking 240 sample cases through the sentencing process. Basic data regarding the defendant and the offence were obtained from the 'court sheet' and social enquiry and school reports were analysed before the hearing. During the hearing we approached prosecuting solicitors for details of the defendants' antecedents and we tried to note everything that may have influenced the final sentence. Thus we made careful note of the clerk's style, the stance adopted by the prosecutor in presenting evidence, any contribution by either a social worker or a probation officer, the part played by the defendant in the proceedings, the mitigation offered by the defending solicitor and, of course, any utterance from the Bench.

After the hearing a questionnaire was administered to the social enquiry report authors. This questionnaire was intended to identify the perceptions of the report writer about their role in the particular case and in terms of providing a service to the court, offering recommendations about sentencing and supervising clients 'in the community'. We received a high response rate, probably facilitated by our long-term presence around the courtroom and our public relations with social services and probation in each area.

Interviewing magistrates

Previous research into decision-making by magistrates has been undertaken mainly through the use of postal questionnaires or simulation exercises (Kapardis 1981). We therefore had no acquired wisdom or research literature to rely on in constructing interview schedules and rehearsing the interview process. Consequently we piloted the schedule in Yellowtown, accepting that it would need revising both initially and perhaps as we moved between court areas. Changes were made to the schedule at various stages, these being mainly concerned with devising a method of quantifying the impact of different factors on the Bench's final decision.

Equally important were the starkly practical problems of timing and administering the interview. The setting and circumstances for conducting over 240 group interviews demanded much of the interviewer's 'art'.

A fairly lengthy schedule provided the basis for semi-structured interviews. Four factors in particular impinged on the interview routine. First, the ever-increasing likelihood of having to re-interview magistrates, second, the unpredictable time limits which respondents sometimes set on the interview, third, the domination of interviews by the senior magistrate and, finally, magistrates' knowledge of the law.

By definition the rotation of magistrates sitting in each PSD meant we would observe them in different combinations and thus be engaged in group interviews where initially no magistrates had been previously interviewed but then, as fieldwork progressed one, two or even three magistrates would be known to us. In Greytown where a resident Stipendiary Magistrate sat we obviously had to interview him several times. The second pressure was less easy to predict and occurred only infrequently. This involved being confronted with a time-limited interview whereby a Bench would invite the researcher into the retiring-room but then one or more magistrates would announce that they had only *x* minutes to spare. In the main this was a reasonable response given some Benches had sat for three or four hours and were feeling tired or emotionally drained. In Yellowtown for instance we sometimes began interviews after 5 pm sharing the building with only the cleaning staff and our interviewees. We dealt with these pressures by agreeing that those questions on the schedule which focused on the specific sample case should receive priority. This gave purpose to the interview for *all* magistrates and allowed those who had answered general questions previously to withdraw or sit back once the first part of the interview was completed. Furthermore if the interview was time limited it was deemed more important to obtain information about the specific case from even 'first-time interviewees', on the grounds that more general questions could be posed equally well at a later date. We also accepted the need to conduct an interview without all members of the Bench present and also to allow one respondent to withdraw rather than close a productive interview if their colleagues were happy to continue.

A third difficulty emerged during fieldwork interviews. There was a definite tendency for the Bench to stay 'in role', with the day's chairperson or senior magistrate orchestrating their responses using phrases such as 'we felt' or 'in our view', implying a complete unanimity of thought. While such a consensus did appear genuine in the majority of situations we did feel that earlier disagreements between magistrates in the retiring-room tended to be glossed over in these situations. We noted for instance that in the absence of the senior magistrate or in solo interviews respondents cited disagreements more often.

There was then a methodological price to be paid for being able to get to the heart of the sentencing decision so directly and immediately. In our analysis of the 240 interviews it must be clearly understood that the more general questions in particular do not normally reflect individual responses but unevenly collective ones, some of which will be repeated views. In the end we have no doubt that the price was worth paying given the richness of the findings and their originality in terms of our understanding of the dynamics of the sentencing process in English criminal justice.

Turning now to the interviews themselves, these lasted between ten minutes and an hour. They usually took place immediately after the Bench (or Stipendiary) had completed their list. A quiet room, normally a retiring-room or lounge was available, although interruptions did occur from time to time in Greytown and Yellowtown. We noted that the Chief Clerk or his deputy sat in on the first couple of interviews we conducted in three of the courts, presumably to make their own check on our line of questioning. However the vast majority of interviews were conducted in uninterrupted privacy and with the confidentiality of individual names of offenders and magistrates guaranteed. Our bona fide status, the fact that we had 'shared' the magistrates' experience by being present throughout their court list and having also read the contents of all the written material presented to them also raised our credibility.

As a consequence interviews were rarely uneasy or difficult to conduct. A potential embarrassment was identified early in the fieldwork however. This concerned posing questions specifically about legislation, It became clear very quickly that some magistrates were not sufficiently familiar with the law generally or the changes in sentencing possibilities brought about in the 1982 Act to be able to answer questions about, for instance, the Section 7(7) Care Order or requirements on supervision and probation orders (see also McLaughlin 1988). We thus negotiated our way into this section of the interview with great care, testing levels of knowledge without causing embarrassment which would jeopardize our rapport with the respondents.

Coding and analysing data

A total of over 800 hours' court observation, 233 'retained and coded' interviews with magistrates, an analysis of 240 social enquiry reports and 57 school reports generated a very large data set. In our data collection we chose initially to include all potentially influential factors and analyse for significance later.

By far the most difficult schedule to code was the one for magistrates' interviews. There were initial changes made, after piloting, to the form of questions asked. We also decided to include some questions about drug misuse for our Yellowtown interviews, given that a discussion of heroin use occurred spontaneously in so many earlier interviews. These revisions made the actual interviewing process across the four courts quite straightforward. However, because we were recording magistrates' explanations, rather than merely offering them the limited choices of a more structured or pre-coded interview schedule, we were faced with a complicated situation when it came to coding and analysis. It became clear that some of our data were at the margins, where quantification had only limited utility. Answers to questions about why a particular sentencing decision was reached or what hopes magistrates had for the offender after sentence often produced a uniqueness of response which defied economical coding. Consequently as the qualitative nature of Chapters 4 and 5 indicate, we felt it appropriate to accept this situation, not as an unresolved methodological problem, but as a reflection of the reality of the sentencing decision as perceived by magistrates.

Issues of targeting and comparability

We established in Chapter 2 that each of our four courts produced, over a number of years, quite distinctive sentencing profiles. After examining a range of 'variables' which might explain these sentencing patterns we concluded that there were no 'external' factors of sufficient influence to explain such differences. We were left therefore with the strong possibility that the differential sentencing was a product of the courtroom process.

Our court samples were not selected on the basis that they would mirror the overall sentencing profile of each court. Instead they were merely designed to isolate 240 offenders 'at some risk of custody'. In judging whether or not a case was at risk of custody a number of criteria were applied: these concerned the nature, frequency and seriousness of offending as well as the defendant's criminal record. However, some local factors were also borne in mind, for example if the offence was the subject of a local 'clampdown' it was acknowledged that this might increase the likelihood of a custodial sentence. Identifying cases 'at some risk of custody' is in fact more difficult than identifying 'definite' custody cases. The danger is that in trying to capture 'either way' high tariff cases the characteristics of the sample and the sentence become too diverse for comparison between courts. Thus before proceeding further it is necessary to look at the sentences imposed in each sample case. We must then assess whether the seriousness of past and present offending, or any other factor, such as age or sex, suggest difficulties for a comparative analysis.

The sentencing outcomes for the 240 cases are laid out in Table 3.1, which shows that about 30 per cent of the cases received custodial sentences revised by the 1982 Act and around 20 per cent received the revised alternatives (i.e. CSO for 16-year-olds, requirements on probation and supervision orders and compensation).

With the exception of the eight conditional discharge cases, which are apparently off target, the remainder of sentences are all middle or high tariff disposals which stand alongside those sentences revised or introduced by the 1982 Act. Indeed as our analysis develops it will become clear that the comparison between these and the 'new' sentences provides much insight into magistrates' perceptions of the meaning and value of different sentences.

Such basic statistics, however, merely confirm that in practice we did identify a sample at some risk of custody. They do not tell us whether this sentencing

Table 3.1

Targeting of all sample cases in order of frequency of result

		Number	Percentage
Community service (including 15 juveniles)	(16–20 years)	47	19.6
Detention centre	(14–16 years)	44	18.3
Youth custody	(15–20 years)	28	11.7
Attendance centre	(14–20 years)	23	9.6
Supervision order with IT or SA	(14–16 years)	21	8.8
Fine	(14–20 years)	21	8.7
Probation order	(17–20 years)	17	7.1
Deferred sentence	(14–20 years)	10	4.2
Conditional discharge	(14–20 years)	8	3.3
Supervision order	(14–16 years)	7	2.9
Probation order with 'package'	(17–20 years)	5	2.1
Care order	(14–16 years)	5	2.1
Crown Court for sentence	(14–20 years)	3	1.2
Compensation order	(14–20 years)	1	0.4
Total		240	100

pattern was representative of each court or a 'justifiable' result in terms of an objective measure of the seriousness of each case. The 1982 Act intended that custody should be used only in certain circumstances and by implication that the new 'alternatives' should also be used only for 'high tariff' sentencing.

Once we look at the sentencing picture for each individual court (see Table 3.2) it becomes clear that we have potentially eight but in particular four quite distinctive sentencing patterns. Furthermore these patterns look, on the surface, to be related to the PSD area and its long-standing overall sentencing profile. Hence, as noted in Chapter 2, Yellowtown magistrates who have traditionally used custody more often than the other courts seem to have utilized youth custody rather often. Bluetown courts have turned to the new custodial sentences least often apparently taking up the new requirement 'packages' attached to supervision orders, with the same enthusiasm for which Redtown has used community service in respect of young adults.

The crucial issue is of course whether this differential sentencing and use of new legislation is a product of courtroom preferences and prejudices or the measurable result of the particular characteristics of each case – particularly the seriousness of the offenders' record and current offence. We can now turn to these issues.

Age, sex and occupational status of sample cases

There were obviously some differences in the distribution for each court but in

Table 3.2.

Primary sentence for each sample case by court

	Juveniles				Young adults				
	Yellowtown	Redtown	Greytown	Bluetown	Yellowtown	Redtown	Greytown	Bluetown	
Conditional discharge	—	2	—	—	2	—	3	1	Conditional discharge
Fine	1	1	5	3	1	2	4	4	Fine
Compensation	—	—	—	—	—	—	—	1	Compensation
Attendance centre	4	5	4	4	—	2	—	4	Attendance centre
Supervision order	1	3	1	2	2	5	6	4	Probation order
Supervision with specified/IT	3	3	5	10	3	1	1	—	Probation with requirements
Care order	1	2	—	1	—	—	—	—	
Resid. cond.	—	1	—	—	—	—	—	—	
Community service (16-year-olds)	4	2	3	6	6	13	5	8	Community service order
Detention centre	6	7	8	3	4	7	5	4	Detention centre
Youth custody (15 years +)	6	3	2	1	8	—	4	4	Youth custody
Deferred sentence	4	1	2	—	2	—	1	—	Deferred sentence
Crown Court	—	—	—	—	2	—	1	—	Crown Court
	30	30	30	30	30	30	30	30	

terms of the eligibility for particular sentences (e.g. detention centre at 14 as against youth custody at 15) the age distribution looks unremarkable. However as there was a concentration of older young adults in Yellowtown it is possible that they had accumulated more substantial criminal records than in the other courts.

There were nineteen females in the sample. This figure was well below the intended target. However, despite our best efforts, the absence of females in the final sample is a clear reflection of the small number of women 'at some risk of custody' appearing before these courts. Five females were present in the overall Yellowtown sample, two in Redtown, five in Greytown and seven in Bluetown. The small numbers and their distribution across the courts makes it very unlikely that the female component of the sample introduces any difficulties into the four court comparison.

A recent study of unemployment and the magistrates' courts by Crow and Simon (1987) has shown that

> unemployed offenders were less often fined, and some moved down tariff to conditional discharge while others moved up, so that at the top end the unemployed went more often into custody, and the employed had a better chance of a prison term being suspended.

We compared the occupational status of each court sample. Differences were obviously minimal amongst the juveniles. However, general trends in regional youth unemployment were reflected in the young adult sample. Only four of the Yellowtown sample were employed as were eight of the Greytown group. At best, as in Redtown and Bluetown, a third of the sample were in some kind of paid employment.

The seriousness of criminal records

Without entering a detailed debate about the principles of sentencing in English criminal justice it is clear that the status of the offenders' criminal record, or antecedents, is a major consideration in the sentencing process. This is apparent in the formal sentencing theory literature (Thomas 1979; Cross 1981), research findings based on court observation (Parker *et al.* 1981) and evaluations of magistrates' decision-making (Devlin 1970; Brody 1976). Indeed it is this principle which lies behind one of the three custody 'safeguards' criteria introduced in Section 1(4) of the CJA, whereby custody should be used only when 'no other method of dealing with the offender is appropriate. . . because he is unable or unwilling to respond to non-custodial penalties'.

Given the possibility that the differential sentencing between the four PSDs generally, and in the sample cases in particular, may be a result of caseloads with dissimilar antecedent weighting, we tried to quantify the seriousness of previous offending for every case. We thus calculated a general seriousness score for all offenders' records, based on the principal offence for each conviction date during the past three years. We allocated each offence to one of five 'score' categories (which are laid out Note 1).

Clearly given the lack of any universally agreed criteria, any system for scoring seriousness we produce is open to criticism (Fitzmaurice and Pease 1986). Furthermore because it must be based on legal labels which appear on charge sheets and criminal records, any such scoring system will fail to get behind these labels to where 'true' seriousness is said to lie (this point was made by the Court of Appeal in the *R*. v. *Bradburn* case, 1985).

Certainly we do not claim that the system we have adopted is foolproof. We have based it more on common agreements which circulate in and around the courts than on a statistically generated set of rules. This is because our numerous attempts to produce a method of improving our scoring system, by producing a formula based on a combination of current offence and criminal history scores, proved unsatisfactory.

However, as the basic indicator of seriousness to be applied even-handedly to each case and each court, we do feel our approach has merit. Consequently we assessed all 240 criminal records and an overall seriousness score for every case was calculated. Each case was then allocated to its court jurisdiction. Note 2 summarizes the overall score patterns and Table 3.3 illustrates this score group rating by court sample. The aggregate scores in the table are produced by giving each of the score groups a value of 1–11 based on seriousness and multiplying the frequency of sample cases with the appropriate value. The calculations are not shown but the aggregate score by court is indicated at the foot of the table.

Dealing with juveniles first, Greytown has the highest aggregate score, closely followed by Yellowtown. Redtown holds the middle ground whereas Bluetown, with two-thirds of the sample being very lightly convicted or first-time offenders, has a much lower aggregate score. The same pattern emerges for young adults but with the Greytown sample being at a considerably higher level than all other courts. Although Bluetown comes closer to the mean for young adults it again has by far the lowest rating.

On the basis of the seriousness of previous offences then, assuming other things to be equal we would expect Greytown magistrates to pass higher tariff sentences, in the court hearings under scrutiny, than the other courts.

Although basing our assessment of criminal records on principal offences is the most objective method of comparing our sample's criminality, there is little doubt that sentencers pay as much, if not more, attention to previous disposals. In terms of objectivity such an approach is fundamentally flawed. Given that almost without exception previous sentences were made by the same Bench or 'home' court, the likelihood of previous, possibly locally defined, sentencing, being cited to reinforce present sentencing of a similar style is considerable. Perhaps the classic example of this process is the making of a second longer custodial sentence for a young offender who received a short custodial sentence for a previous offence but in the eyes of the Bench has obviously not learnt his lesson. This cyclical process was identified by Parker *et al*. (1981) in relation to

Table 3.3

Seriousness rating of each court based on previous offences by sample cases

Score group	Juveniles				Young adults			
	Yellowtown	Redtown	Greytown	Bluetown	Yellowtown	Redtown	Greytown	Bluetown
1	10	10	7	20	10	13	4	5
2	6	9	9	6	8	4	6	8
3	2	2	4	—	—	6	3	2
4	7	3	2	3	5	5	5	3
5	—	3	3	1	1	1	4	1
6	4	2	2	—	1	1	3	1
7	—	—	2	—	—	—	2	—
8	—	—	—	—	3	—	2	—
9	—	1	1	—	1	—	1	—
10	—	—	—	—	1	—	—	—
11	1	—	—	—	—	—	—	—
Aggregate score	91	82	95	49	100	70	122	60

Table 3.4

Sample cases with custodial sentences[a] prior to present offences

	Juveniles				Young adults			
	Yellowtown	*Redtown*	*Greytown*	*Bluetown*	*Yellowtown*	*Redtown*	*Greytown*	*Bluetown*[b]
No previous custodial sentence	18	27	24	28	16	24	15	25
Detention centre	9	3	6	2	7	4	8	3
Youth custody or Borstal	3	—	—	—	3	—	4	—
Detention centre and YC or Borstal	—	—	—	—	4	2	2	1
Prison	—	—	—	—	—	—	1	—

Notes: [a] Made during past three years
[b] One not known

second-time offenders sentenced for car taking who had received detention centre sentences for their first offence.

In order to distinguish between seriousness based on offending and seriousness based on previous 'in house' sentencing we looked at both the number of previous custodial sentences made against the sample and the tariff position of each case based on previous sentencing (see Note 3). Table 3.4 presents the frequency and nature of previous custodial sentences for each court's sample.

This picture is not the one we would expect to emerge. In Yellowtown, for both juveniles and adults, the number of previous custodial sentences seemed somewhat higher than we might expect when compared with the Greytown profile, which on the basis of previous offence seriousness, should have attracted the highest rates of custodial sentences.

In the same way the tariff positions for each case illustrated in Table 3.5 (see Note 3) not only are an indication of the seriousness of previous offence, but also are a reflection of the local sentencing practices of recent years. Thus again Yellowtown juveniles and young adults were apparently at more risk of custody (i.e. in categories 4–6) in current proceedings, using this measure, than could be expected using the more objective 'seriousness score' noted in Table 3.3. The main reason for this is the frequency of 'previous tariff jump' cases in Yellowtown – the product of using high tariff sentences 'early' in delinquent careers. The sentencing in the other courts shows little discrepancy in terms of a rank ordering of the courts.

The nature and seriousness of current offences

As we might expect, the types of offences included in the sample were fairly serious crime categories, with the unauthorized taking of cars, burglaries in commercial premises and dwellings, physical assaults and general theft predominating (see Note 4). Note 5 indicates the number of current offences against each case by court. The most striking features are that Bluetown juveniles, closely followed by Redtown's, faced more charges than those in Yellowtown and Greytown and that young adults in Bluetown were sentenced for very many more current offences than their peers in the other three courts.

Table 3.6 deals with the seriousness of the current offences, based on the same formula used to assess previous offences. The aggregate totals give the seriousness score for the offences to be sentenced by each court. Again, Bluetown closely followed by Redtown had higher overall scores than the other two courts.

Conclusion

There may well be significant factors within the courtroom process, such as the standard of legal representation or the impact of reports, which might explain the differences in sentencing by PSD. We will look at these matters in later chapters. In this chapter we have dealt with the age, sex, occupational status,

Table 3.5

Tariff position of sample cases prior to present offence (based on past three years' sentencing)

Tariff position	Juveniles				Young adults			
	Yellowtown	Redtown	Greytown	Bluetown	Yellowtown	Redtown	Greytown	Bluetown
1 No previous	2	3	2	12	1	4	1	7
2 Low tariff climbing	14	17	15	14	8	16	7	13
3 Middle tariff climbing	1	6	6	2	6	4	5	5
4 Previous tariff jump	4	2	—	1	5	—	—	1
5 Post-custody/care plateau	4	1	4	—	4	2	8	—
6 High tariff	5	1	3	1	6	4	9	4

Table 3.6

Seriousness of current offences for samples by court

Seriousness score group	Juveniles				Young adults			
	Yellowtown	Redtown	Greytown	Bluetown	Yellowtown	Redtown	Greytown	Bluetown
1	10	8	6	5	15	15	11	5
2	5	7	9	8	6	4	9	13
3	1	1	1	2	2	2	6	5
4	8	3	11	3	4	5	1	5
5	—	5	1	6	1	1	1	1
6	1	—	—	4	1	—	1	1
7	—	3	1	—	1	1	—	—
8	4	—	1	—	—	1	1	—
9	—	1	—	1	—	1	—	—
10	—	1	—	—	—	—	—	—
11	1	—	—	—	—	—	—	—
12	—	1	—	—	—	—	—	—
13	—	—	—	1	—	—	—	—
14	—	—	—	—	—	—	—	—
15	—	—	—	—	—	—	—	—
	105	114	91	117	67	75	70	77

seriousness of previous offending, previous sentencing, and the seriousness of current offences. These are all matters which are immutable: the current case arrives, for better or worse, with these credentials. We have for the present regarded age, sex and occupational status as 'neutral' and concentrated upon measuring the seriousness of past and present offending. An objective assessment of these two measures particularly when combined implies several things.

First, it shows that our court samples are indeed comparable and that while some account must be taken of the low seriousness score for Bluetown sample's previous offences, there is otherwise no reason to be tentative in making comparisons. While Bluetown and Redtown have lower antecedent ratings they have higher current offence seriousness ratings than Greytown and Yellow-town. On the basis of our assessments, using these two key measures, we would expect Greytown to be making the most use of high tariff sentences closely followed by the other three courts, perhaps with Yellowtown very slightly 'ahead' of the other two. Generally speaking these measures do not provide any reason to predict widely divergent sentencing in the four courts.

Second, the comparison between the seriousness of previous offences score and the 'prior use of custody' and 'tariff positions' for each court suggests that the earlier sentencing of the sample cases by each local court impinges on the present decision. By reflecting not only the seriousness of previous offending but also the earlier sentencing preferences and perhaps prejudices of the same group of magistrates, the tariff position for the sample cases, as they face current charges, looks likely to place the Yellowtown sample in particular at a greater risk of custody. By the same token the greater reliance placed on community-based disposals in recent years, for instance by Redtown, is likely to be reflected in the 'previous use of custody' and 'tariff position' scores for this sample.

Third, the actual sentencing produced by each court in respect of the sample cases under scrutiny is substantially different and is not an obvious reflection of the seriousness of past and present offending. We would expect Greytown with the highest combined previous and present offending aggregate scores to produce the highest custody rate and the other courts to be broadly similar in their use of custody. However, while Greytown's magistrates resorted to custody in 30 per cent of the sample cases, Yellowtown, who one would expect to use less than this, actually resorted to custody in 43 per cent of cases. Bluetown magistrates on the other hand, who had the most serious current offences before them, used custody in only 20 per cent of cases.

While a different scoring system would conceivably alter the aggregate scores for each court it is highly unlikely that it would reduce the differences between them. It may be however that the differential sentencing was due to the 'hidden' seriousness which the legal labels on the defendant's charge sheet or criminal record cannot refer to but which magistrates can, on the day, penetrate. This possibility must remain on our agenda to be pursued in a later chapter.

We have not got to the heart of the matter therefore. Sentencing remains a mystery even when we look at the seriousness of previous offending and present offence. However, there are some leads to follow. First, the post-1982 sentencing practices as portrayed in the sample cases processed by each PSD are remarkably consistent with their overall pre-Act 'historical' sentencing practices as described in Chapter 2. This is firm evidence of the durability and pervasiveness of local sentencing traditions. These same traditions were responsible for the results of our 'previous custody–tariff position' analysis, which showed that past sentencing reinforces present sentencing in the local setting.

Clearly therefore we will succeed in finding out why these differences occur and endure and thus how new legislation affects local sentencing only by focusing upon the courtroom and perhaps the retiring-room. Hence we now turn to a detailed analysis of our interviews with the magistrates in the four courts under study.

Notes

Note 1   Categories of seriousness by offence

Score	Seriousness of offence
20	GBH – Malicious wounding Robbery, Demand with menaces Burglary of dwelling – aggravated burglary Category A drugs Category B and C drugs for resale Arson (over £1,000)
8	Burglary of unoccupied dwelling, commercial premises or school Criminal damage over £1,000 Theft over £1,000 UTMV Arson under £1,000 Unspecified burglary
4	Burglary of void premises Attempt burglary Theft – £400/£1,000 Deception – Fraud – Handling Theft from person by inducement Reckless driving Criminal damage £400/£1,000 Assault ABH
2	Theft £50/£400 Trespass on enclosed premises Going equipped Attempted TWOC

Score	Seriousness of offence
	Interfering with motor vehicle
	Breach of order
	Category B and C drugs for private use
	Criminal damage £50/£400
1	Theft − less than £50
	Criminal damage − less than £50
	Road Traffic Act
	Allowing to be carried
	Offensive weapon
	Breach of Bail Act
	Public order
	Unspecified theft
	Unspecified criminal damage

Note 2

Seriousness of criminal records: score pattern for overall sample

Score group	Value	Frequency	%
1	0−5	75	31.3
2	6−10	61	25.4
3	11−15	20	8.3
4	16−20	41	17.1
5	21−25	61	6.7
6	26−30	8	3.3
7	31−35	5	2.1
8	36−40	7	2.9
9	41−45	3	1.2
10	46−50	1	0.4
11	51−55	—	0.0
12	56−60	2	0.8
13	61−65	—	0.0
14	66−70	—	0.0
15	71−75	1	0.4
		240	100

Note 3

The tariff positions were interpreted in the following way

'No previous'
No previous convictions

'Low tariff climbing'
An offender with 1–3 convictions normally of discharge or small fine

'Middle tariff climbing'
Offenders with 2–4 convictions which will have included attendance centre or supervision – probation orders and/or large fines

'Previous tariff jump'
Offenders who will have received either custody or an 'alternative' such as community service on a first or second offence, presumably due to the nature of the offence

'Post-custody/care plateau'
Offenders who have already been in care or custody but whose last sentence was not high tariff, this being an atypical position from which future sentencing is difficult to predict

'High tariff'
Offenders who have already received several disposals which have most recently involved custody, supervision or probation packages, or community service: these offenders are in practice at risk of custody on any future court appearances

Note 4

Principal offences for which sample cases were sentenced

	Juveniles				Young adults				Total
	Yellow-town	Redtown	Greytown	Bluetown	Yellow-town	Redtown	Greytown	Bluetown	
UTMV	1	2	8	6	4	—	8	7	36
Burglary of commercial premises	5	—	6	6	1	7	3	3	31
Burglary in occupied dwelling	7	3	4	1	3	2	1	2	23
Theft from shop	—	5	3	2	7	1	1	2	21
General theft	—	5	—	—	5	2	2	3	17
Minor assault	1	1	1	5	1	4	2	1	16
Burglary in unoccupied dwelling	1	2	2	—	3	1	—	4	13
Criminal damage/arson	2	3	—	3	—	2	1	2	13
Serious assault	4	—	2	3	—	1	—	—	10
Theft from vehicle	2	2	—	—	1	1	1	2	9
Road traffic offence	3	—	1	—	—	2	—	1	7
Robbery/demand with menaces	2	2	—	—	—	1	—	—	5
Handling	1	1	—	—	—	1	1	1	5
Other (frequencies < 5)	1	4	3	4	5	5	10	2	34
	30	30	30	30	30	30	30	30	240

Note 5

The number of current offences for sentencing by sample

	Juveniles				Young adults			
	Yellowtown	Redtown	Greytown	Bluetown	Yellowtown	Redtown	Greytown	Bluetown
1	13	7	11	6	11	14	15	7
2	10	11	8	9	7	7	7	7
3	3	7	5	7	7	5	4	5
4	2	2	2	2	3	1	2	5
5	—	1	1	2	—	1	1	2
6	1	—	1	3	1	2	—	—
7	—	2	—	1	1	—	—	—
8	—	—	—	—	—	—	—	1
9	1	—	1	—	—	—	—	1
10	—	—	1	—	—	—	1	2
Total	65	77	70	81	71	64	64	103

4 Upholding the law of the land?

Oh, God! You're not going to interview them about that last case! If you do, you'll never come back. Their decision was not influenced by any of the legislation of the last twenty years!

(A clerk, Redtown)

Magistrates undertake, when they are sworn in as Justices, to uphold the law of the land without fear or favour. Yet it is clear from the material presented in the last two chapters, as well as from other studies quoted there, that upholding the law has different meanings in different parts of the land, at least as far as sentencing is concerned. The legal framework is effective in defining what sentences are available to be used but, beyond that, Criminal Justice Acts, like any other legislation, have to be interpreted in practice. This chapter reports on magistrates' responses to the changes brought about by the 1982 Act. Their views of the substantive changes in available sentencing options are obviously of importance here, but there is also a question about why some changes were welcomed, others were regretted, and some apparently significant changes were considered to have made no difference at all to sentencing. This mixed reception can be explained in part by magistrates' perceptions of the sentencing task more generally and the chapter goes on to consider how the interpretation of the Act at local level is shaped by the social, as well as legal, context in which sentencing takes place.

The CJA and the codification of common sense

Sentencing is about common sense and nous more than anything.

(Magistrate, Yellowtown)

One of the important features of the 1982 Act was the introduction of restrictions on the use of custody under Section 1(4). The Benches interviewed in the sample cases were asked if the Act, particularly in respect of this subsection, had made any difference to the way they reached their sentencing decisions. Discounting one panel which claimed never to have heard of the Act, two-thirds of the thirty-six Benches replying to this question said it had made little difference.[1]   Part of the explanation for this, mentioned by some magistrates, rests in the difficulty of keeping up with the complexity of the law and of assimilating changes. Thus it was clear from our courtroom observation that some Benches were still struggling with the implementation of the Bail Act, some three years after its enactment, while clerks were already preoccupied with the then forthcoming Police and Criminal Evidence Act. The problem of finding time to learn about new ideas was thus given as a reason for 'tending to go for traditional patterns of sentencing'.

For over half of the Benches, however, the main reason for the lack of change in sentencing was that the Act 'only codifies what we did anyway' in respect of custody. The Act was dismissed by one Justice in Greytown as 'a load of verbiage':

> What it comes down to is gravity of offence and previous record. It doesn't make any difference. Custody was never used lightly.

The criteria in Section 1(4) were described by another magistrate as 'the sorts of things people had in mind anyway. It doesn't need spelling out to responsible people.' As far as most Benches were concerned, custody was only ever used where it was really necessary and this part of the Act was therefore regarded as quite superfluous. The only difference which most magistrates noted was that they now have to state their reasons for using custody and their responses indicated that Section 1(4) is indeed superfluous to the sentencing process in the majority of cases.

Although a minority of Benches said that the criteria did make them think more carefully and systematically about using custody, the public statement of reasons was seen by most respondents as a merely cosmetic change. As one Bench in Bluetown put it:

> It hasn't changed the way we think or sentence. It just has to be referred to at the sentencing stage, usually because the clerk reminds us.

They added that they were usually able to make one of the criteria 'fit OK' and evidently concurred with many of their colleagues in viewing the criteria as stated in the Act as vague enough to allow most eventualities to be covered (cf Burney 1985a; Reynolds 1985):

> It has made a small difference in that sometimes we want to use custody and can't find a suitable reason. But the loophole in the Act is 'the protection of the public'. You can usually fit it into that.
>
> (Magistrate, Yellowtown)

This method of negotiating the criteria was illustrated clearly in the comments made by magistrates dealing with a sample case in the same court:

> When we sentenced, we said ninety days because non-custodial measures hadn't worked. We wanted to say a 'very serious offence' but we didn't feel we could because we weren't using custody for the co-defendant.

It is clear that the legal requirement to state reasons for a custodial penalty was often a matter which was both separate from and subsequent to the decision to use custody.

While it was apparent in some cases that the clerk had attempted to insert the Section 1(4) criteria into the sentencing process, it was also obvious that clerks on occasions colluded with the use of the criteria as *ex post facto* constructions, as in the following conversation which took place between the clerk and the chairperson of the Bench which had just dealt with a sample case in Redtown:

> *Chair:* 'I didn't formally announce reasons.'
> *Clerk:* 'Oh, that's all right. I entered them in the book.'
> *Chair:* 'Which one did you choose?'
> *Clerk:* 'All of them.'

Clerks may have their own reasons for not encouraging magistrates to explain their decisions very fully in court and magistrates in three of the courts said that they were told to say as little as possible when announcing sentence. One reason is that clerks may wish to protect lay magistrates from the embarrassment of 'getting it wrong' in public. Another reason mentioned by magistrates themselves was the strategic one of minimizing Appeals: 'the more reasons you give, the greater the grounds for Appeal'. This was linked with magistrates' distrust of judges' sentencing, which will be discussed in more detail later.

There were then two distinct rationales operating in relation to the use of custody. One was the criteria set out in the legislation and the other was magistrates' actual decision-making process. Although magistrates claimed that the Act was no more than a codification of their existing practice, it was clear that the two forms of decision-making did sometimes conflict. Where the two forms of rationale were in conflict, 'getting round' the legal form was a more likely resolution than a change in the magistrates' own view that custody was appropriate. One clear implication here is that if legal criteria intended to limit the use of custody are to have any 'bite' they need to be much more rigorously defined than they were in the 1982 Act: the fuller explanations of sentencing required in subsequent legislation will, hopefully, have more impact. Otherwise magistrates' 'common sense' about the use of custody will continue to prevail. The 1982 Act, in so far as it extended magistrates' custodial sentencing powers, widened the scope for exercising magisterial common sense.

The necessity of custody

> Custody is the last resort. It is necessary to protect the public.
>
> (Magistrate, Yellowtown)

> Custody is a natural progression, the ultimate deterrent. The thinking has always been that you should try everything else first.
>
> (Magistrate, Yellowtown)

Magistrates believe that there is a hard core of cases for whom nothing but custody will do. Although they claimed that this had not been changed by the Act, it would seem that in some courts at least the size of this hard core group had grown since its implementation. This must reflect the use made of the increased powers in respect of custodial sentences which the CJA accorded to magistrates. The vast majority (92 per cent) of the seventy-five Benches who commented on these new powers expressed satisfaction. For some, this was on grounds of general principle: 'Perhaps it's just because we like having more power', as one magistrate in Yellowtown remarked. But this specific element in the CJA was given a particularly positive reception because it was thought better for defendants to be sentenced by magistrates rather than by judges in Crown Court.

The reduction in the number of committals consequent upon the 1982 Act was regretted by a few magistrates in Yellowtown because defendants no longer tremble at 'the full panoply of the law', but more commonly the change was seen as beneficial. Among the benefits mentioned were the reduction in delays resulting from committal and that crime could now be dealt with locally rather than at a geographically removed Crown Court. However, the main benefit, as far as magistrates were concerned, was the transfer of power from what was believed to be an over-lenient judiciary.[2] As a Yellowtown magistrate put it, 'the judge might let them off'. Two-thirds of the eighty-six Benches who responded to a question about whether judges sentence differently from magistrates believed judges to be more lenient. It must be said that judges, in their sentencing capacity, were not well thought of by the magistrates we interviewed. Our respondents had an apparently endless fund of stories about cases in which the judge had not given the anticipated sentence. Although it was recognized that judges might deal with a more serious caseload so that what appeared heinous to magistrates might be relatively small beans to a judge, the magistrates made many comments to the effect that judges are largely out of touch, 'living in a different world', 'more concerned about poaching than about burglary' and simply 'not streetwise', especially as far as juveniles are concerned. Quite how 'streetwise' a largely middle-aged and middle-class magistracy is remains a matter for some speculation!

While welcoming an extension of their own powers, a minority of Benches did express reservations about the new youth custody order. One concern here was about young people spending time in prison while awaiting allocation to a youth custody centre:

> Abolishing Borstals has meant that young people go to prison with adults in effect.
>
> (Magistrate, Greytown)

Other reservations focused on the nature of the youth custody regime itself. For a few Benches there was an almost sentimental attachment to tradition here, as in the comment from a Bluetown magistrate, who felt

> there is an old-fashioned attachment to Borstal. We do not feel quite the same way about youth custody.

The new regime, without the training element of the old Borstal system, was also seen as a less positive and constructive sentence. For magistrates in Yellowtown in particular, this was interpreted as meaning that the system had 'gone soft'. As one described a visit to a youth custody centre:

> They were smoking in the classroom, propping up the walls. And they looked at you, you know. No discipline. I was appalled.

Nevertheless, such reservations were evidently not strong enough to prevent magistrates in this court from using this disposal.

Nationally youth custody (YC) sentences have increased whereas the rise in detention centre (DC) orders has not matched the fears expressed by some at the time the Act was passed. Clearly magistrates have little confidence, in reality, in the 'short sharp shock'. However, they duly repeated the rhetoric which surrounded this disposal. Over half of the eighty-eight Benches who gave their views on the new shorter sentences were positive about them. Most of these Benches believed firmly in the greater impact of the shorter sentence: 'It's drummed into us that it's the first two weeks that are effective'. Responses to custody were clearly considered to follow the law of diminishing returns, as we were repeatedly told that it is the first clang of the gate which has the sharp and shocking effect.

> It's like the army; to begin with everyone wants to go home but eventually they begin to enjoy it,

according to a magistrate in Yellowtown, where several Benches expressed a desire for the power to make sentences even shorter than the current three-week minimum.

In contrast, one of the reservations expressed by a significant minority of Benches about the new short sentence concerned the ineffectiveness of a short period in custody. A period of three weeks or so was not considered long enough for it to 'work':

> Just time for them to be processed in and processed out. There's no time to achieve anything,

said one Greytown Justice while a colleague in Redtown considered that

> Custody should only be used where there is a need to protect the community and protecting the community for two weeks [i.e. taking remission into account] is clearly not worthwhile. It tends to be used as an alternative to a non-custodial measure and not as an alternative to longer periods in custody. The short sharp shock is a nonsense.

Condemned by these respondents as too short, the short DC order was condemned by other magistrates as insufficiently sharp or shocking:

> I agree with the short sharp shock but I wish these places weren't geared to them enjoying themselves so much.
>
> (Magistrate, Yellowtown)

> We did think of sending him to the holiday camp at [the local DC].
>
> (Magistrate, Redtown)

The belief that 'DC's gone soft now' was one criticism voiced about the regime in these establishments. The other was that new DC regime was not very constructive when compared to YC. While none of the magistrates interviewed made any reference to the Home Office report on the stricter DC regimes (Home Office 1984), it was this type of regime in particular which attracted criticism:

> I like the short sharp shock, but not the Yorkshire variety [New Hall in Yorkshire was one of the original experimental centres]. That has taken away the positive element.
>
> (Magistrate, Bluetown)

> The more rigid DCs are less constructive than the training regimes [in YC centres]. With all that PE that they do, all they do is turn out fitter criminals − so that they can run away to evade arrest!
>
> (Magistrate, Yellowtown)

What was common to both the welcoming and the critical comments about the shorter custodial sentences was that DC was not really seen as providing some of the things which magistrates saw as desirable in a custodial sentence. It was considered not long enough to be punishment, not long enough or sufficiently constructive for rehabilitation and too short to protect the public. While magistrates may have expressed some doubts about the YC in terms of its supposed 'softness' and lack of training component compared with the old Borstal regime, DC was seen as even less likely to provide what was wanted. DC, in the magistrates' eyes, seemed to perform a different role in the repertoire of available penalties.

Short detention centre sentences were not seen as a replacement for longer custodial sentences on more heavily convicted or serious offenders. They were seen as most useful at an early stage of a defendant's criminal career, 'if you have the courage to use them early'. Despite their claims that custody is used only as a last resort, in keeping with Section 1(4) of the CJA, many magistrates also subscribed to a 'nip them in the bud' theory of when DC should be used. They were apparently quite unaware of the high reconviction rates which suggest that DC does not provide an effective nip in the bud (for example, prison statistics show that 67 per cent of those sentenced to DC in 1982 were reconvicted within two years: (Stern 1987) quite apart from any other deleterious effects of a single custodial sentence on the individual concern (cf Ashworth 1983). However, it was a theory which was reinforced by prison department staff in detention centres. Most magistrates had visited a DC at some point during their training and staff in these establishments carried high credibility. 'When we went to the detention centre, the governor said. . .' was the preface to many statements that this is a form of sentence most suited to defendants at an early stage of their criminal career. Where the language used to describe DC regimes was that of 'holiday camps' and 'superior boarding schools', and the early use of custody no longer countered by a 'long' minimum sentence, it is not surprising that some Benches believed that DC was used where a custodial sentence would previously have been ruled out. As one put it,

> Borstal was often too long for a juvenile so you didn't use custody, but now you will, but with a shorter sentence.
>
> (Magistrate, Bluetown)

Thus custody was not an undifferentiated form of penalty in magistrates' eyes. Youth custody was seen as appropriate where real punishment, sustained training or the protection of the public was at stake. Magistrates welcomed the transfer of power to ensure the imposition of such a sentence from what many Benches saw as a 'soft', or at best unreliable, higher court. Detention centre on the other hand, and despite the dangers of criminal contamination, was meant to 'put the frighteners' on the less highly convicted offender at a much earlier stage. This differentiation is clearly seen in the use made of 'four months and a day' YC sentences, which, although contrary to the notion of a continuum of custodial sentencing envisaged in the 1982 Act, ensured that a defendant was subject to what the Bench regarded as the 'right' regime in the case. How the 'right' regime is selected in each case is not of course given in law, but again is part of magisterial 'common sense'. The differentiation of the two regimes may also go some way towards explaining why magistrates were at once able to say that custody is the 'last resort' and at the same time to say that DC should be used at an early stage: there is a sense in which only the longer sentences were really 'counted' as having the properties of a custodial penalty. Although there were substantive criticisms of both DC and YC regimes, magistrates welcomed the power to ensure that custody was actually used where they themselves thought it should be, without judges' interference. They also enjoyed the power to have more say about what sort of regime a defendant should be subjected to, albeit that this was quite contrary to the intention behind the Act. Thus magistrates welcomed this part of the Act because it allowed them more power to assert the 'common sense' of sentencing. Conversely the loss of powers was interpreted as a loss of an important element of flexibility in sentencing.

Losing power: the case of the suspended sentence

> It's no great loss. They're either custody or they're not.
>
> (Magistrate, Bluetown)

Although technically the suspended sentence is a custodial penalty and is counted as such in official statistics, the way in which our respondents talked about its loss for the 17–20 age group made clear that this was not their view. Nearly a third of the eighty-two Benches who commented on this particular aspect of the 1982 Act said it had made no difference to them because they had made only occasional use of the suspended sentence for this age group anyway. The reasons they gave for this, of which the following two illustrations are typical, are very interesting:

> It creates problems if they come back to court and you are then tied to sending them down. It should be custody if it's custody and something else if it's not.
>
> (Magistrate, Greytown)

> If it's custody then it should be that.
>
> (Magistrate, Yellowtown)

For this substantial minority of respondents, then, custody is custody and nothing else should substitute for it.

However, the majority of the Benches interviewed expressed strong regret about the 'real loss' which this aspect of the Act had entailed, describing it as 'scandalous', with several Benches expressing incomprehension of 'what they can have been thinking of when they did that!'. Partly this clearly reflected magistrates' dislikes of any encroachment on their powers:

> It's a big loss. Anything that denigrates magistrates by removing powers is bad. Magistrates are intelligent and trained and should be allowed the discretion to exercise their intelligence and training.

More than the affront to magisterial dignity, the loss of any sentencing option meant a loss of flexibility. Specifically in relation to the suspended sentence, this meant the loss of an option which was believed to have strong deterrent properties inherent in it. Frequently our respondents likened it to the Sword of Damocles hanging 'like an axe held over their heads with a piece of string', as one Yellowtown Justice put it. Others saw it as valuable in 'returning responsibility to the offender'. The assumption of the rational responsibility of offenders for their offences, which underpins this type of argument, is a very questionable one (Bottoms 1981), but was uncritically adhered to by many of our respondents. Regardless of the underlying philosophical assumptions, the deterrence argument is heavily undermined by the high rates of activation of suspended sentences. But again, the magistrates we spoke to showed no awareness of this and a strong shared 'common-sense' belief in the unique deterrent properties of the suspended sentence remained.

Conditional discharges and deferred sentences were said to be used to the same effect, even though magistrates were quite well aware that these options should not be used in this way. In this situation, the law was regarded as something to be subverted or, as magistrates preferred to phrase it, to be 'got round' in order to achieve the desired result. Thus one senior Justice proudly recounted how he had given a stiff fine and a conditional discharge on two concurrent charges in a recent case, contrary to the clerk's advice that this was bad sentencing policy, so that the defendant would be punished and also 'have something hanging over his head'. The objectives of deterrence and individual responsibility in these instances took precedence over the letter and spirit of the law.

Implicitly the properties ascribed to the suspended sentence and its occasional, weaker, substitutes were somewhat different from those ascribed to custodial sentences. Deterrence here was thought to be effected through individual responsibility rather then the shock of a custodial sentence. Nor was the suspended sentence referred to as a punishment in itself and clearly it could not provide either the training or the protection for the public which custodial sentences were seen to offer. This might begin to suggest that the suspended sentence had been seen as appropriate for a rather different range of cases, and indeed the cases in which magistrates felt its loss most keenly were not generally those in which a custodial sentence was being considered at all, as the following comments from two benches illustrate:

> Anything held over their heads is better than a fine.

> We need an alternative punishment now that fines are no longer viable.

The use of the suspended sentence in lieu of a fine was made quite explicit by some magistrates:

> I don't know why they took it away. It was a good deterrent, especially where the defendant doesn't have the means for a heavy financial penalty for which he may end up in prison for non-payment. The state is hard on low-income people and I've got a social conscience. I don't want them to go to prison for non-payment of fines.

It was not clear whether this magistrate's conscience was less troubled by the thought of people ending up in prison on the activation of a suspended sentence or that he was simply unaware of the 30–40 per cent likelihood that this would be the result (about a third of the suspended sentences imposed in 1984 were subsequently activated, for example: Stern 1987). Neither were these respondents, charged to uphold the law of the land, troubled by the illegality of this use of suspension in lieu of a fine, completely contrary to Section 22(2) of the powers of the Criminal Court Act 1973.

Nevertheless, a great many of the magistrates we spoke to were very conscious of the difficulties of unemployed defendants in paying fines. They looked for an alternative penalty, feeling themselves to be caught between imposing amounts small enough to be paid off within a reasonable amount of time (a year is usually considered to be the maximum) but large enough to reflect the gravity of the offence, particularly relative to the amounts imposed for motoring offences. As one Greytown magistrate explained it:

> There is a real crisis in sentencing because of unemployment. Magistrates have few options between fines and custody. We can't impose meaningful fines because people can't pay them and we don't want to use custody except as the very end of the line. There is not enough in between.

This, as well as the common-sense belief in its deterrent effect, is clearly a major reason why the loss of the suspended sentence for 17–20-year-olds is so deeply regretted by magistrates. This aspect of the Act was largely unpopular because it restricted magistrates' powers to deal with what they saw as a major practical problem of sentencing. The need to deal with this problem led to a certain amount of subversion of the law relating to other existing penalties and also structured the response to other changes in the 1982 Act.

Most obviously, the problems which many magistrates identified in using financial penalties might be expected to recur in respect of the new power to impose a compensation order as a principal disposal. Most respondents (four-fifths of eighty-two Benches) were very positive about compensation in principle, although some felt its scope to be too narrow, not allowing recompense for the sheer shock of finding one's home burgled, for example. But only half said that they used a compensation order as the chief or sole penalty and the anxieties expressed in relation to the defendants' inability to pay meaningful amounts were reiterated here. One Bench suggested that a new power to defer payment of compensation until such time as the defendant obtained work would provide some welcome flexibility. Others feared that claims are sometimes over-inflated for insurance purposes, so that the amounts involved would add injustice to defendants' inability to pay. This was one issue on which there was a considerable difference of opinion between the four courts. Yellowtown Benches were less enthusiastic about compensation: only a sixth of the respondents here thought it should be the primary penalty. In Redtown almost all the respondents expressed a willingness to use it in this way. Nevertheless, this new power did not generally seem to be viewed as a viable alternative to fining defendants and the pressure to find another alternative thus remained. It would not be surprising to find that the new powers intended as alternative to custody were used to fill this role.

Alternatives to custody?

> There is no alternative to custody. Custody is custody. All you can do is put in steps that can be taken before custody is imposed.
>
> (Magistrate, Redtown)

As explained in the first chapter, the 1982 Act built upon and strengthened Orders involving social work supervision for both juveniles and young adults, as well as extending the community service order to 16-year-olds. To some extent therefore, magistrates' views of their new powers in respect of non-custodial sentences were coloured by their previous knowledge of supervision offered by probation officers and social workers and of community service for adults.

Thus magistrates were already familiar with additional requirements in probation orders and generally they showed little awareness of the use of Schedule 11(4)(a) requirements beyond the medical or psychiatric treatment requirements previously available to them. However, half (thirty of the fifty-eight) of the Benches responding to this question approved of these powers, although only seven (12 per cent) said that they would use them in place of custody. For most, individualized additional requirements were not seen as providing a sufficient measure of either the discipline or the punishment which would put a probation order on a par with custody. Probation was still seen as basically about helping people and not tough enough for the more heavily convicted offender, even with additional requirements of this type. Requirements of a restraining or negative type were seen as unrealistic and unnecessary as well as antithetical to the helping role of probation. The only exceptions to this were a few Benches who showed a certain amount of confusion between these requirements and the conditions which can be imposed in relation to bail. More typical views of additional requirements were:

> Probation orders are there to help people. It shouldn't be an alternative to custody because it isn't punishment.

> Probation should be about helping people. If you start putting restrictions in, they're likely to get broken and it's difficult to keep help going if the probation officer has to bring them back to court.

The power to impose (4) (a) requirements appeared to have had little impact on magistrates' perceptions of what probation orders are for.

Requirements under subsection (4) (b), by contrast, were regarded with more enthusiasm. Day centre 'packages' were popular amongst those who had heard of them, with thirty-five (61 per cent) of these Benches expressing approval. Most of the critical comments related to the unavailability or inadequacy of local provision, again suggesting a positive view of the schemes and that their expansion would be welcomed by magistrates. 'Packages' were welcomed as strengthening the probation order by providing discipline and training:

> It's like Outward Bound. It's good because of the discipline.

> Anything that gets them out of bed before 9 am and out of the pub at lunchtime is good. It's a form of occupational therapy − stops them thinking about more crimes. The devil makes work for idle hands.

> It's a good variation on probation. More positive than just reporting to the probation officer once a week, especially for the unemployed. You should put in your report that there should be more day centres. There is a need for training for the unemployed. Do you know what I'd like to do? I'd like to be able to sentence people to two years of technical college!

'Packages' may have been regarded as 'one up from probation', as one magistrate described them, providing additional discipline, but this was not generally seen as sufficient to replace a custodial penalty. Some Benches were critical of the local day centre schemes on these grounds:

> It should be more like the factory, like the production line. Instead it encourages people to lay in. They don't have to be there till 9.15 and they finish at 3 and they can do what they like while they're there. There isn't enough compulsion or corrective influence. It's OK for first and second offenders who are unemployed.

What is clear from both the approving and the critical comments illustrated here is that day centres were regarded as primarily appropriate for the unemployed, at once avoiding the problems of fining those on a low income and, more positively, providing a specific form of work experience and work discipline, although not in a measure that some magistrates would like to have seen.

Similar themes of help versus discipline were apparent in magistrates' views of intermediate treatment and specified activities requirements in supervision orders for juveniles. As was noted in Chapter 2, the distinction between these two types of additions was not always clear, and which one was used seemed to depend upon the history of IT in particular areas and the availability of current 'packages'. Hence the two types of requirements are best considered together, although separate questions were put to magistrates in the interviews. Overall they viewed additional requirements as useful, for two main reasons. First, supervision orders were still seen by some magistrates as primarily welfare orientated. In Bluetown in particular, magistrates viewed additional requirements as compensatory for social deprivation. For example:

> I sometimes think IT is a bit too soft. But on my good days, when I'm feeling positive, I think it's very good. By the luck of the draw, these kids get good or bad parents. The good parents almost automatically get their kids into things, you know – like the scouts or sports or hobbies. Perhaps for this boy it will be compensation.

This was more then just *noblesse oblige*, as it also reflected the second reason why magistrates generally favoured specified activities requirements in particular. This was that magistrates were able to assume more control over what happens in supervision orders: in part they were concerned to specify the activities of the supervisor as well as the supervised, particularly in those courts where magistrates felt little confidence in local authority social workers (Harris and Webb 1987). This mistrust was well illustrated in the comment of a magistrate in Yellowtown on a sample case in which the Bench felt they had to make a choice between the care order recommended in the social enquiry report (SER) and a 'short' DC sentence. Having been informed by the social services department's court officer that a residential Community Home place would not be immediately available, they opted for the maximum DC sentence of four months:

> He'll just be lodged in [the local assessment centre] for assessment and would probably stay there and possibly be returned home. We trust Mr [the court officer]: he always tells us the truth about the availability

of places. But we are powerless in relation to the local authority. We feel we are being manipulated by the authority with this sort of recommendation. We're aware of the devious nature of the social services department.

Where magistrates believed that 'at the most, twelve months supervision would mean two interviews', as one in Bluetown told us, it is not surprising that any increase in control over this process was welcomed.

This same lack of confidence in social services departments was also apparent in the positive comments made on the new power to include a charge and control condition in a care order. The positive reception for this was hardly surprising in view of the criticisms of the 1969 Act expressed by the Magistrates' Association (see Chapter 1). However, there was also a continued concern with the discretion exercised by the local authority and a feeling that the new power would have little effect because of other pressures arising from lack of resources. Thus pressure to keep children at home was felt from SERs and in any case, as one magistrate pointed out, the Bench has no redress if supervision and care orders were not carried through properly.

Perhaps surprisingly, in view of this mistrust of social workers, there was no mention of any doubts about the frequency with which breach proceedings would be brought. In this respect at least, local authority social workers enjoyed as much confidence from the Bench as did their colleagues in the probation service in respect of additional requirements under Schedule 11, where only two Benches expressed anxiety about whether defendants would actually be brought back to court for non-compliance. More generally, however, probation officers were trusted more than social workers, as magistrates' opinions of social enquiry reports revealed (see Chapter 5).

What disturbed magistrates more about additional requirements in supervision orders was their inability to make a custodial sentence in the event of breach of the additional requirements. They were anxious that

> If the lads at [the local IT centre] found out that they couldn't be given custody for not doing the Order, they'd run amok!
>
> (Magistrate, Greytown)

The solution for some Benches was to try to ensure that 'the lads' didn't find out. Thus magistrates dealing with one of the sample cases in Yellowtown expressed considerable annoyance about a clerk who had taken his responsibility to explain matters to the defendant to include spelling out the consequences of non-compliance in full detail in open court. The Order would, they felt, be taken less seriously in consequence.

This aspect of the Act undermined the confidence of many magistrates in this disposal, but there was also the fear that additional requirements for juveniles constituted a 'soft option', lacking discipline and training:

> It would be better if it was like Outward Bound or something like that. These groups are like a knitting circle. They just sit round and discuss

> their problems. That sort of thing is probably all right for sociologists
> and people like that, but these kids just have a laugh about it and think
> it's a let off.
>
> (Magistrate, Greytown)

Not only might it be a 'soft option', but also some magistrates feared that it
could be pleasurable enough to constitute a reward for delinquency, particularly where this involved such 'treats' as professional squash lessons arranged
by the probation service.

> You have to be careful to avoid sending the child who murdered its
> parents to the orphans' Christmas party,

as one magistrate in Bluetown succinctly, if somewhat bizarrely, put it .
   Despite these reservations and despite some complaints about the inadequacy
of local provision in Yellowtown (which, although it had alternative to custody
IT schemes on offer, had not yet obtained DHSS funding at the time the fieldwork was carried out), additional requirements for juveniles were welcomed.
This was particularly so in Redtown, where some magistrates complained that
they were not able to use specified activity requirements as much as they would
have liked because, as one put it, 'you can't use it if the professionals won't
recommend it'. One reason why professionals may not make such recommendations often is the fear of tariff slippage, but in fact Redtown's magistrates were considerably more receptive towards the use of specified
activity requirements as an alternative to custody than their colleagues in other
courts. For example, one Bench here defined IT as being for

> those petty offenders who've been through the system, who've had
> everything, who've been to DC and that hasn't worked.

In Bluetown, too, the scheme offered to the court as a specified activity
requirement was viewed by some of the Bench as alternative to custody,
offering an element of training and punishment:

> It's not what they do or discuss that matters. That won't make much
> difference. It's their attendance, 90 days, 3 days a week. It's a lot. Like
> custody, they have to be somewhere.

Opinion in Bluetown was, however, divided on this point, with about half of
the Bench sharing the reservations of most magistrates in the other two courts
about the 'soft option' or else seeing this type of disposal primarily in welfare
terms. Community supervision for juveniles thus seemed to occupy a more
ambiguous position as an alternative to custody than did Schedule 11(4)(b) for
young adults. Orders with specified activities could thus be described as 'a
flexible sentence; not necessarily an alternative to custody'.
   Community service (CS) orders for 16-year-olds also occupied an ambiguous
role, according to our respondents: an ambiguity which was sustained by the
differing interpretations made by the clerks who advised the magistrates in the

sample courts. Although a few Benches felt that it was not an appropriate disposal for this age group, the majority welcomed its extended availability, with a few saying that it was more suitable for this age group than for older offenders. But only just over a quarter of the fifty-seven Benches who commented on CS said it was an alternative to custody and, as with additional requirements in supervision orders, these respondents came mostly from Redtown. Inevitably magistrates' views of the use of CS for juveniles were coloured by their perceptions of the sentence in general. Thus some regarded it as 'pathetic' and were sceptical about 'the mickey mouse work that's available', a reservation which was also expressed by magistrates who otherwise welcomed the introduction of CS into juvenile court. Yellowtown magistrates in particular were doubtful about whether CS was 'strict enough and well structured enough', fearing that it might be a 'soft option', 'rather weak', with 'not enough hard work and discipline' and 'too much like YTS' (youth training schemes for the unemployed). The impression given by some magistrates here was that they would have been happier if CS looked more like chain gang labour: 'out on the Rock [a local coastal landmark] at dawn on a cold winter morning' as one suggested. Other Benches, in all the courts, held a widely shared image of CS as being mainly about 'gardening in window boxes':

> I do wish they'd be more imaginative. I can't think of anything worse than gardening and decorating for old people,

as a Bluetown magistrate complained. Types of work were not thought to be matched very well to offenders, so that 'a six-foot navvy putting on records at an old people's home' would have been 'far happier digging a trench'. This image of CS as being about work with old people put some magistrates off using it for more serious offenders, in case the recipients of the service might be placed at risk. The urge to protect the public from the activities of offenders on CS was also fed by the circulation of a number of (probably apocryphal) stories such as the one about the theft of lead flashing from a church being decorated by a CS team in Redtown. For these kinds of reasons, many Benches, particularly in Yellowtown, would have liked much more control over the allocation of tasks:

> A list of schemes in order of severity so that we could select ones to match a particular offender at sentence.

Again, as with supervison orders, there is evidence of a reluctance to delegate power to the professionals who enforce the Orders made by the court and, as with custodial penalties, a desire to specify the sentence given as precisely as possible.

For these reasons, many magistrates said that the community service order is a disposal which must be used selectively, being 'not suitable for the violent ones' for example. Particular care was to be exercised with juveniles:

> You have to be very careful because juveniles aren't by nature very mature. They must have the right attitude.

In sum, according to a Yellowtown Bench:

> It needs to be made on an individual basis rather than as a blanket alternative to custody.

Community service thus occupied a very ambiguous status, being viewed as an alternative to custody on some occasions but not on others, which could of course have very serious implications if, for example, a panel accepting of CS as an alternative were dealing with a breach of an Order imposed by a Bench which had taken a different view.

Most commonly, CS was seen as a way of stretching out the tariff, a 'stepping stone on the way to custody', a 'useful stop-gap between the supervision order or attendance centre and custody'.

> It's a useful way of keeping the hardened offender out of DC. . . . It fills the gap, the big gap, between attendance centre and detention centre. It's used when you're considering custody,

explained a member of the Bluetown Bench. Seen as making up for the loss of flexibility with the removal of the suspended sentence, it was clear that CS was placed quite high on the tariff by some, 'a bridging last chance sentence'. If it is recalled that the suspended sentence was missed because of the difficulty in imposing heavy fines on the unemployed in particular, it is not surprising to find that community service was also seen as useful in filling that gap. For example:

> Community service orders and conditional discharges will become more important because of unemployment and the consequent difficulties over fines.

Like the Schedule 11 'packages', CS was viewed as a form of work experience for the unemployed, 'getting them involved in something and settling them into a pattern of work'. Whatever criticisms magistrates had of CS, it was welcomed as another possible solution to what was perceived as the real problem in sentencing, the middle range of cases where a large fine might be deemed inappropriate but before custody was defined as necessary. While CS and supervision orders with additional requirements were sometimes seen as alternatives to a custodial penalty (particularly in Redtown), they did not fulfil this role in any blanket kind of way and for many magistrates (particularly those in Yellowtown), indeed, the very idea of an 'alternative' was unthinkable.

The impact of the Criminal Justice Act

Most magistrates, as we have seen, did not see the Act as having altered the way in which they reached their sentencing decisions. The grounds for using custody remained the same as before, even if the formal announcement in open court conformed with the criteria in the Act. 'Alternatives' might be used as such, but seemed more likely to be used to solve other problems which magistrates identified in practical sentencing. Part of the explanation for the uneven impact of the Act may rest in the kind of mental somersault which it asked sentencers to perform: having satisfied themselves that a case is most appropriately dealt with by a custodial penalty, they are then required to go back and look for an alternative. This is not an easy path of thought: as one magistrate put it, 'it's as if you're not sure about your decision'. But this is only a part of the explanation, since it was clear that for many of our respondents, the line of reasoning required by the Act was an addendum to the actual reasoning whereby the sentencing decision was reached. In this respect, the Act was incorporated into existing patterns of decision-making.

However, changes in the structure of custodial sentences available to magistrates were welcomed on the grounds that they increased available powers, ensuring that custodial sentences would be imposed where the Bench thought it necessary and without the risk of the judges taking an alternative course of action. Conversely those parts of the Act which meant a curtailment of power were criticized (i.e. the loss of the suspended sentence) as meaning not only a diminution of power but also of a flexibility which would allow the 'right' result to be reached. The new 'alternatives' were welcomed first, as increasing flexibility in the middle range of cases where fining was seen as difficult, and second, as providing magistrates with more control over the professionals who administer the Orders of the court. Only in Redtown were they really seen as alternative to custody. Power, flexibility and control were thus the keywords in magistrates' responses to the changes brought by the CJA: the legislative framework was ignored, subverted or welcomed in so far as it accentuated these capacities. The purposes to which power, flexibility and control were put are not given by the legislation itself and also those purposes apparently differed between the four PSDs, as the sentencing patterns discussed in Chapter 2 indicated. This suggests magistrates' definitions of the sentencing task, and particularly any differences between the four PSDs, need to be considered further.

Philosophies of sentencing

> Magistrates are not concerned with the philosophy of sentencing. Though at the end of the day they may do something everyone would applaud, they may not be able to articulate why they have done so.
>
> (Chairman, Yellowtown Bench)

Many of our respondents would probably have considered it unreasonable to expect a largely lay magistracy to be *au fait* with debates within penal philosophy, regarding their own practical experience as of more value than penological theory or research. Nevertheless, the competing and contradictory claims of retribution, rehabilitation deterrence, incapacitation and restitution (Packer 1969; Walker 1972; Gross and Von Hirsch 1981) have, in some way, to be resolved at the practical level.

Although previous research has cast doubt on the extent to which, in themselves, individually held philosophies explain sentencing behaviour (Hogarth 1971), it might have been possible to identify differences in broad philosophical outlook between the four PSDs. As one method of looking at this aspect of sentencing practice, we asked magistrates about what they hoped the penalties imposed in the sample cases would achieve. The hopes which were expressed were quite diverse, but overall there was an emphasis on the defendant and the defendant's needs, rather than on the victim or on society at large. In most cases, the main hope was that the defendant would in some way benefit from the sentence, although these were not necessarily ways that might readily have been recognized by defendants as being in their own interest! Although Yellowtown juvenile Bench and Bluetown adult court expressed retributive objectives more often than their counterparts and there were differences within each PSD, the differences were not very marked. None of the courts adhered exclusively to a single objective or philosophy. Not surprisingly, the classic penal philosophies rarely appeared in pure form in what magistrates said about individual cases: most of their declared hopes were more hybrid in nature. No clear differences of philosophical approach could be found which might explain the disparities in sentencing between the PSDs. Even if marked differences had been apparent, a further difficulty in explaining sentencing disparities between the courts in terms of differences in penal philosophy was that there was no simple relation between objectives and the sentence chosen, although some relationships could be discerned.

Individual deterrence

Magistrates generally were keen on what would, in more formal terms, be described as individual deterrence. Thus the most commonly expressed hope overall, but particularly for the young adults, was that the defendant would be stopped in his/her tracks (mentioned in seventy-nine cases: 35 per cent). This type of sentiment was expressed in comments such as:

> He's in danger of becoming a very sophisticated young criminal. Innocent looking but he expects all his own way. He's already having private tuition because he doesn't like school. We hope a short sharp shock will pull him up.
>
> (Greytown)

> He's on the edge, on the brink and this sentence [6 months YC for S.47 assault, burglary and theft] might be enough to stop him.
>
> (Yellowtown)

> It will hit his pocket and I hope he thinks twice before doing anything so stupid again.
>
> (Yellowtown)

Although expressed in terms of what the defendant 'needs', there was also quite a punitive aspect to this objective. A short DC sentence might well have seemed an obvious vehicle for it and indeed over half of these cases did result in a custodial penalty. However, these included YC sentences of six months as well as the 'short sharp shock', and almost as many defendants received non-custodial penalties.

Rehabilitation

Rehabilitation through more direct help for the defendant was also fairly high on the agenda for the sample as a whole. Magistrates hoped that the defendant would get help in just over a quarter of the sample cases (28 per cent) and a sentence involving social work supervision, which might seem the logical outcome, was made in just over half (34: 53 per cent) of these. For example, a Greytown Bench, which had made a probation order on a 19-year-old for offences of handling and deception while subject to a deferred sentence, hoped that:

> She'll get her housing and other problems sorted out with help. She has committed further offences while on probation and on a deferred sentence, but we hope she's beginning to sort her life out.

But in almost as many 'help' cases, other types of penalties were seen as appropriate. As another Greytown Bench explained a sentence of three months' DC plus a compensation order of £100 on a 15-year-old:

> It doesn't mean we're not trying to help him. There are many caring and capable people working in detention centres who will try and help the lad. It's not only [the local IT centre] where they can help him. It's not like sending him to [the local prison]. He will get help and training in DC.

Magistrates found it quite possible to justify a wide range of sentences on the basis of helping the defendant. Indeed Yellowtown magistrates sometimes made YC sentences on the basis that this would help defendants break their patterns of heroin use. However, a more specific form of the rehabilitative ideal, for which custody was not seen as an appropriate means, was expressed in a small number of cases (11: 5 per cent) in which the hope was that the defendant's time would be occupied and work experience gained and 'alternatives' to custody, in the shape of CS or Schedule 11 packages, were used.

Retribution

In contrast with rehabilitative aims, retributive aims might be expected to result in custodial sentencing more often. Retribution was an objective in a quarter of the sample cases (58: 26 per cent), but appeared to be particularly important to magistrates in Bluetown's adult court, where it was mentioned in over half of the cases. Typical of the responses of this type were comments such as:

> It's a punitive sentence [YC 6 months]. I don't expect it to do him any good.
>
> (Greytown)

> Oh, I don't believe it will do them any good [YC 6 months]. I don't go along with all this prison for rehabilitation nonsense.
>
> (Bluetown)

But in almost half of the cases in which magistrates wanted to exact retribution (28: 48 per cent) a non-custodial penalty was seen as sufficient.

General deterrence

Hopes which were concerned more with society at large than with the individual defendant were not mentioned very often. Although deterrence was an important objective, it did not usually take the form of general deterrence. Yellowtown and Bluetown Benches mentioned the latter slightly more often than their colleagues elsewhere, but the principle was articulated in its purest form by a magistrate in Redtown who hoped that the sentence just given would

> allow a few people to sleep easy in their beds. This lad is a total menace in the locality. I hope it sets an example in the area – it's ridden with crime. The sentence will go round the village. There are a lot of people on the edge of crime. This sentence may make them step back from the edge.

Not only was this not a widely shared aim in the sentencing of the sample cases, being mentioned in only twenty (9 per cent), but it did not fit neatly with a single type of sentence either, although a custodial penalty was given in three-fifths of this group of cases.

Incapacitation

Similarly incapacitation or containment was mentioned in very few cases and where it did occur, it was a very secondary consideration: 'at least it will keep him off the streets for a few weeks' was an addendum rather than a major hope. This is interesting in view of the fact that magistrates did frequently give the protection of the public as a publicly stated reason for imposing custody (see Chapter 5). Nor did magistrates set very much store on the community in general in terms of restitution, despite the number of community service orders imposed in the sample cases.

Non-specific aims

Many of the hopes which magistrates voiced did not, however, fit easily into any classic typology. Around a fifth of the Benches interviewed (42: 19 per cent) entertained no specific hopes, had not thought about the issue or did not really expect the sentence to achieve anything in that they thought the defendant would re-offend. Others expressed hopes of a rather general, even vague, nature: that 'the defendant will keep out of trouble' (43: 19 per cent) or would be given 'a push in the right direction', especially at what was seen as the crucial transition from childhood to adulthood (33: 15 per cent). The following comments illustrate these types of responses:

> We hope he'll find happiness in his foster placement and keep out of trouble.
>
> (Bluetown)

> We hope he'll learn something about how to avoid further trouble and what he stands to lose by further offences.
>
> (Redtown)

> He is a young man at the crossroads, on the verge of full adulthood. It's up to him to choose which way he'll go. We hope the probation officer will help him straighten himself out.
>
> (Greytown)

These more general sentencing aims were not usually associated with a custodial sentence.

Other objectives were more specific, but encompassed several mixed aims. For example the hope that the defendant would experience discipline could be read as reformation through an unpleasant experience, as purely punitive, as a form of deterrence or as a combination of these:

> It's punishment but also rehabilitation through the discipline and regimentation of [4 months'] DC.
>
> (Yellowtown)

> He needs discipline; needs to learn self-discipline so that he becomes responsible for his own actions [9 weeks' DC].
>
> (Redtown)

> Regular discipline will be good for his work. It might make him realize that there are rules [24 hours attendance centre].
>
> (Bluetown)

This general experience of discipline was seen as most appropriately provided by a non-custodial penalty in the majority of cases but was also attached to nearly a quarter of the custodial penalties imposed. Other hopes included that the defendant would break his/her drugs habit, which was mentioned most often in Yellowtown's adult court, that the defendant would acquire literacy skills and the 'real hope' of one Greytown Bench for a woman of 20 and her co-defendant aged 22:

> The real hope with girls like these, presentable girls, is that they'll find a man to take them on, look after them and their children.
>
> (Greytown)

Perhaps fortunately for these two defendants, marriage was not one of the alternatives to custody created by the CJA! A custodial penalty was imposed in seven (41 per cent) of the cases in which this residual category of 'other' hopes was expressed.

Despite the fact that there were some differences in penal ideology between the courts, these were not clear and it was difficult to predict the type of sentence which would follow on from the adoption of any single penal objective, even where this could be identified. This is not surprising since even where sentencers may personally adhere to one particular type of penal philosophy, their personal views are not expressed in a vacuum but only within specific social and organizational, as well as legal, contexts (cf Hogarth 1971). One consideration which has been identified as of potential significance here is the nature of the local community and magistrates' involvement in it (Hood 1962; Burney 1979). In order to examine this issue, we asked magistrates about their perception of their role and the pressures and expectations they experienced in it.

The role of the magistrate

> You've got the Court of Appeal telling you it's a court of law and you think it's a people's court, but then people don't like what you do either.
>
> (Magistrate, Greytown)

Like many others, magistrates see themselves as a maligned and misunderstood group, attempting, within the legal framework, to balance various interests, but actually pleasing no one. The magistrate's task was most commonly defined as the maintenance of a balance between the often competing interests of the defendant and the public (37 of the Benches responding to this question: 27 per cent). But the defendant's side of this equation was mentioned far less often and then mostly by Greytown Benches. The responses from this court were more varied than those in the other courts and included references to the necessity for impartiality between the police and the defendant in the conduct of trials, and a differentiation between juvenile court (where more stress can be put on the defendant's needs) and adult court. The issue of balance, although very high on the agenda, was expressed in a rather different way in Redtown, where magistrates felt that they had to keep a balance between sections of the community. Justices here spoke of the pressure:

> To respond to political crimes in a fair and even-handed way.

> Many of my friends are miners and I find it hard to pass harsh sentences because I think it might be my friends who are sitting at the back of the court.

In the other courts, there was a strong feeling that magistrates should look to the protection of the public. Yellowtown magistrates in particular emphasized this, giving it the same sort of importance as the idea of maintaining balance.

'Our prime function is to protect the public' was a declaration made by more than one Bench here and this was a view shared by colleagues in Bluetown's adult court.

Interestingly, the courts in which this emphasis on the protection of the public was greatest were those with the higher custody rates and those which voiced more retributive objectives. They were also the courts where magistrates felt most heavily pressured by public opinion about crime: 'We're representing the man in the street' was the definition of his role offered by a Yellowtown JP. 'It's what society expects. There would have been an outcry if we had done anything else', explained another in relation to a six-month YC sentence for a serious wounding. Magistrates in these courts certainly believed that the public considered them too lenient. Although the Benches we interviewed may have been right in believing that the public support harsher sentences for specific offences such as burglary, evidence from the British Crime Survey has shown that people generally hold this view in the belief that sentencing levels are lower than they actually are: actual sentencing levels are broadly in accordance with public expectation (e.g. Hough and Moxon 1988). Magistrates' claims to represent public opinion cannot be taken at simple face value.

Magistrates themselves sometimes recognized that the 'public opinion' they claimed to represent is not a simple phenomenon. Thus they felt free to depart from it in some cases on the grounds that the public do not have the full facts:

> People always complain to you about the differences but they use press reports which are no good because they don't tell you if the bloke's got a record or shows remorse.
>
> (Yellowtown)

Public opinion was also considered to be 'distorted' by press misrepresentation of sentencing decisions and this, again, was a particular complaint of Yellowtown's juvenile and Bluetown's adult panel, the courts which placed most emphasis on public opinion as a pressure on sentencing practice. The claim to represent the public thus appeared to have no substantial foundation in the reality of public expectations and in any case these could be readily overridden on the grounds that the public had been misled by the media. 'Public opinion' thus seemed to operate more as a justification for a particular pattern of sentencing than to constitute an explanation for it. 'Public opinion' was no more defined by the public than the 'defendant's interest' was defined by the defendant: both were constructed by sentencers.

What passes under the guise of public opinion may well be the opinion of a particular social group. The suggestion made by Ashworth *et al.* (1984), that judges' understandings of public opinion may be coloured by the narrow social class composition of the judiciary, would also be valid, to a lesser degree, in respect of the magistracy (Baldwin 1976; Burney 1979; Kapardis 1981). This was also borne out in what some of our respondents indicated about how public opinion made itself felt: from what some said, it seemed that its main expression was what their friends said over dinner! Ashworth *et al.* also suggested the operation of what Fitzmaurice and Pease (1986) have identified as a manifestation in sentencing practice of a more general psychological effect, 'false consensus bias', from which magistrates would clearly be no more immune than judges. This is the tendency for people to equate 'public' opinion with their own, to assume that their own views are generally held by all 'right-thinking people'.

This was an assumption which these JPs clearly seemed to make. However the balance between various interests was drawn, magistrates believed that they had got it more or less right across the Bench as a whole, although individuals or small coteries might be referred to as 'Attila the Hun', 'the do-gooders' or 'the hang 'em and flog 'em brigade' (and thus, in effect, be dismissed as extremists). Questions about how magistrates thought the sentencing patterns in their own court compared with other courts often elicited responses such as 'it's a fair Bench', a 'good Bench', a 'representative cross-section of opinion' rather than the anticipated responses in terms of leniency/severity. Only one panel viewed their Bench as tending to use custody quite a lot. About a quarter (25 Benches: 28 per cent) saw themselves as liberal in their sentencing, but this included one of the more punitive of the Yellowtown magistrates who described herself and her colleagues as 'a bunch of softies'! Just over half of the Greytown magistrates also felt theirs was a lenient Bench, but this description usually was made in a critical spirit and several of these comments were made in direct criticism of the court's Stipendiary Magistrate:

> I can't speak for the Bench as a whole. Some members are very lenient, and not just the lay magistrates. The Stip. we've got now is useless and some people think that he's responsible for the increase in crime in Greytown. Some magistrates say they'd never sent anyone down. It's just stupid to think like that.

The vast majority of Benches, however, saw themselves as 'middle of the road', neither lenient nor ready to use custody a lot, achieving a fair balance between the interests of the public and those of the defendant. The problem is that what constituted 'a fair balance' was not defined in the same way in the four PSDs: 'middle-of-the-road' sentencing had substantially different meanings. The notion of 'false consensus bias' is helpful only up to a point in explaining this: while it may explaim the mechanisms whereby particular sentencing practices can be justified and sustained, it does not explain the substantive character of those practices. The apparent contradiction between the view of each Bench that it had 'got it right' and the variations in sentencing patterns between the courts needs further explanation. It could, of course, be that there is no contradiction once the particular character of local crime is taken into account: that is the balance could be defined as 'right' in the context of local conditions.

Local crime and local justice

There are two immediate problems with this type of explanation, however.

First, Chapter 2 showed that the patterns of crime dealt with by the four PSDs were not substantially different. Second, magistrates did not actually reason in the way suggested at the end of the last section. Their satisfaction with their own sentencing patterns was largely based upon ignorance rather than a reasoned account of the specific nature of crime in the locality. Magistrates generally placed little value on inter-Bench consistency and showed minimal awareness of sentencing patterns outside their own PSD (cf Tarling 1979). The only comparisons which were made were with immediately neighbouring courts or related to the higher levels of fines for motoring offences which might be imposed 'in Surrey', the archetypical stockbroker belt. Nevertheless, the four Benches did have quite different views about the nature and level of crime in their locality and these different perceptions did seem to be linked with the use of custody in the courts.

A fifth of the ninety Benches who commented on the nature of local crime believed it to be mostly of a serious nature, with magistrates in all the courts expressing particular concern about burglary:

> Burglary is the offence we all dread because it can happen to us.
>
> (Magistrate, Yellowtown)

> I go home and look to see the marks round the door, see if it's open. We all know someone who has been burgled.
>
> (Magistrate, Greytown)

Magistrates in Yellowtown were particularly disturbed by burglary because of its relationship to drug use. The drugs factor was seen as a significant element in Yellowtown's crime (cf Parker *et al.* 1988 for a study in the same region) and the 'epidemic' of heroin use would, we were told, 'ravage the countryside'. Yellowtown magistrates believed that local crime was increasing at an alarming rate both numerically ('the only thriving industry on Merseyside') and geographically ('In the old days all the crime was at the north end; now it's all over the borough') as well as becoming more serious ('It used to be stealing chocolate biscuits from Woolworth's and now it's burglary'). It was clear that magistrates in Yellowtown felt themselves to be much more under threat from crime than their colleagues elsewhere. Bluetown was the most similar to Yellowtown, with Benches here also believing that they had a problem with serious crime and that crime, particularly burglary, was increasing. They were divided on how slight or substantial the increase was, with some feeling that Bluetown had less of a problem than other neighbouring courts. But generally there was much less of a sense of threat in this PSD. Unlike their colleagues in Yellowtown, Bluetown magistrates believed that crime was heavily, and perhaps safely, concentrated in one part of the PSD, an 'overspill' council estate. As one respondent put it:

> Most of the crime – and the work of the Care Court – comes from there. It's all so much more visible with the working classes: we cover it up more effectively.

In Greytown, opinion was much more divided. A high proportion of Benches here believed crime in the area to be mostly of a serious nature and shared Yellowtown's sense of threat ('There's a war on and we're losing'). But nearly a quarter said they deal mostly with what one described as 'the pestilential nuisance of small time crime related to poverty and unemployment'. Redtown Justices were the least alarmed. They also saw local crime as serious, but over half of the respondents here saw the miners' dispute as a significant feature at the time of the research, mentioning the increase in street disturbances and picket line offences but also an increase in more 'routine' crime such as burglary. Crime was seen as increasing, but only slightly and was thought still to be at a lower level than in neighbouring areas.

There were then quite major differences in how local crime was *perceived*. These different perceptions seem to owe more to the social characteristics of the areas in question than to objective differences in the extent or character of their crime (cf Chapter 2). Yellowtown and Bluetown were both socially divided communities, but Yellowtown's middle classes, without the physical separation between themselves and the poorer sections of the community characteristic of Bluetown, felt much more under threat. It might also be that their strong sense of a recent sharp escalation in crime contributed to their more punitive attitudes to the new young criminals appearing in their juvenile court. In Bluetown, such fears were ameliorated by the welfarist sense of *noblesse oblige* apparent in magistrates' comments about supervision orders, referred to earlier. Some of Greytown's Benches took a similar view to those of Yellowtown and the sentencing here might well have been more severe had it not been for the presence of the Stipendiary Magistrate and of a number of magistrates whose perceptions were more in line with Redtown's view of crime. Redtown magistrates' view that crime was not reaching threatening proportions, perhaps accompanied by a sense that it could be dealt with within a strong and relatively homogeneous community, meant that they were much more willing to look for alternatives to custody.

This suggests that differences in perceptions of local crime are important in explaining sentencing variation. The question which arises, however, is how these perceptions and beliefs and the sentencing patterns associated with them are sustained. One possible explanation might be the existence of locally adopted Bench policies, such as clampdowns on specific types of offence. Our respondents did indeed refer to such policies. Thus Yellowtown magistrates said that there was a policy of thinking about custody in cases involving drug-related burglary, while Greytown respondents considered the taking of motor vehicles as a particular problem. Bluetown Benches were concerned about inter-school gang fights and in Redtown the Bench felt it had to clamp down on 'town centre trouble'. But it was also clear that these policies were not always adhered to and that actually neither their own nor their colleagues' previous sentencing decisions had very much impact on magistrates' sentencing of the sample cases. Intra-Bench consistency was no more of an issue for most magistrates than inter-court consistency.

A few of the panels interviewed (11: 12 per cent), particularly those in Yellowtown, said that they thought their Bench was already consistent. But a number of Yellowtown magistrates, perhaps because of the size of the Bench there, said that they did not know enough about their colleagues' sentencing to answer or said that they had not given the matter any thought. The vast majority of magistrates in all the courts did not believe that they were consistent and only a minority (6: 6 per cent) thought that they should be. Consistency was seen as a salient issue only in respect of the fines imposed on motoring offenders. The largest single response, from almost a third of the Benches interviewed, was that some framework of consistency was needed but in the end it is more important to judge every case on its merits. Altogether, three-fifths of the respondents stressed the individuality of each case. The following were typical replies:

> Magistrates get a lot of criticism for not being consistent. Consistency is important but it never ought to be a case of looking up the offence in a book in order to fix the penalty.
>
> (Magistrate, Redtown)

> It's rough and ready justice I suppose, but you can't standardize it without making it so rigid it becomes unfair.
>
> (Magistrate, Greytown)

> Sentencing is a very personal thing. It has to be directed to the individual.
>
> (Magistrate, Yellowtown)

Consistency need not, of course, imply rigidity (Bottomley 1973), but this equation was one which many magistrates seemed to make. Decisions taken by colleagues even in their own court were largely discounted.

At first sight, this seems to contradict the suggestions made by previous researchers who have concluded that membership of a particular Bench with its own sentencing traditions may be an important influence on magistrates. However, the responses given to another of our questions suggest something of how this 'Bench effect' (Tarling 1979) may operate. When asked about the impact of their own sentencing decisions in previous cases similar to those in the research sample, the vast majority of Benches said that precedent, in this sense, had not been an influence. In part, the explanations which they gave were in terms of an ideology of professional detachment. As one magistrate put it:

> When I first started as a magistrate, I used to cry over some cases, but I learned not to worry. You concentrate in court and then forget about it.
>
> (Magistrate, Greytown)

Alongside this went a belief that sentencing is a matter of experience. Previous cases were not important as overt reference points, but rather as an 'accumulated wisdom', 'unconsciously' working on current cases. As one new magistrate in Yellowtown told us, 'You can't really learn about the application of penalties to particular cases from training; it's the sort of thing you get from more experienced colleagues' (cf Chambers 1982). This suggests that senior magistrates can exert a considerable influence on junior colleagues (cf Burney 1979; also see Chapter 5) and this may be the mechanism whereby the 'sentencing culture' of a particular court is maintained. But it also, more fundamentally, suggests the prevalence of a specific view of the sentencing task as an art, an aesthetic beyond rational exegesis.

The craft of the sentencer

This conception of sentencing is explored further in subsequent chapters, but it is already clear that it is a markedly different view from the rationality of legal thinking implied in the oath to uphold the law of the land without fear or favour. Rather than determining the sentencing process, the legal framework operates as a resource for the achievement of other objectives (cf Bittner 1967) and thus, conversely, on occasion, as a handicap which has to be overcome in order for those objectives to be met. This explains why elements of the CJA which increased sentencing powers were welcomed (especially in relation to custody), while other elements which removed flexibility (notably the loss of the suspended sentence for 17–20-year-olds) were much regretted. The new powers in respect of custody were welcomed as allowing magistrates to ensure that custody was used where it was 'really necessary', allowing magisterial 'common sense' to prevail over what was considered to be judicial unreliability. For many magistrates, custody, like other penalties, was considered to have its own unique qualities for which there is no substitute. The new 'alternatives' to custody seem largely to have been welcomed as a resource for dealing with what magistrates saw as an effective limitation on the use of the fine, arising from high unemployment, rather than as substitutes for incarceration. The Act thus received a mixed response according to whether it extended or restricted the power, control and flexibility regarded as necessary to deal properly with the pragmatic problems of sentencing, of matching penalty to offence and offender.

The appropriateness of particular penalties in individual cases, like the objectives of sentencing more generally, were defined neither by law, by penological research nor penal philosophy. Magistrates saw themselves as striving for a balance between public interests and those of individual defendants, but the nature of those interests was not actually defined by either the public or by defendants. The substance of those interests as well as the balance between them is defined by the magistrates. Despite the differences in sentencing produced by the balance reached in the four PSDs, most magistrates were convinced that their Bench had got it right. This confidence was largely sustained in ignorance of how other Benches sentence and, in many cases, ignorance of how other panels in the same Bench sentence. Nor was it sustained by a knowledge of the specific nature of local crime patterns in comparison to other areas or to national figures. However, magistrates' *perceptions* of local crime, and specifically the extent to which they felt threatened by a rising tide of crime, did seem to be linked with the patterns of custodial sentencing. These patterns did not seem to follow from the consistent implementation of local Bench policies, however: indeed, consistency was very often rejected as equivalent to rigidity. Sentencing patterns seem rather to be produced and reproduced through a process akin to 'professional socialization', through watching more experienced magistrates at work in individual cases. At this level too, sentencing is a matter of professional pragmatics, the 'common sense' of the experienced practitioner applied to the individual case.

Magistrates' views of the CJA thus indicated more about how they perceived the sentencing task than about the substantive nature of sentencing options. Their definition of this task as one of judging what is appropriate in the individual case means that the process of decision making in the sample cases is a central concern. We look at this process in more detail in the next chapter.

Notes

1 The number of Benches responding to each of the general questions in the interview schedule varied. The reasons for this, as explained in Chapter 3, were that when the full interview could not be carried out, priority was given to questions about the specific sample case.
2 It would seem from the research carried out by Asworth *et al.* (1984) that suspicions of leniency between the magistracy and the judiciary are reciprocal!

5 True believers:
the professional ideology
of the lay magistrate

Theory or policy of sentencing must be regarded with suspicion. Every case, like each finger print, is different, and should, so far as possible, be approached without preconceptions of any kind.

(Bartle 1985: 30)

In the last chapter we showed that magistrates believe that general legal or other principles cannot govern sentencing, unmediated by the circumstances of each individual case. An appropriate disposal can be arrived at only once the circumstances of the particular case are known and understood. Sentencers are, however, heavily dependent on information provided by others in order to arrive at an understanding of the individual case.

Generally magistrates have no knowledge of the case prior to the actual court session. On beginning the sentencing process for a specific case, their first impressions stem from the allegations on the charge sheet and the appearance of the defendant who is brought to stand before them, perhaps accompanied to court by friends or family. The details of the offence are filled out by the prosecution, at which point the case may begin to sound more or less serious than it appeared on the court list. The number and type of previous convictions will be shown on the defendant's antecedent record. If the defendant is legally represented, a plea in mitigation on the defendant's behalf may give a different version of the offence and perhaps some information on the defendant's social situation. Other information on the offender's social circumstances and on the offence may come in a social enquiry report (SER), along perhaps with an assessment of the likely effects of a particular penalty being imposed and a recommendation for an appropriate disposal. There may also be other reports, from school in the case of juveniles, or medical or psychiatric reports. Magistrates have then to weigh all these factors, perhaps advised by their clerk, in the light of their own philosophies and perceptions of their role and arrive at a choice of sentence.

Clearly they are expected to absorb and assess a great deal of information within a very short space of time. Our objective in what follows is not to describe and interpret courtroom interaction as such (e.g. Carlen 1976) but to elucidate magistrates' perspectives on it. We therefore consider what happens when the 'common sense' of the magistracy meets not only the particular defendant but also the various, possibly conflicting, professional perspectives on the case held by other courtroom actors. Since many of these participants have an interest in influencing the Bench towards a particular kind of outcome, how do magistrates sift and evaluate the information presented to them?

Influences on sentencing

One approach to this question is to look at which factors influenced the magistrates' sentencing decision. The most frequently mentioned factors mentioned by the Benches dealing with the sample cases are shown for each court in Table 5.1. Some differences between the four PSDs are evident from the table, for example, that the Greytown takes a more straightforwardly tariff orientation while factors related to local problems were reported to be more influential in Yellowtown adult court, reflecting the concern with drug-related crime, noted in Chapter 4. However, there is a broad similarity between the courts in the emphasis placed on certain factors. As Table 5.1 shows, the most frequently mentioned influences in all the courts were SERs (mentioned in 79 per cent of the cases in which they were available) and school reports (76 per cent of the cases in which they were available) on the one hand, and, on the other, magistrates' own assessments of both the defendant's personality (158: 68 per cent of cases) and his or her propensity to commit further offences (125: 54 per cent). Seriousness of offence was, as might have been expected, an important influence (148: 64 per cent), but antecedent record (95: 41 per cent) and protection of the public (81: 31 per cent) were mentioned much less frequently. Generally, then, the criteria on the use of custody set down in the CJA were less important than the inputs from reports and from magistrates' own constructions of the defendant's character. Inputs from other court professionals, particularly defence lawyers and, to a lesser extent, the prosecution, were also more important than the defendant's previous record or the need to protect the public.

The pattern shown by this analysis of which factors were said to have influenced the sentencing of the sample cases thus appears to confirm magistrates' claims that the circumstances of the individual case are important. Factors related to the need to ensure Bench consistency and to reflect public opinion or the need to protect the public seemed generally to have had less influence.

The same pattern was apparent when the influence of the various factors was analysed not simply in terms of frequency but in terms of relative weighting. In order to analyse the strength of the different potential influences, a distinction was made between 'major' influences, that is factors which were described by the magistrates in that way or which were said to have led to a more or less severe disposal, and 'minor' influences, that is factors which, though discussed and weighed, were said to have had a much smaller or 'neutral' effect. The results of

Table 5.1

Most frequently mentioned influences on sentencing

Juveniles

Yellowtown	%	Redtown	%	Greytown	%	Bluetown	%
SER[a]	93	Moral assessment	90	SER	73	SER	87
School report[b]	86	SER	83	Seriousness of offence	70	School report	87
Seriousness of offence	53	Risk of further offending	80	School report	50	Moral assessment	87
Antecedent record	50	School report	74	Moral assessment	50	Risk of further offences	87
Moral assessment[c]	47	Seriousness of offence	70	Antecedent record	47	Defence	83

Young adults

Yellowtown	%	Redtown	%	Greytown	%	Bluetown	%
Moral assessment	66	SER	91	SER	67	Defence	97
SER	62	Prosecution	91	Seriousness of offence	53	Moral assessment	93
Seriousness of offence	38	Moral assessment	79	Antecedent record	47	Prosecution	93
Defence[d]		Seriousness of offence	79	Moral assessment	33	Risk of further offences	93
Risk of further offences	} 34						
Protection of public							
Drug-related offending							

All juveniles	%	All young adults	%	All cases	%
SER	83	SER	77	SER	79
School report	76	Moral assessment	67	School report	76
Moral assessment	68	Seriousness of offence	63	Moral assessment	68
Seriousness of offence	64	Defence	60	Seriousness of offence	64
Risk of further offences	56	Risk of further offences	51	Defence	55

Notes: [a] % is expressed as a proportion of cases in which a school report was available.
[b] % is expressed as a proportion of cases in which a SER was available.
[c] The Bench's assessment of the defendant's character.
[d] % is expressed as a proportion of cases in which the defendant was legally represented.

this analysis are shown in Table 5.2. Again there are some variations between the courts, with Greytown's stress on antecedent record adding further force to the suggestion that this court tended to go for tariff sentencing, an approach which, although on a shorter tariff, was also evident in Yellowtown's juvenile court. In general, however, several of the most frequently mentioned factors (as shown in Table 5.1) were also the most important 'major' influences.

Reports have a very strong influence, and a particularly interesting and important finding is that school reports emerged as the most important influence on sentencing in percentage terms. They were mentioned as a 'major' influence in almost two-thirds of the cases in which they were available. For juvenile defendants, then, school reports assumed great significance. While reports were influential, magistrates also appeared to give much the same weight to their own assessments of the defendant. Antecedent record and the protection of the public seem to have had a less decisive effect in the cases where they were influential factors. Rather surprisingly, this was also true of the seriousness of the offence which was referred to as a 'major' influence on the sentencing of only 8 per cent of the sample cases. This was the only exception to the general rule that the most frequently mentioned factors were also the strongest influences. It may be that respondents did not mention this factor so often because they took it as axiomatic and too 'obvious' to mention: seriousness of offence was mentioned more frequently when Benches were asked to summarize their reasons for choosing the specific sentence given, as we shall see later. Possibly, 'influences' on sentencing were discussed from a 'baseline' of a penalty which had already suggested itself to the Bench on the basis of the type of offence. While the influence of the nature of the offence, and possibly also other factors may be underestimated in this analysis, it is quite clear that reports and magistrates' own assessments were important factors in sentencing.

Another problem, related to the possibility that the influences examined here were effective only after a basic decision had already been reached, is that the substantive nature of each influence is difficult to determine. The various 'major' factors could lead to either a more or less severe outcome. Whether any individual factor has one effect rather than another is a function not only of the factor itself but also of the situation in which it operates. Thus, for example, a Bench that readily thinks of custody offers more scope for being influenced away from this 'remedy' than one which is inclined to less severe penalties from the beginning. Although problematic, the results of an analysis of how the various factors influenced the sentencers in the sample cases are shown in Table 5.3. It is interesting to note that the factors which magistrates said had most influence were often those which led them to consider a lower tariff penalty. SERs, magistrates' own assessment of the defendant, and, unsurprisingly, the defence lawyers' pleas in mitigation all had this effect in many cases. However, the impact of these factors was not consistent. Thus magistrates' views of the defendants' character also resulted in a higher tariff penalty in a quarter of the cases. Rather surprisingly, Table 5.3 shows that the factors which are supposed

Table 5.2

Most frequently mentioned major influences on sentencing

Juveniles

Yellowtown	%	Redtown	%	Greytown	%	Bluetown	%
School report[a]	79	Moral assessment	80	SER	60	Risk of further offences	70
SER[b]	66	Risk of further offences	67	Moral assessment	50	Moral assessment	67
Moral assessment[c]	40	School report	63	Defence	30	SER	60
Risk of further offences	37	SER	62	Other	30	School report	59
Defence[d]	26	Prosecution	57	School report	25	Defence	45

Young adults

Yellowtown	%	Redtown	%	Greytown	%	Bluetown	%
Moral assessment	66	Prosecution	83	Moral assessment	67	Risk of further offences	80
SER	62	Risk of further offences	80	SER	50	SER	46
Risk of further offences	34	SER	71	Other	27	Prosecution	43
Defence	23	Moral assessment	67	Defence	21	Moral assessment	33
Other	17	Clerk	17	Antecedent record / Prosecution	10	Defence	30

All juveniles	%	All young adults	%	All cases	%
School report	63	Moral assessment	70	School report	63
SER	61	SER	56	SER	58
Moral assessment	59	Risk of further offences	48	Moral assessment	57
Risk of further offences	47	Prosecution	35	Risk of further offences	47
Defence	30	Defence	22	Prosecution	32
				Defence	26

Notes: [a] % is expressed as a proportion of cases in which a school report was available.
[b] % is expressed as a proportion of cases in which a SER was available.
[c] The Bench's assessment of the defendant's character.
[d] % is expressed as a proportion of cases in which the defendant was legally represented.

to be the most welfare orientated were in fact also frequently mentioned as influences 'up tariff'. A third of the school reports presented on the sample cases had this effect, a disturbingly high proportion (Sumner *et al.* 1988; NACRO 1988a). A further and equally disturbing finding was that SERs were referred to as having the same effect in thirty-three (14 per cent) cases and that the percentage for juveniles (17 per cent) was higher than for young adults (12 per cent). This effect of SERs was noticeably more marked in Yellowtown. The effect of reports on the severity of the outcome of the case does, of course, need to be considered alongside an analysis of content and we consider the substance of the reports presented in the sample cases in Chapters 7 and 8.

There are some problems with interpreting the references which magistrates made to the various possible influences on their sentencing decisions, but it seems from this analysis that they were strongly influenced by the information which they received in court, particularly from reports. But magistrates clearly did not take these inputs at face value. Their own judgements about the defendant were an important influence on the outcome of the case. Just how significant these judgements were is even more apparent from the comments which Benches made about the various types of information presented to them in court. Some of this information was clearly considered to be irrelevant, unreliable or, indeed, misleading to sentencers trying to arrive at an appropriate result.

Subjective knowledge: social enquiry reports

SERs provide a useful starting-point since the comments made about SERs are also very illuminating of how magistrates more generally sift and sort the information which they receive. Despite the fact that SERs were so often referred to as a key influence on the sentencing of the sample cases, it was clear that they were also used with caution. Some Benches considered that the amount of 'irrelevant' information made SERs pretty useless:

> There's a lot of silly twaddle in SERs and there are too many of them. I don't want to know where they were born or at what age they went to school. I want to know what can be done for them.
>
> (Greytown)

Benches like this one will no doubt welcome change in SER preparation in line with recent Home Office guidelines (Home Office 1986). Others, however, considered a focus on the defendant's 'background' to be of more importance than the recommendations contained in the reports. Many magistrates were critical of recommendations in SERs and quite resentful of what they saw as a usurping of their power.

> I object to social workers making recommendations in SERs. It really gets up my nose when solicitors say, 'If you have it in mind to *comply* with the social enquiry report. . .' A lamentable lack of tact on their

Table 5.3A

Effect of major influences on sentence: towards a more severe sentence

Juveniles

Yellowtown	%	*Redtown*	%	*Greytown*	%	*Bluetown*	%
School report	36	School report	42	Moral assessment	27	School report	32
SER	27	Prosecution	40	SER	20	Moral assessment	27
Moral assessment ⎫	17	Risk of further offences	37	Prosecution	13	Risk of further offences	27
Risk of further offences ⎬							
Previous record							

Young adults

Yellowtown	%	*Redtown*	%	*Greytown*	%	*Bluetown*	%
SER	21	Prosecution	79	Moral assessment	13	Risk of further offences	43
Moral assessment	17	Moral assessment	42	SER	10	Prosecution	37
Risk of further offences	10	Risk of further offences	40	Previous record	10	Moral assessment	27

All juveniles	%	*All young adults*	%	*All cases*	%
School report	34	Prosecution	34	School report	34
Moral assessment	26	Risk of further offences	26	Prosecution	25
Risk of further offences	21	Moral assessment	21	Moral assessment	25
				Risk of further offences	23

Table 5.3B

Effect of major influences on sentence: towards a more lenient sentence

Juveniles

Yellowtown	%	Redtown	%	Greytown	%	Bluetown	%
School report	43	SER	47	SER	40	SER	53
SER	37	Moral assessment	47	Defence	27	Moral assessment	53
Moral assessment	} 23	Risk of further offences	30	School report	25	Defence	} 43
Defence						Risk of further offences	

Young adults

Yellowtown	%	Redtown	%	Greytown	%	Bluetown	%
Moral assessment	48	SER	58	SER	40	Moral assessment	43
SER	41	Risk of further offences	29	Moral assessment	20	SER	40
Risk of further offences	21	Moral assessment	25	Defence	20	Risk of further offences	37

All juveniles	%	All young adults	%	All cases	%
SER	44	SER	44	SER	44
Moral assessment	37	Moral assessment	35	Moral assessment	36
Risk of further offences	} 26	Risk of further offences	23	School report	29
Defence				Risk of further offences	24

part. It appears to the defendant and the public that the probation service is running the court.

(Bluetown)

There are magistrates who accept the recommendations every time and therefore in effect the probation officer is determining sentence. I saw one that said custody would be totally wrong in a particular case. What was totally wrong is that a probation officer should make such a recommendation.

(Greytown)

Even when the existence of recommendations was found acceptable they were often considered to be 'unrealistic', with the absence of recommendations for custodial sentences often referred to as symptomatic of this. Magistrates attributed some of this lack of 'realism' to a tendency of report authors to side with their clients:

I don't know what side the probation officers are on, ours or the defendant's. They are supposed to be objective but I think they are after leniency.

(Redtown)

There's too much emphasis on SERs these days. The information used to come out in court anyway through asking questions. But sometimes they're useful provided the SER author doesn't try and wipe your eye. Probation officers must have more information because they visit the home. But they must become prejudiced when they get to know people and want to do the best for their client.

(Yellowtown)

They won't say that they're suggesting custody. I suppose it's difficult when they've got to work with the family afterwards. They don't want them saying, 'My probation officer got me sent down'.

(Greytown)

Another cause of 'unrealistic' recommendations was located in the composition of the social work profession. Stereotypes verging on caricatures, and with a strong element of sexism in particular, came into play here:

[SERs] are very useful for the background but you never get recommendations that say 'This bugger's a real villain and should go to jail'. It used to be different because a lot of probation officers were ex-servicemen. Now you get dolly birds of 22 fresh off their social studies courses – very attractive young women some of them too – and they write things like he's been in to see me twice a week while he's been on probation. Of course he has! I would too if I was getting the chance to chat up an attractive young woman twice a week.

(Greytown)

Probation officers' reports are more realistic and concise than social workers'. Some social workers are very put out if you don't accept their recommendations, but they're often not realistic, recommending conditional discharges all the time. The best social workers have been lost to early retirement. The new breed of whizz kids go to Keele for two years, have their brains removed, get a plastic card with their picture on it and think they're a social worker.

(Greytown)

I can remember that probation officer hitch-hiking round Europe with a guitar and a little rucksack. He had hair down to his shoulders and a beard down to his navel. *People of that kind are likely to take a lenient view of crime.*

(Redtown: emphasis added)

It seems that it is a particular attitude and experience which magistrates expect from probation officers and social workers. In that sense, report authors are as subject to 'moral assessment' as defendants are and individuals (even young women!) can come to be trusted by the Bench:

Sometimes probation officers think too much about their client and not enough about the offence, but this one wasn't like that. You get to know the names of the probation officers and who you can trust.

(Yellowtown)

Social workers were seen as less realistic than probation officers and the greatest invective was directed against them. A particularly striking example occurred in Greytown, where one juvenile court Bench said that they would not actually have followed the recommendation for attendance centre in one case if it had come from a local authority social worker rather than a probation officer. Probation officers were not, however, immune from this type of critique.

Magistrates thus treated reports with a degree of suspicion, basically around the themes of their being subjective, too much on the defendant's side and 'unrealistic'. It was, however, precisely those aspects of SERs which magistrates saw as weaknesses which were, paradoxically, identified as strengths. The fact that the report author is closer to the defendant and has a more intimate knowledge than magistrates themselves was commonly seen as the most useful feature of the report. However, the knowledge which the Bench acquired was not always quite what the SER author may have intended to impart. For example, one report author's contention that a refusal to reveal the names of accomplices to the police showed strength of character was not read by magistrates as something for which the defendant should be awarded any 'brownie points'. Magistrates, then, found SERs valuable as an aid to their own assessments of the defendant's character. If the report author could be trusted, so much the better. If not, the Bench still felt that it had the skill and insight to 'decode' and re-code the content.

Objective knowledge: school reports

School reports were considered very useful and important in the cases in which they were available and clearly had a significant influence on sentencing. The content of these reports is examined in Chapter 7, but for the moment the focus is on how magistrates saw them and why they were so well received in comparison with other sorts of information available to the Bench.

One reason for this may be that juvenile court panels seem to have attracted a number of teachers, particularly in Yellowtown and Bluetown: indeed on one occasion the author of a school report submitted to Bluetown juvenile court had to stand down from the Bench while the case was dealt with. The occupational composition of the juvenile panel may be one factor which increases the credibility of school reports, but they were also regarded as more reliable than SERs in providing information about the defendant's character. In Yellowtown in particular, we were often told that

> Generally we take more notice of school reports because schools have them all the time and know them well. Social enquiry reports are only based on what the parents tell the social worker.
>
> (Yellowtown)

Considered in the light of what has been said about social enquiry reports, it is not surprising that school reports were taken as a more reliable source of information. As we show in Chapter 7, the content of school reports is often very damning and thus these reports are much less open to charges of being 'subjective', that is on the defendant's side. School reports, also in contrast to social enquiry reports, very rarely make explicit recommendations (Burgin 1988) and thus are less likely to tread on sentencers' toes to be dismissed as 'unrealistic'. Their importance to magistrates seemed to rest upon the idea that they contained a very thorough and 'objective' view of the defendant's character and thus made a useful contribution to sentencers' own assessments.

In both school reports and social enquiry reports, the magistrates seemed to be looking for information which was based upon a detailed knowledge of the defendant, and which they could also regard as 'objective'. School reports were considered to exhibit both characteristics, whereas SER authors were considered capable of being hoodwinked by defendants and, anyway, likely to be too much on the defendant's side. The same suspicions were felt *a fortiori* about defence lawyers.

'Worse than their clients': defence lawyers

> Barristers and solicitors will try and tell you black is white: it's their job. Probation officers and social workers sometimes do the same – they don't always tell you the truth.
>
> (Magistrate, Greytown)

Most of our sample cases were represented by solicitors and only very few by barristers, but magistrates did not indicate that they differentiated between the two branches of the legal profession. Magistrates clearly expected that defence lawyers should do their best for their clients and quite a few felt that this responsibility was not always well discharged. Indeed, Benches dealing with several of the sample cases said that they were left with the impression that the defence would have sent the defendant down for longer than they did! On the other hand, one of the few complimentary remarks about a solicitor was made by a Bench who were impressed by the 'honesty' and 'balanced approach' shown by the discussion of custody in the plea in mitigation. But the predominant feeling among the magistrates we interviewed was that defence lawyers are too much on the defendant's side and so not to be trusted.

> I never believe anything defence solicitors say anyway. They're worse than their clients some of them.
>
> (Magistrate, Yellowtown)

Most Benches did understand that advocates may 'code' statements to the court in order to resolve their dilemma and to carry out their client's instructions (Shapland 1981):

> 'They'll say things like a burglary at three in the afternoon isn't as serious as one at night. I suppose if you're in bed asleep it's worse from that point of view. But you can't suggest that therefore it's not serious if it's in daytime. But solicitors say that sort of thing a bit tongue in cheek.'
> 'Yes. They say things like "I am instructed that" or "My client tells me that", and you think "Aye, aye! What's going on here?"'
>
> (Conversation between Greytown magistrates)

What defence lawyers said had thus to be translated, although the new message was not always what was intended, as in the case in which the Bench felt that the defence solicitor had made things much worse for his client, a young man whose failure to attend community service appointments was explained to the court as the result of his lack of an alarm clock, combined with an inability to get up in the mornings! Information helpful to an assessment of the defendant's character was sometimes extracted from pleas of mitigation but in general it seemed that they were to be taken with a pinch of salt, if indeed they were worth listening to at all:

> Sometimes you can say 'We're minded to follow the recommendation in the Social Enquiry Report' and that shuts them up.
>
> (Magistrate, Yellowtown)

One of the reasons why mitigations were not considered worth listening to was that, regardless of whether or not they were seen as biased, they were generally thought to provide little additional information for the court. In so far as advocates mitigate on the basis of the defendant's social situation, they were considered as little more than interpreters of SERs. In so far as they presented legal arguments, they were regarded as less reliable than the clerk of the court.

Some magistrates took the view that the defence was not merely a rather superfluous source of information, but that the presence of a legal representative was actually a hindrance to the course of justice. In Yellowtown, in particular, there were references made to 'unprepared advocates who ask for adjournments on the slightest ground', thus causing delays in the administration of justice. But more pertinently, and particularly in juvenile courts, a number of Benches considered that the presence of a defence lawyer inhibited their own assessment of the case.

> It is often easier to get to the bottom of a case when he's [sic] not legally represented. If there is a solicitor, the defendant often plays little part in the proceedings.
>
> (Magistrate, Redtown)

> Sometimes I wish defence lawyers weren't there in juvenile court because they'll stand up and tell you black is white if that's what their instructions are. Of course people have a right to legal representation but we would get more at the truth by talking to juveniles directly.
>
> (Magistrate, Yellowtown)

Defence lawyers were, therefore, generally perceived as inhibiting magistrates' search for 'the truth' of the case. At worst they 'distorted' it by presenting only the defendant's side, or, by their mere presence, they obstructed the possibility of direct communication with the defendant. In any event, they were often redundant because the information given was available anyway from the SER or from the clerk.

The facts of the case: the prosecution

Prosecutors occupy a somewhat different position from the professional groups discussed so far in that they do not have any direct influence on sentencing as such (although an inexperienced prosecutor in Greytown did attempt this on one occasion!). Nevertheless, as providers of key information about the details and circumstances of the offence, they have an important role at an earlier stage of the court proceedings in fleshing the bones of the legal category on the charge sheet. An offence could be made to sound much worse by the inclusion of 'frightening details' or it could sound much less serious than it first appeared, as the following examples illustrate:

> Taking the motor cycle because he wanted the exhaust pipes made the TWOC [taking a vehicle without consent but without the intention to permanently deprive the owner of it which would make it theft] sound as close to theft as you can get.
>
> (Magistrate, Redtown)

> The prosecutor made it sound like a prank rather than a real crime.
>
> (Magistrate, Redtown)

Prosecutors are thus potentially powerful influences on the court and this potential was often fulfilled in Redtown. Here, the chief prosecutor, who often presented cases himself, was very adept at playing offences up or down and magistrates took notice of his cues in their own consideration of sentence. For example:

> The prosecution were not at all determined in this case. He must have felt the same way that we did, that he [the defendant] needed help.
>
> (Magistrate, Redtown)

In the other courts, however, as we have seen, the prosecution was not mentioned by magistrates as an influential source of information in the sample cases. In Bluetown in particular, a number of critical comments were voiced about the inefficiency of prosecuting solicitors, which may be one reason for their apparent lack of influence. But it is interesting to note that the critical comments made about the prosecution related only to professional competence and efficiency: there were no comments about potential bias in the information given by prosecutors. Prosecutors were never referred to as on the side of those instructing them, that is the police. (It should be noted in this context that the research was carried out just prior to the introduction of the independent Crown Prosecution Service.) It may well be that prosecutors, distanced from the offender in terms of the source of information and distanced from the sentencing process in terms of making any recommendation to the court, were seen by magistrates as a source of unbiased information.

Taking advice: the role of the clerk

Objectivity is traditionally a requirement of the clerk, who is supposed to provide legal advice, but not to influence sentencing. Nevertheless, clerks also occupy a very powerful position in relation to sentencing (cf Darbyshire 1984). Their role in the training of magistrates, within the general outline curriculum set by the Lord Chancellor's department, gives them a high degree of influence, of which magistrates, with minimal knowledge of practice in other courts, may not even be aware. In individual cases, the dividing line between offering advice and having an influence on sentencing is obviously a rather thin and unclear one (e.g. Justices' Clerks' Society 1980: 30–5) and, again, lay magistrates may be in weak position to challenge such advice.

Clerks in the sample courts certainly had ways of letting their views be known, as in a burglary case in the Redtown sample, where the clerk was said to have 'got his book out when he felt we were straying away from custody'. The influence of clerks was most apparent in Redtown, where it was not uncommon for the clerk, and certain clerks in particular, to retire with the magistrates. In the three other courts, the usual practice was for the clerk to be called into the retiring-room later. Their role in individual cases in these courts seemed more usually to take the form of preventing magistrates from imposing proposed sentences than making positive suggestions about what should be done. Where magistrates suggested that the clerk had discouraged a particular course of action, this was usually on the grounds that what they wanted to do would have been 'bad sentencing policy'. This happened more often in Bluetown where magistrates were keen on helping defendants as well as punishing them. In one case, their enthusiasm for these two objectives led the Bench to suggest a period of youth custody combined with a supervision order with an IT requirement 'to help him when he comes out'! It may have been clerks' responses to suggestions like this which led another member of the Bluetown Bench to the view that 'magistrates are the puppet of the clerk. There are one or two strong magistrates who stand up to the clerk'. Similarly a Greytown justice discussing a sample case said:

> The clerk advised us that it was only the second offence and not all the options had been tried. I wonder whether I shouldn't have stood up to him. If I'd been sitting with a more experienced magistrate – Mr X [her colleague on that day] is new to the juvenile Bench – then perhaps we might have.

> (Magistrate, Greytown)

Although the power relationship between magistrates and clerks will vary between courts and, indeed, between individuals, most magistrates interviewed did not mention the clerk as a major influence on their sentencing decision, and the number of cases in which clerks were said to have influenced the Bench towards a more severe disposal was very small. Clerks' apparently infrequent interventions in individual cases, though sometimes resented by magistrates, were not generally seen as biased in any particular direction. It must be remembered, however, that magistrates may be quite unaware of the more indirect general influence exerted through clerks' responsibility for training at local level. The very limited experience and knowledge of other courts which magistrates have means that they have little basis for comparison: the particular local interpretation of sentencing policy and practice with which they are presented during training can thus become definitive as far as they are concerned.

The search for truth

It would seem from magistrates' perceptions of what influenced their sentencing decisions in these 240 cases that the role of some of the court professionals is rather limited. SERs and pleas in mitigation were seen as biased, yet they provided knowledge which magistrates would not otherwise have had. Benches had therefore to 'de-code' the knowledge of the defendant, which they felt to be crucial, from sources which could not necessarily be trusted to be objective. Sources of information which seem to attract more confidence from the Bench, the prosecution and the clerk, provided information about the offence or about the legal framework, but not about the defendant. School reports were unique in that they were seen to offer detailed knowledge of the defendant and an objectivity, which, as we shall see in a later chapter, derives from the prevalence of negative comment about the defendant in their content. Ironically this information comes from the professional group which most rarely presents its information to the court in person and whose information is, with the exception of the clerk's advice in the retiring-room, the least open to scrutiny by the defendant. Most cases, even amongst juveniles, have however to be dealt with without a school report and magistrates are faced with the problem of finding out the details of the individual case when the only sources of information cannot be trusted. Unsurprisingly they rely on their own judgement to ascertain the 'true character' of the case.

In part, of course, these judgements must be based on information gleaned from others, from reading between the lines of the SER, for example. But there was also an element of a very direct assessment of the defendant's appearance and demeanour (cf Stewart 1980; Hedderman 1988). Despite the multiplicity of ways in which the experience of being in the alien and often confusing environment of a courtroom might affect a defendant's manner and behaviour (e.g. Carlen 1976), magistrates believed in their ability to assess the defendant's character in this situation. For example,

> It's amazing what you get from the patients – sorry, customers. The way their eyes look at you, wondering 'What am I going to get'.
>
> (Magistrate, Greytown)

> Funny things influence you sitting up there. Sometimes you judge a son by what the father looks like.
>
> (Magistrate, Redtown)

Symbolic aspects of courtroom behaviour and interaction were combined with other sources of information in more or less complex ways. Dissonance might have to be resolved, as in the case of a 19-year-old man appearing in Greytown court whose physical appearance totally belied the SER description of him as 'timid and sensitive'. The Bench dealing with this case said afterwards that they thought of custody because of his appearance and attitude in court, but in this case they had been swayed by the SER:

> You couldn't imagine anyone looking less timid and sensitive! But the probation officer's the one that knows him and has talked to him. I nearly dropped through the floor when I found out he had a wife and baby!
>
> (Magistrate, Greytown)

Written information could undermine immediate impressions in ways less helpful to the defendant. For example, one of the most damning epithets commonly used in school reports is 'plausible', which places the defendant in a 'no win' situation. Signs of remorse, fear or other similar emotions are likely to be interpreted as merely an act, while lack of them will clearly not be interpreted in the defendant's favour.

The combination of immediate impression and more detailed information produced, in many cases, an overall moral assessment of the defendant:

> That girl had no intention of going to school. She had her story off pat — 'It's my nerves!' Then when she turned away and I saw her split skirt and high heels, I thought 'You'll be on the game in a year or two.'
>
> (Magistrate, Redtown)

> He was putting on a good act, standing there as if butter wouldn't melt. . .!
>
> (Magistrate, Greytown)

> He wasn't like the other lad. He was towed along by other people. We feel he was really led astray.
>
> (Magistrate, Redtown)

Magistrates said that their sentencing was influenced by their judgements of the defendant's character in no fewer than 158 (68 per cent) of the sample cases. This is clearly an important element in sentencing which is easily underestimated in research techniques utilizing paper sentencing exercises (see e.g. Kapardis and Farrington 1981; Corbett 1987).

The importance of character judgements is, however, even greater when a further related aspect of it is considered, namely the predictive factor of the likelihood of further offending. Magistrates certainly did not assess this by reference to reconviction rates for various age groups or for various disposals or any other such objective criteria. Rather this assessment took the form of 'we will/won't see him or her again':

> He'll be back. He struck me as a seasoned tough nut. He will be back.
>
> (Magistrate, Bluetown)

Assessments of this type influenced sentencing in 110 (47 per cent) of the sample cases.

If these two sets of responses are taken together and the purposes for which SERs and school reports are seen as useful are also borne in mind, it seems that sentencing is more influenced by magistrates' own moral judgements of the defendant's character than by anything else. These moral judgements assume importance because of a belief that few of the courtroom actors who make sentencing recommendations to them can be trusted as free of bias in favour of the defendant. Magistrates see themselves as having a unique position in relation to the competing definitions of the case offered during the courtroom process. As one respondent put it:

> Magistrates are the only strata of people running the court who have a responsibility to the community. That's why Bench decisions can sometimes appear extreme. Other agencies like social workers, probation officers and lawyers are representing the interests of their clients. It's

only magistrates who look to the interests of the community. We have to show that crime doesn't pay.

(Magistrate, Yellowtown)

Sentencing decisions cannot, therefore, be expected to be consonant with the views of the court professionals. But, as we showed in the previous chapter, sentencing will not necessarily reflect public opinion either, or even magistrates' perceptions of what is in the interests of the community. For magistrates, unlike other members of the public, share with the professionals a detailed knowledge of the particular case, to which the public at large do not have access. On this view, magistrates, and magistrates alone, are in a position to determine what is the true balance in each case.

This perception of the magisterial role contains certain dangers. First, there is a risk that it could place sentencing outside any accountability or criticism: no one else can 'know' because no one else has the same knowledge or has the same duties. Second, the insistence that the balance has to be struck for each case on its individual merits may mean that it is difficult to ensure any level of consistency in the way cases are dealt with. These dangers are particularly acute in the light of what has been said about the influence of magistrates' own moral assessments of defendants on sentencing. It becomes very important to look at which factors carried the day in the sentencing of the sample cases and particularly at how important the moral assessment of the defendant was to the outcome. The next section, therefore, looks at the magistrates' reasons for the sentences imposed.

Accounting for the sentence

Striking the balance

It might be thought that finding the right balance in each case would be a rather difficult matter, given the multiplicity of factors which need to be considered and the range of sentences available. However, the Benches interviewed seemed to reach their decisions with remarkably little disagreement and difficulty.

Most Benches said that their decision had been completely unanimous, but it is likely that the degree of disagreement was underestimated. Some Benches said that they were all agreed, but it became apparent during the interview that there had been some disagreement before accord was finally reached (cf Burney 1979). Collective responsibility seemed to be the general unstated rule, but we found that magistrates were more likely to talk about disagreements when interviewed alone or without the senior magistrate present, especially where the senior magistrate had overruled them. This happened more in Yellowtown than in the other courts. Mostly, where disputes were revealed, they were overcome within a set of informal rules (e.g. where there was a 2 to 1 majority in favour of custody, the third person's view would be recognized by an adjustment of length of sentence). Major disagreements were seldom revealed, but these few instances indicated the power of the senior magistrate on the day.

Only just under a third of the sample cases were described as causing particular difficulty. These included cases involving co-defendants whom the magistrates thought should receive dissimilar disposals and cases where the defendant was in especially fraught personal circumstances, with drug-related cases also being mentioned as difficult by Yellowtown magistrates. Problems also sometimes, though not invariably, arose when the Bench was unable to impose its first choice of sentence: often because the first choice was an illegal sentence such as a suspended prison sentence on a young adult, but sometimes because of lack of facilities, particularly of community service places (a not uncommon problem in many parts of the country). Although quite a range of factors was said to have made a case particularly difficult, the most common theme in magistrates' comments on this question was that difficult cases were often those in which the conflict between the public interest and that of the defendant was most acute. Accounts of sentencing in these cases usually involved a big 'But. . .'. An illustration of this type of reasoning is the case of a 16-year-old boy who appeared in Yellowtown juvenile court for two offences of burglary, with a further similar offence taken into consideration, having previously had two separate three-month DC sentences. The Bench said that they would normally have given six months' youth custody for a drug-related burglary of a dwelling-house, but in this case the boy was being given a chance to settle with new foster parents in the hope that this would help him break his drug addiction. After much discussion, the Bench opted for a deferred sentence, but felt that their decision was a 'risky' one because of possible further offending and because of the departure from public expectation.

Cases like this are clearly very different from the type which we shall refer to in Chapter 6, in which custody was felt to be absolutely necessary and nothing else could be considered. Equally they are different from those in which custody was simply not an issue at all. Although this middle group of either way cases were considered problematic, what is perhaps more surprising is how straightforward magistrates found it to decide the balance in the majority of cases (65 per cent of decisions were said not to have been difficult). This is perhaps less surprising when it is realized that only a small number of factors were decisive in the reasons for the imposition of the particular sentences in the sample cases.

The rationale of sentencing

Magistrates were asked to give their reasons for selecting the sentence they imposed in each case and up to six reasons were coded for analysis. The most frequently mentioned reasons for each court and each age group are shown in Table 5.4. This shows that a relatively small group of factors were mentioned as informing magistrates' decision-making in the majority of cases, particularly since some of the less frequently mentioned reasons can be quite closely related to the small group which was most often mentioned, as will become clear in the

Table 5.4

Main reasons given for sentence

Juveniles

Yellowtown	%	*Redtown*	%	*Greytown*	%	*Bluetown*	%
Seriousness of offence	53	Seriousness of offence	60	Seriousness of offence	70	Seriousness of offence	63
School performance	50	Moral assessment	50	Welfare/family concerns	40	Moral assessment	60
Moral assessment	40	Welfare/family concerns	43	Antecedent record	37	Welfare/family concerns	50
'Hands were tied'	37	School performance	26	SER recommendation	17	'Hands were tied'	37
Welfare/family concerns	30	'Hands were tied'	23	Protection of public	17	Antecedent record	30

Young adults

Yellowtown	%	*Redtown*	%	*Greytown*	%	*Bluetown*	%
Seriousness of offence	66	Seriousness of offence	63	Seriousness of offence	47	Seriousness of offence	60
SER recommendation	31	Moral assessment	33	Antecedent record	47	'Hands were tied'	33
Antecedent record	24	Defendant needs a jolt	25	'Hands were tied'	33	Moral assessment	23
Protection of public	24	Defendant flouted court's authority	21	SER recommendation	27	Antecedent record	23
Local clampdown	17	Antecedent record	21	Avoiding specific penalty	23	SER recommendation	20

All juveniles	%	*All young adults*	%	*All cases*	%
Seriousness of offence	62	Seriousness of offence	58	Seriousness of offence	60
Moral assessment	41	Antecedent record	29	Moral assessment	32
Welfare/family concerns	41	'Hands were tied'	26	Welfare/family concerns	28
'Hands were tied'	28	SER recommendation	24	Antecedent record	27
School performance	27	Moral assessment	22	'Hands were tied'	27

discussion which follows. This pattern was broadly similar in all four courts, although some differences in orientation were apparent.

As might have been expected, seriousness of offence was the most frequently mentioned reason for the sentencing given. The fact that this factor was, by contrast, mentioned less often as an influence on sentencing may be, as suggested earlier, because it is taken as a starting-point for sentencing. This may also explain the otherwise remarkable fact that it was not mentioned as a reason for sentence in over one-third of this sample of cases in which there was a risk of custody.

Offences could be assessed as more or less serious either because of the nature of the charge (e.g. burglary or offences involving violence) or because of the details revealed in court. For example

> We thought about Crown Court committal. We had to consider whether if the other lads involved had been charged they would all have gone into custody and we decided they would. It was a vicious assault − he kicked him in the face. And someone was going to suffer.
>
> (Bluetown)

> From the outside it might look rather harsh [three months' DC] but compared with the other case it was at opposite ends of the offence. The other boy was just messing about whereas this one was a real theft. It's like the difference between an elderly lady who doesn't pay for a bobbin of cotton through sheer forgetfulness and someone who goes into Harrod's and makes a career out of stealing. They're both shoplifting, but they're entirely different.
>
> (Greytown)

> The burglaries were serious but they weren't of a dwelling-house and so it wasn't quite so bad. We weren't really thinking of custody as there was supervision with IT which is quite demanding now, so that was an obvious choice.
>
> (Greytown)

The interpretation of seriousness of the offence in relation to the particular offence in question rather than the general category is in line with Court of Appeal rulings (e.g. *R.* v. *Bradbourn* 1985). However, there is, perhaps inevitably, a moral element in delineating what makes an offence a more or less serious one of its type. The most striking example was Yellowtown's attitude to drug-related offences, summarized in the following comment on a sentence of four months' youth custody on a young woman:

> There are a number of offences here *but you have to treat it as one offence really − drug-taking.*
>
> (emphasis added)

Other examples of exacerbating factors included a Yellowtown magistrate's view that 'we're always inclined to be a bit harder where a breach of trust is involved' and cases involving elderly victims: for example a custodial sentence was imposed in Redtown on two youngsters for an attempt to sell an old and short-sighted man some dirt as if it were coal.

The nature of the defendant's previous record would also be expected to be an important determinant of sentence. It was, however, much less important than the current offence, being given as a reason in 27 per cent of the 240 cases. This was a more important reason in the sentencing of young adults, who, of course, might be expected to have longer records, on average, simply on grounds of their age. Previous convictions were also important for Greytown defendants, also reflecting the greater likelihood of their having more serious records compared with defendants in the other PSDs (see Chapter 2). Mostly the previous record became a reason for sentence when it was a bad one, but fewer or less serious prior convictions were also used to justify a less severe sentence.

There were indications that not just the length of the record and the nature of the offences on it were taken into account. In determining the current sentence, magistrates also considered previous types of disposal. There did not seem to be a rigid set of prescriptions about this, but in a number of cases, Benches felt that they had to go up tariff:

> He's had DC already, so it had to be youth custody.
>
> (Magistrate, Yellowtown)

> We don't like using attendance centre a second time because obviously if they re-offend it hasn't worked.
>
> (Magistrate, Greytown)

Although there were exceptions to this pattern, the tendency to impose a more severe sentence on each reconviction makes the ambiguity of community service orders (CSOs), in particular, an important mechanism for escalation through the tariff.

Following this logic, the court may impose a custodial sentence on the grounds of the defendant's unwillingness or failure to respond to non-custodial penalties. For example after imposing a five-months' youth custody sentence without an SER, a Bluetown Bench said that the defendant, who had previously had two CSOs, had 'worked right through the menu – a report would have made no difference'. The imposition of a particular sentence, because of a feeling that the defendant has had his/her chance, is therefore closely related to the impact of the antecedent record. So also were cases involving a breach of a court order. Breaches of bail as well as failure to keep to the terms of sentence evoked strong feelings amongst magistrates:

> I would have been quite happy to send him down, well not happy, but it wouldn't have been unjust in any way. To commit an offence six days after being put on community service shows you what his attitude is. You could have sent him down on the basis that he is unwilling to respond.
>
> (Magistrate, Bluetown)

The common theme was that the authority of the court was being ignored or flouted.

A slightly different concern with the defendant's criminal record was where the Bench wanted to take preventive measures, to avoid a short or less serious record from becoming worse. In a small number of cases, magistrates had decided to give the defendant a jolt, 'a salutary shock in his own interests' as one Greytown Bench summarized their thinking.

The third major factor which might have been expected to be important although it was not mentioned as a frequent influence on sentencing, was the protection of the public. This was not commonly cited as a reason for sentence in the interviews with magistrates. Yellowtown magistrates were more likely to explain their sentencing decisions in these terms, but it seemed that what they had in mind was deterrence rather then containment, although the latter was an element in some cases. It is arguable that the powers available to magistrates are not sufficient to protect the public in any meaningful sense, but as we saw in Chapter 4, Yellowtown justices held a much more alarmist view of local crime than their colleagues elsewhere, particularly in respect of drug-related cases, and such local clampdowns on specific offences can be seen as closely related to the protection of the public.

Given that our sample consisted of cases where there was a risk of custody and that the possible reasons for sentence considered so far relate closely to the criteria on the use of custody in the 1982 Act, it is a little surprising that these three factors were not mentioned in more sample cases. Even more alarmingly, a factor which has no legal relevance to the decision to use custody formed an important part of the rationale for the sentence in a third of the sample cases. Magistrates' own moral assessments of the defendants were more than an important influence on sentencing: they were actually a key element in it, especially for juveniles. Some of these judgements were positive in tone:

> He didn't seem a violent boy. Carrying the knife didn't seem to have any criminal intent behind it.
>
> (Magistrate, Yellowtown)

More positive moral assessments also appeared in the form of wanting to give the defendant a chance, although this was a reason for sentence in a much smaller proportion of cases. An illustration of this type of reasoning was from a Bench who said they wanted to

> give him a chance after his unhappy home background and prevent him becoming someone who'll be backwards and forwards to court for years; if he'd been an adult, the offences would have been overriding. He'd have gone away.
>
> (Magistrate, Yellowtown)

But other judgements on the defendant's character were much more damning:

> Weak. A dreg. He'd had all the soft options: probation, community service, more probation. Time to cool his heels.
>
> (Magistrate, Yellowtown)

> He's already a hardened little thief. He really needs a shake up. Something to pull him back.
>
> (Magistrate, Bluetown)

These kinds of assessments could be powerful enough to tip the balance towards a custodial sentence. Thus a Greytown juvenile Bench said that they felt they had 'no alternative' but to send a 15-year-old to detention centre for an offence of taking a car without consent, given what they had learned of his character from the SER. They thought he was 'a bully' and 'needed a short sharp shock to help him curb his temper'.

Moral assessments applied not only to the defendant, but also extended to friends or relatives who came to court to provide support: a particularly common phenomenon in Greytown, where one Bench were impressed by the fact that a woman had bothered to come to court with her 19-year-old son:

> If he'd had a bunch of his cronies nudging each other on the back row of the court, we might have viewed it differently and leaned more towards custody.
>
> (Magistrate, Greytown)

Clearly some Benches took a broader view of the defendant and this was particularly so where family background was an important consideration.

More welfare-orientated reasons, relating to family background in particular, were, not surprisingly, more evident in juvenile than in adult courts. Despite the drift away from welfare implicit in the 1982 Act, considerations of this type informed the sentencing decision in just over a quarter of all cases and two-fifths of the juvenile court sample. Bluetown magistrates in particular emphasized welfare considerations for juveniles, but not for young adults: 'at 17, welfare is not a priority: society has to show its abhorrence', as one put it. Welfare reasons were also invoked more frequently in relation to female defendants (10 of 19: 52 per cent) than male (44 of 214: 21 per cent) (cf Edwards 1984). Mostly the concerns were with family problems but a 'good' family background did also have some bearing on sentence in some cases. Assessments of family situation, like assessments of the defendant, were largely moral categorizations, based on a very specific ideology of the family, which seemed to be carried particularly strongly by Bluetown magistrates (cf Chapter 4 for their comments on what can be provided for young people by IT and specified activities requirements). Typical of the way this factor emerged in explanations of sentence was:

> A weak boy without decent parental guidance. His father has completely abandoned his responsibilities and his mother's on valium. He needs the guidance of supervision – another model.

(Magistrate, Bluetown)

Moral assessments of defendants and their families thus carried through from being an important influence on sentencing to being a determinant reason for sentence.

We have already shown that reports presented to the court were seen as useful in providing information on which magistrates could base their own judgements. Recommendations made in SERs were said to be less important an influence on sentencing. Nevertheless, the SER recommendation was referred to as a reason for sentence in 24 per cent of the cases involving young adults and 19 per cent of juveniles. This may seem disappointingly low for report writers who aim to influence sentencing. They may not be any more encouraged by the reasons which those Benches who did follow the recommendations gave for doing so. Of the fifty cases in which the SER recommendation was followed, magistrates in sixteen said it was because of the high quality of the report. In seventeen the recommendation was followed almost by default because nothing else which was appropriate and available sprang to mind, and in the remainder, it was followed simply on principle. As one Greytown Bench explained this principle:

> We have to treat the probation service as the professionals, although this report didn't make very clear what was wanted or why.

This demonstrates again the dangers of assuming that a high rate of accord between SER recommendations and outcome is evident that SER recommendations are actively influencing sentencing. The rate at which recommendations are accepted may reflect no more than authors' skills in anticipating what the Bench is likely to do. This issue of 'second guessing' by report authors, which is taken up again in Chapter 8, is difficult to disentangle, but the way in which 'second guessing' can maintain a particular sentencing pattern was well illustrated by the following comment from a magistrate in Yellowtown on a report with an implicit recommendation for a custodial sentence:

> An SER which had presented any other recommendation wouldn't have made any difference. He's had IT and CS. If the SER had said anything else, I'd have had hysterics.

(Magistrate, Yellowtown)

On a slightly more optimistic note, the explanation for sentence in sixteen cases referenced the availability of a realistic alternative to custody. These would generally have been recommended in the SER, especially since some Benches felt it was not open to them to consider IT or CSO if it was not mentioned in the report. However, these sixteen cases represent a low number in comparison with the objectives of report authors and the types of recommendations made in the sample cases, which are discussed further in Chapter 8.

School reports, by contrast, emerged from magistrates' explanations of their sentencing decisions as extremely powerful documents. School performance was mentioned as a reason for sentence in as many as a quarter of the cases in which a school report was available. This was one issue on which a striking and important difference between the courts was apparent. School performance was not mentioned in the account of the sentencing process in any of the cases in Greytown, where information about this aspect of the defendant's life was generally included in the SER rather than in a separate document. In Yellowtown, on the other hand, school performance was only slightly less important than the seriousness of the offence. It was, indeed, sometimes unclear for which of these the defendant was being sentenced. To take an example not from Yellowtown, but from Bluetown, a 15-year-old youth was sentenced to six months' youth custody for what was admittedly a serious assault. Yet the account of the reasons for imposing that sentence made strong reference to 'the seeds of concern' in the school report: what this amounted to was that the boy 'couldn't accept authority in the school football team'. This disciplinary problem in school became part of the rationale for the imposition of the maximum sentence available to the court. This example bears out the suggestion made earlier that school reports provide Benches with a valuable source of information on which to base judgements of the defendant's character: a 14-year-old who is assessed on the basis of his school report as 'a potential future mugger' runs the risk of being dealt with accordingly.

Although this section has looked at the main reasons for sentence in the sample cases, it should be noted that in a significant minority of cases (27 per cent), the Bench felt that there was little to explain since they had 'had no choice'. In some of these cases, there was a genuine legal constraint; for example, following the Court of Appeal ruling in the case of *R.* v. *Gillam*, in 1980, a custodial sentence could not be passed where a previous Bench had adjourned the case for an assessment of the defendant's suitability for community service, if the defendant was then assessed as suitable and work was available. (Because of this ruling, some Benches were careful to request that 'all options' be considered when adjourning for an SER.) But in many of the 'no choice' cases, it was not clear that such constraints were operative. Half of the 'no choice' cases involved more than one defendant and the sentence passed on a co-defendant was said to have meant that the same sentence had to be imposed in the sample case. But this was by no means a rigid rule, with other Benches saying that passing different sentences on co-defendants was not a problem because, as one Greytown magistrate put it, 'individualized cases need individualized treatment'. In 10 per cent of the sample, the restriction on the final choice of sentence was even less evident: the process of reasoning in these might best be described as sentencing by default. Having gone through a list of available options and rejected most of them on one ground or another, the

Bench then claimed that there had been 'no option' but to impose the one that remained. An illustration of this process was the case of a 15-year-old with no previous findings of guilt, who was dealt with for offences of arson, burglary and theft in Yellowtown's juvenile court. As he was already in care under civil proceedings, the Bench felt that a supervision or a care order would be redundant. A fine was considered inappropriate, given the nature of the offences, as was a conditional discharge which would have been thought too lenient: 'it would have been misread; you can imagine what the papers would say', explained one of the magistrates dealing with the case. Custody was rejected because it was the boy's first conviction and the Bench feared that it would lead to contamination by criminal influences. In the end sentence was deferred, the Bench saying that there was no other choice. Magistrates' hands are thus tied to the extent that they feel bound by other pressures.

In an important minority of cases, these pressures included the wish to avoid inflicting the secondary consequences which might have resulted from the imposition of a particular penalty. This mainly took two forms: the wish to avoid the possibility of a custodial sentence turning the offender into a more hardened criminal and the wish to avoid the use of financial penalties. Comments made in the first type of case included:

> Custody might have turned him into a big lout.
>
> (Magistrate, Bluetown)

> It was me who thought he should go down. He had failed to comply with three court orders. I saw he had some trauma in his background and a short, sharp shock might have upset recent progress at home, at work and at the attendance centre. And he has just started paying his fine. If we had sent him into custody, it would have meant starting from square one.
>
> (Magistrate, Bluetown)

The second type of case in which the avoidance of particular penalties was an issue involved monetary penalties. It was said by some Benches to be counter-productive to impose fines on defendants on low incomes or without employment who could not pay them. Although many Benches seemed unconcerned about this aspect (for example the case in Bluetown of a fine of £190 on a 20-year-old for an offence of taking a vehicle without consent despite the fact that he had £500 worth of outstanding fines already), several Benches were explicitly concerned to avoid an indirect custodial sentence for fine default. The defendant's ability to pay was very much related to employment status and this was taken into account in deciding sentence in a fifth of all cases (although, of course, some of our juvenile court sample were not of an employable age). As one Greytown magistrate noted in an interview:

> You can't do anything which would undermine somebody who gets a job in this area.

Their fears about the loss of the defendant's job had turned the Bench in this case not only away from custody but also away from community service, and a fine was seen as the most suitable penalty because 'he'll be earning good money and can pay a steep fine. He'll be punished and keep his job'. In another case in Greytown, the Bench said that everything pointed towards custody: offences of taking cars, which was seen as a significant local problem, as well as burglary, on top of a bad previous record. Although this 16-year-old was described by the magistrate as 'a shocker', he had just got a job:

> If he'd lost his job because of a custodial sentence now, it would have been like sentencing him to a life of permanent unemployment.
>
> (Magistrate, Greytown)

This does of course raise the question of whether unemployed defendants are more likely to be given a custodial sentence and this issue did concern some magistrates:

> It's a very serious offence and the public needs to be protected. Someone could have been hurt. So we did consider custody but decided against it because he's a hard working young man. He works seven days a week so it would be wrong to expect him to do community service. With the loss of earnings from not being able to drive [after disqualification], we wondered if he'd be able to pay the fine [£500 for an offence of drunk driving]. . . . We talked about whether we'd have dealt with him differently if he had been unemployed. I don't think so. We would have fined him less. Had he been unemployed, we might have done a community service order. Had he been older we might have done a suspended sentence. That would have been the right thing.
>
> (Magistrate, Greytown)

This bears out what was suggested by magistrates' comments on the use of probation day centre 'packages' and of community service (see Chapter 4), namely that these 'alternatives' to custody are more readily used for the un-employed, even if they are not more likely to be sent into custody (cf Crow and Simon 1987). This may, of course, have the effect of making a custodial sentence more likely in the event of further offending.

Other reasons for sentence which were relevant to only a small number of cases included a small group in which a pathology/treatment model was invoked and these were primarily cases in Yellowtown, where the offences were thought to be related to the defendant's drug use. Local factors also emerged in the explanation of sentencing in Redtown, where the offence occurred in the context of a major industrial dispute, and in Bluetown, where local police practice favoured cautioning. In Bluetown also, there was more of an emphasis on the desirability of compensation to the victim and reparation to society, although this was offered as an explanation in only ten cases. This is a surprisingly low figure in view of the claims that sentencing is responsive to public opinion and of evidence that compensation and reparation are an important element in what the public wants from the criminal justice system (e.g. Hough and Mayhew 1983; Hough and Moxon 1988). Finally there were two cases in which sentencing seemed to have been by divine inspiration rather than by any logic which could be articulated: the sentence imposed just 'seemed like the right thing'.

Explaining the sentence

It should be evident from the quotations used to illustrate the foregoing analysis of magistrates' reasons for sentence that many factors interact and combine in explanations of why a particular decision was made. However, a small number of factors appeared to be drawn upon more often in the rationale of sentencing. The seriousness of the offence, the need to protect the public and the defendant's antecedent record are statutorily defined as relevant to the decision to use custody. It is therefore not surprising that the nature of the offence and, to a lesser extent, the defendant's record appeared to be very important reasons for sentence in a sample of cases selected on the grounds that there was a risk of a custodial sentence. What is more surprising is the weight given to magistrates' own moral assessments. It is also surprising to find that school reports carried a very high weighting compared to social enquiry reports, which are prepared by professionals with some expertise in criminal justice matters.

Nor does an examination of the reasons which magistrates gave to explain their sentencing decisions go very far to explain the variations in sentencing patterns and particularly the variations in custody rates between the sample courts. Differences between the courts could be discerned. Greytown Benches tended to take more of a straightforward tariff approach, sentencing mainly on the basis of the offence and the defendant's record. Redtown magistrates were concerned primarily with moral assessments once the seriousness of the offence had been taken into account. Bluetown's juvenile defendants were more likely to be dealt with on the basis of magistrates' moral assessments and welfare considerations, but young adults in Bluetown faced more tariff-orientated sentencing. In Yellowtown the protection of the public was paramount, particularly where the problem of drug-related crime was an issue.

As Table 5.5 shows, certain types of rationale were more often used to explain a custodial sentence. But none was inexorably linked with this type of disposal. Thus only just over half of those who received their sentence because of the seriousness of the offence were sent into custody and a fifth of those defendants from whom the public was thought to need protection were dealt with by means of a non-custodial penalty.

It might be suggested therefore, first, that sentencing in the sample cases was not decided only on criteria which are open to scrutiny, and second, that similar sorts of reasoning produced quite disparate outcomes. In Chapter 6, we consider whether the decision to use custody was any exception to this.

Table 5.5

Reasons for sentence by type of sentence in sample cases

	Custodial	1982 Alternatives	Other	Total
Serious offence	57	31	21	109
	(52%)	(28%)	(19%)	(100%)
Less serious offence	2	12	17	31
	(6%)	(39%)	(55%)	(100%)
Positive moral assessment	1	16	18	35
	(3%)	(46%)	(51%)	(100%)
Negative moral assessment	23	6	10	39
	(59%)	(15%)	(26%)	(100%)
Hands were tied	18	21	23	62
	(29%)	(34%)	(37%)	(100%)
No welfare/family problems	1	5	13	9
	(5%)	(26%)	(68%)	(100%)
Welfare/family problems	4	11	31	46
	(9%)	(24%)	(67%)	(100%)
Bad antecedent record	25	11	11	47
	(53%)	(23%)	(23%)	(100%)
Not bad antecedent record	—	8	7	15
		(53%)	(47%)	(100%)
School performance poor	4	4	4	12
	(33%)	(33%)	(33%)	(100%)
School performance not poor	—	3	1	4
		(75%)	(25%)	(100%)
Followed SER recommendation	9	19	22	50
	(18%)	(38%)	(44%)	(100%)
Avoid secondary consequences	1	15	18	34
	(3%)	(44%)	(53%)	(100%)
Protection of the public	24	2	4	30
	(80%)	(7%)	(13%)	(100%)
Defendant needs a jolt	9	8	9	26
	(35%)	(31%)	(35%)	(100%)
Flouted court's authority	15	1	9	25
	(58%)	(4%)	(35%)	(100%)
Avoiding penalty, e.g. fine	6	4	11	21
	(29%)	(19%)	(52%)	(100%)
Defendant's employment status	1	10	10	21
	(5%)	(48%)	(48%)	(100%)
Give defendant a chance	1	6	10	17
	(6%)	(35%)	(59%)	(100%)
Realistic alternative to custody available	—	14	2	16
		(88%)	(13%)	(100%)
Local clampdown	8	3	3	14
	(57%)	(21%)	(21%)	(100%)
Pathology/treatment model	4	3	6	13
	(31%)	(25%)	(46%)	(100%)
Defendant had chances	10	—	1	11
	(91%)		(9%)	(100%)
Other	2	10	16	28
	(7%)	(36%)	(57%)	(100%)
Total no. reasons	221	220	271	712
	(31%)	(31%)	(38%)	(100%)
No. cases	72	70	91	233
	(31%)	(30%)	(39%)	(100%)

Conclusion

This chapter has continued the concerns of Chapter 4 in examining the influence of various factors on the sentencing of the sample cases. In Chapter 4 we showed that magistrates believed that legislation has to be interpreted in the light of 'common sense'. This common sense is exercised by magistrates as representatives of the public, but members of the public who are uniquely placed in having access to detailed information about the individual case. In Chapter 5 we have considered how magistrates acquired and interpreted information about individual cases and balanced the interests of the defendant against those of the public. Clearly the nature of the offence and relevant characteristics of the defendant, such as previous record, were influential as was information provided by various professional groups involved in the court-room process. In the end, however, sentencers relied very much on their own personal judgements of the defendant's character. Who the defendant is thought to be, as well as what he or she has done, is a central factor in the sentencing decision. It is no wonder that sentencing patterns are so difficult to explain when at the heart of the process is the belief that sentencers, and they alone, are uniquely placed to understand not only the uniqueness of the events which constitute the offence, but also the character of the individual who has committed it. Sentencing, in this sense, is something of a mystery.

In an older sense of the term, 'mystery' is perhaps an accurate description of how many magistrates see their role. The craft of sentencing is seen as an esoteric one, acquired through the experience of sitting with senior colleagues and involving a specific form of knowledge and expertise unavailable to others. A recent publication by a Metropolitan Stipendiary Magistrate offering 'practical advice' to the newly appointed Justice of the Peace takes this further. The author mentions three qualities which a magistrate should have. As well as a working knowledge of the criminal law and available sentencing options, the magistrate should have the 'gift' of 'a sound judicial sense' and, finally, the 'crucial' 'gift of sound judgement'. The author uses the term 'gift' advisedly because

> I do not believe that it can be developed if it has never been present in the first place. Good judgement is the ability to evaluate evidence, assess witnessess and, having reached a correct conclusion, pass a sentence which does not err in principle. A sentence which does not err in principle is one which is neither too severe or too lenient, and which is wholly appropriate having regard to the facts of the offence and the history of the offender.
>
> (Bartle 1985: 9)

While none of those we interviewed described sentencing as an innate skill (if indeed omniscience can be described as a skill!), there was a general adherence to what might, were it not for the fact that all but one of our respondents was an amateur, be called the professional ideology of the lay magistrate.

The basis of this ideology is the belief in the uniqueness of the magisterial role and in the uniqueness of each case. This is an ideology which precludes any questioning of specific decisions: the public cannot question because it does not know the detailed facts of each case; the professionals in the courtroom cannot question because they are partial and anyway do not have the same responsibilities to the public. The idea that 'every case is different' and must be 'judged on its merits' further compounds the inaccessibility of the sentencing process. On one level, it is of course true that every case is different. But on another, it could be read as straying from any notion of justice as the principle of comparing cases on relevant criteria, treating like cases alike and dissimilar cases differently. The preceding chapter highlighted one cause for concern in this respect in that it showed that magistrates have a sublime disregard for the principle of treating like cases alike. Most did not even refer back to their own previous decisions, much less those of the colleagues, and even less to decisions made in other localities. Consistency was equated with rigidity.

The material discussed in this chapter points to a further cause for concern in terms of the criteria used to differentiate cases. Magistrates' moral judgements of the defendant's character not only appear explicitly, but also pervade their interpretations of other considerations, such as the defendant's family circumstances or the significance of information given in school and social enquiry reports. It could be argued, rightly, that moral issues cannot be divorced from sentencing, from deciding whether burglary is worse than assault, for example. But such questions would at least stand public debate in a way that some of the comments quoted in this chapter almost certainly would not. Indeed, the pervasive ideology of the unique role of the magistrate and the ideology of the uniqueness of each case place sentencing beyond questioning and thus actually serve to prohibit such debate. At a national level this makes the management of magistrates' justice, with its highly punitive character, well nigh impossible, as the present prison crisis illustrates (see Chapter 9).

For individuals at risk of losing their liberty, the issue is no less serious. However, the magistrates we interviewed did maintain that their use of custody was in line with the criteria set down in legislation. The reasons given for using custody did reference these criteria most commonly. Perhaps it could be argued that the use of custody, at least, suffers less from an inconsistency which might also be viewed as arbitrariness. Chapter 6 looks further at consistency and inconsistency in the use of custody in the four courts to assess whether this really is the case.

6 The custody decision: can it be defined?

> With those that like using custody, you can legislate till kingdom come and it wouldn't make any difference.
>
> (Magistrate, Greytown)

Introduction

Chapter 4 examined general factors outside the courtroom which influenced magistrates in their choice of sentence. Chapter 5 moved on to look at the 'on the day' courtroom influences on sentence. This chapter concentrates on the reasons magistrates gave for using custody. We examine the magistrates' own reasons for sentence in relation to what we have termed the 'custody potential' of the sample cases. The sample cases will be compared on a number of criteria in order to see if the magistrates' reasons concur with the empirical data. This exercise further demonstrates how magisterial common sense is as influential as some of the strict legal requirements in the sentencing practice of the lower courts. The magistrates' own snap moral judgements about defendants are shown to be a critical factor in the custody decision, a finding which leads us to a deeper understanding of how it was that magistrates in our four areas dealt with very similar kinds of cases in quite different ways.

Table 5.4 (p.105) which deals with all 240 cases shows that the magistrates' moral assessment of the defendant was the second most important reason for sentence. Indeed the 'seriousness of the offence' was the only other factor found to be more important. The reasons given for the seventy-two cases in which a custodial sentence was passed reveal a similar picture (see Table 6.1). Here the magistrates' three most important reasons were broadly in keeping with the criteria laid down by contemporary legislation, provided a bad antecedent record is regarded as an indication that the defendant is unable or unwilling to respond to non-custodial penalties. Seriousness of the offence again emerges as being by far the most important reason and was mentioned in twice as many cases as either of the other two criteria. Perhaps more surprisingly the magistrates gave their negative moral assessments of the

Table 6.1

Reasons given for custodial sentences[a]

Very serious offence	57	(79%)
Bad antecedent record	25	(35%)
Protection of the public	24	(33%)
Negative moral assessment	23	(32%)
Hands were tied	18	(25%)
Breach of order/flout court's authority	15	(21%)
Defendant had chances	10	(14%)
Defendant needs jolt	9	(13%)
Followed SER recommendation	9	(13%)
Local clampdown	8	(11%)
Avoid specific penalty, e.g. fine	6	(8%)
Welfare/family problems	4	(6%)
Poor school performance	4	(6%)
Pathology/treatment model	4	(6%)
Other	6	(7%)
Total number of cases	72	

Note: [a] Up to six reasons could be recorded for each case.

defendants virtually as much significance as either the need to protect the public or the defendant's criminal record.

This finding confirms the significance of the magistrates' estimation of the defendant's moral status in the custody decision, providing an important clue to the origins of the courts' different sentencing patterns. Clearly moral assessment, typically involving the magistrates' views about whether or not a particular defendant will re-offend, is a matter of personal judgement in itself the result of guess work.

Before moving on to a more detailed analysis of the magistrates' approach to the custody decision it is necessary to make some observations about the use of custody as opposed to non-custodial penalties.

Are there alternatives to custody?

Chapter 4 suggested that magistrates attached different meanings and purposes to available sentences, particularly non-custodial measures. Our conversations with court officals revealed a wide range of opinions regarding the use of the 'alternative' sentencing options. Bluetown's clerk was adamant that community service was never intended as a strict alternative to custody; Redtown's clerks regarded this view of community service as 'heresy'. If the Justices' legal advisors held completely opposing views, it is hardly surprising that their magistrates pursued quite different sentencing practices in relation to alternatives to custody. In a sense the criteria for custody developed in recent CJAs have compounded some of the difficulties associated with the 'alternative' sentences and their relationship to custody. Strictly speaking magistrates should first decide that a custodial penalty is necessary before moving on to consider the 'alternative' sentences. One or more of the 'custody triggers' have now to be pressed before a custodial sentence is imposed: having decided that

> no other method of dealing with him is appropriate because . . . he has a history of failing to respond to non-custodial penalties or because a custodial sentence is necessary for the protection of the public from serious harm or because the offence was so serious that a non-custodial sentence cannot be justified,

it is surely illogical to back-track and pass a sentence that leaves the defendant at large in the community. 'Proper' use of alternatives is, therefore, impossible without a double-think, since 'alternatives' ought only to be initiated after the decision has been made that there is no alternative.

Given the existence of this 'double-bind' it is hardly surprising that magistrates tend not to think in terms of custody and its alternatives, prefering instead a common-sense division of penalties into custodial and non-custodial sentences. One magistrate put it succinctly:

> There are no alternatives to custody; there are only custodial sentences and non-custodial sentences.

This dichotomized way of regarding sentences provides the framework for a much simpler sentencing process along the lines of what some American penologists call the 'in-out decision' (Wilkins 1980; Kress 1980). Despite our selection procedure to identify cases at risk of custody, there were some cases where the magistrates did not appear to have raised the question of custody at all. Generally speaking though, the core question of whether or not a case deserved custody was raised and answered at an early stage in the Benches' deliberations. Sentencers quickly separated off the most and least serious cases, leaving a middle band of offenders 'at the threshold' for whom custody was a possibility but not a certainty. In order to carry out the analysis undertaken in this chapter we attempted to gauge where the magistrates placed each case in relation to custody. The likelihood of custody or 'custody potential' was ascertained by asking the magistrates to recount what had actually been said in the retiring-room earlier in the day when sentence was determined. In cases where a custodial sentence had been passed we asked the Bench if custody had been their immediate conclusion, or whether any other options had been considered. Magistrates themselves referred to 'definite custody' cases, and we have borrowed this term. Cases in which consideration was given to both custodial and non-custodial sentences were coded as 'threshold'. Similarly, in cases where a non-custodial penalty was made, we inquired if other sentences, including custody, had been considered. If custody had been a genuine possibility the case was again coded as 'threshold'; if it had not it was placed in a 'not custody at all' category.

This tripartite division of cases according to their custody potential – definite custody, threshold, and not custody – is used repeatedly throughout this chapter. The threshold group was two limbed; a small minority lost their liberty ('threshold custody') but the majority did not ('threshold not custody'). This classification provided us with an important analytical tool that has enabled us to examine the relationship between custody potential, reasons for sentence and actual sentence. The application of our criteria also teases out some revealing similarities and differences between the courts.

The tripartite division of cases

Table 6.2 shows how the magistrates regarded the cases in relation to custody. The two most distinct groups were definite custody (25 per cent) and non-custody (36 per cent) cases. In between these two groups were the threshold cases, fifteen (6 per cent) of whom went into custody while seventy-three (30 per cent) retained their liberty. The magistrates' views were not obtained in seven (3 per cent) of cases.

Perhaps the most striking feature of the data is the number of cases in Yellowtown where the magistrates expressed no doubts about the use of custody (38 per cent). The magistrates in Redtown and Greytown felt that custody was inevitable in only about 22 per cent of cases and Bluetown felt this way about a relatively small number of offenders (18 per cent). Given that the samples were of comparable offenders (see Chapter 3) these disparities suggest that 'definite custody' is in part a locally defined phenomenon. The concept of the universal custody case appears to be under some threat and may represent only a very small number of the most serious cases dealt with by magistrates.

Approximately 40 per cent of the sample in Redtown, Greytown and Bluetown were defined as threshold: this group was much smaller in Yellowtown (18 per cent). Only a small number of threshold cases went into custody from each of the courts. Bluetown seemed prepared to give almost all

Table 6.2

Magistrates' estimation of custody potential

	Yellowtown	Redtown	Greytown	Bluetown	Total
Definite custody	21	13	14	11	59
Threshold custody	4	4	6	1	15
Threshold not custody	14	19	18	22	73
Not custody	20	18	22	26	86
Not known	1	6	—	—	7
Total	60	60	60	60	240

its threshold cases the 'benefit of the doubt' and all bar one were given non-custodial penalties.

The non-custodial cases were fairly evenly spread across the eight courts; the low figure in Redtown adult court is almost certainly the result of there being no magistrates' interviews in six cases, all of which were probably at the lower end of the scale of seriousness.

Taken overall the magistrates' assessment of custody potential was remarkably similar for the juvenile and adult samples. In terms of definite custody cases Yellowtown and Greytown treated juveniles and adults in an almost identical way. Given the rather different briefs of the two tribunals, it is perhaps surprising that the magistrates did not seem to differentiate between adults and juveniles in this fundamental respect (although this may be a consequence of the 1982 CJA treating 15–20-year-olds as equally culpable). The overall picture is, however, somewhat misleading because Bluetown and Redtown behaved in opposite ways. As we have already seen, Redtown sometimes flew in the face of normal expectations and the court was at its most punitive when dealing with juveniles. Bluetown behaved more conventionally and was more lenient towards its younger offenders: the explanation for this disparate behaviour probably lay in an ideological split between the juvenile and adult panels whereby liberal-minded Bluetown magistrates tended to gravitate towards the juvenile Bench. Conversely in Redtown there were a handful of rather punitive senior magistrates on the juvenile panel who, although out of line with many of their colleagues, sat very regularly.

From our interviews with magistrates it is clear that they discuss whether or not the case deserves custody quite early in their deliberations, and much of the more detailed discussion that follows hinges upon this pivotal choice. While magistrates certainly did not use the vocabulary of a 'tripartite division of cases' this model does seem to be a fair reflection of the sentencing process in the sample cases. Clearly it is important to establish how the magistrates used this implicit sentencing tool and in the following section we will attempt to discern the basis upon which the magistrates assessed the seriousness, and presumably therefore the custody potential, of the sample cases.

The magistrates' reasons for their choice of sentence and their assessment of custodial potential

This section attempts to isolate the important factors that the magistrates brought into play when judging the seriousness and, therefore, the custody potential of cases. In Table 6.3 the custody potential groups are cross-tabulated with the magistrates' reasons for sentence, so identifying the factors most closely associated with a custodial decision. The magistrates' reasons were grouped as in Chapter 5 (Tables 5.1, 5.2 and 5.3). As stated previously, a sentence was often not decided on the basis of one reason alone and the coding of responses allowed Benches to give up to six reasons for each of their decisions.

Table 6.3

Magistrates' reasons for sentence associated with a high risk of custody

	Definite custody	*Threshold custody*	*Threshold not custody*	*Not custody*	*All cases*
Serious offence	46 (78%)	12 (80%)	30 (41%)	21 (24%)	109 (47%)
Bad antecedent record	19 (32%)	6 (40%)	14 (19%)	8 (9%)	47 (20%)
Negative moral assessment	19 (32%)	6 (40%)	6 (8%)	8 (9%)	39 (17%)
Protection of public	23 (39%)	2 (13%)	3 (4%)	2 (2%)	30 (13%)
Breach of order/flouted court's authority	13 (22%)	3 (20%)	5 (5%)	4 (5%)	25 (11%)
Local clampdown	7 (12%)	1 (7%)	4 (5%)	2 (2%)	14 (6%)
Defendant had chances	9 (15%)	1 (7%)	1 (1%)	0	11 (5%)

Magistrates' reasons for sentence associated with a low risk of custody

	Definite custody	*Threshold custody*	*Threshold not custody*	*Not custody*	*All cases*
Welfare/family problems	4 (8%)	0	14 (19%)	28 (33%)	46 (20%)
Followed SER recommendation	6 (10%)	2 (13%)	19 (26%)	17 (20%)	44 (19%)
Positive moral assessment	1 (2%)	0	14 (19%)	20 (23%)	35 (15%)
Avoiding secondary consequences	0	1 (7%)	26 (36%)	7 (8%)	34 (15%)
Less serious offence	1 (2%)	1 (7%)	11 (15%)	18 (21%)	31 (13%)
No welfare problems	1 (2%)	0	12 (16%)	13 (15%)	26 (11%)
Defendant's employment situation	1 (2%)	0	13 (17%)	7 (8%)	21 (9%)
Give a defendant a chance	1 (2%)	0	11 (15%)	5 (6%)	17 (7%)
Realistic alternative to custody available	0	0	15 (21%)	1 (1%)	16 (7%)
No bad antecedent record	0	0	6 (8%)	9 (9%)	15 (6%)
School performance not poor	0	0	3 (4%)	1 (1%)	4 (2%)

Magistrates' reasons for sentence apparently not associated with the risk of custody

	Definite custody	*Threshold custody*	*Threshold not custody*	*Not custody*	*All cases*
Hands were tied	10 (17%)	3 (20%)	8 (11%)	14 (16%)	35 (15%)
Defendant needs a jolt	6 (10%)	3 (20%)	7 (10%)	10 (12%)	26 (11%)
Avoiding penalty (e.g. fine)	4 (8%)	2 (13%)	3 (4%)	12 (14%)	21 (9%)
Pathology/treatment model	4 (8%)	0	4 (5%)	5 (6%)	13 (6%)
School performance poor	4 (8%)	1 (7%)	2 (3%)	5 (6%)	12 (5%)
Other	6 (10%)	1 (7%)	18 (25%)	16 (19%)	41 (18%)
Number of reasons	185	45	249	233	712
Number of cases	59	15	73	86	233
	(100%)	(100%)	(100%)	(100%)	(100%)

Note: Up to six reasons were recorded for each sample case. The numbers give the percentage of cases in which the reason for sentence was given for each custody potential group. For example the seriousness of the offence was given as a reason for sentence in 78% of definite custody cases, and 47% of the total sample (27 cases). Positive moral assessment was given as reason in 19% of threshold-not custody cases, and 15% of the total sample of cases.

Some reasons were associated with an increased likelihood of custody, others were instrumental in directing the magistrates away from custody and a third group seemed to have little bearing on the risk of custody.

Reasons associated with a high risk of custody

As previously noted the three formal triggers for custody, together with 'negative moral assessments', emerge as being particularly influential in steering the magistrates towards using custody. The seriousness of the offence was the single most important reason behind custodial sentencing; it was mentioned in 80 per cent of all cases that received custodial penalties.

The magistrates' moral judgements of the defendants seems to have been as influential in the decision to use custody as either a serious criminal record or the need to protect the public. Interestingly, cases where the magistrates perceived a need to protect the public or which involved an offence that was the subject of a local clampdown, were predominantly categorized as definite custody rather than threshold. Defendants who flouted the court's authority, usually by re-offending or breaching a previous court order, also encouraged the Bench to use custody.

Reasons associated with a low risk of custody

Bearing in mind the crucial role of the seriousness of the current offence in custodial sentencing, it is perhaps surprising to find that a 'less serious offence' was given as a reason for the imposition of the non-custodial penalty in only twenty-nine (18 per cent) cases. Similarly the absence of a serious criminal record eliminated the risk of custody in only fifteen (17 per cent) cases. The importance of positive moral assessments in non-custodial sentencing is, of course, the corollary of negative moral assessments in cases with a high risk of custody.

Perhaps the most stiking feature of this group is the ambiguous role of welfare/family problems: for while problems of this kind generally tended to lead magistrates away from custody, in a smaller number of cases the absence of welfare/family problems had a similar effect! The magistrates were also reluctant to disrupt defendants' employment prospects: this was a factor in diverting thirteen (18 per cent) threshold cases away from custody. Similarly fear of the secondary consequences of imprisonment was given as a reason for twenty-six (36 per cent) threshold cases receiving non-custodial penalties. In contrast the availability of a realistic alternative to custody was influential in comparatively few threshold cases (16: 21 per cent)

Reasons that are not associated with risk of custody

Perhaps the most notable aspect of this third group of factors is the finding that the penal philosophy of the 'short sharp shock', expressed here as 'the defendant needs a jolt', was not closely associated with a high risk of custody: in seventeen (65 per cent) of the cases in which this was given as a reason defendants retained their liberty. Equally surprising the reasons categorized as pathology/treatment model had little discernible influence on the custody decision.

'Seriousness' and custody potential: testing the fit

Quantifying seriousness

Having looked at the magistrates' account of their reasons for their choice of sentence, and related these to custody potential, we now consider how far the magistrates' estimation of seriousness was borne out by the characteristics of the cases. This analysis was undertaken by applying a series of 'objective' tests to the immutable facts of the cases in order to establish how these related to the magistrates' tripartite division of cases. The seriousness of current offending, previous record, the protection of the public and the magistrates' moral assessments of defendants stand out as being highly significant in custodial sentencing. Inevitably the application of objective criteria is problematic, for while it is possible to devise theoretical tools to gauge the approximate seriousness of past and present offending, the need to protect the public is more difficult to measure and moral assessment almost certainly defies objective analysis of this kind. The magistrates', and indeed anyone's, moral assessment of defendants is essentially a matter of subjective judgement. Reasons for such judgements are located as much in the beliefs and prejudices of the individual as in the characteristics of the defendants: moral assessment is not, therefore, susceptible to the type of analysis attempted here.

In this section an objective measure of the seriousness of the cases in respect of the three formal criteria for custody is cross-tabulated with the magistrates' tripartite division of cases. If the magistrates actually sentenced for the reasons they articulated then one would expect this exercise to reveal a progression whereby the most serious were categorized as definite custody, and the least serious as non-custodial cases: the threshold cases would, of course, lay between either extreme. Similarly if these notions of seriousness were applied consistently then a similar pattern would occur within each court.

The seriousness of current offending

In Table 6.4 the seriousness of the current offences, calculated in the way described in Chapter 3, were cross-tabulated with the magistrates' assessment of custody potential. The aggregate total for each column was divided by the number of cases in each category of custody potential in order to arrive at an average score.

Viewed overall there does not seem to be a strong relationship between the seriousness of the offence and custody potential. Surprisingly since the courts

Table 6.4

Seriousness of current offence score by custody potential

	Juveniles (14–16)				
	Definite custody	*Threshold custody*	*Threshold not custody*	*Not custody*	*Not known*
Yellowtown	4.0	2.5	4.6	2.3	—
Redtown	5.3	3.0	5.2	2.3	—
Greytown	4.3	3.3	3.0	2.2	—
Bluetown	4.0	—	4.2	3.5	—
Total	4.4	2.2	4.3	2.6	—

	Adults (17–20)				
	Definite custody	*Threshold custody*	*Threshold not custody*	*Not custody*	*Not known*
Yellowtown	2.1	2.5	3.0	1.4	7.0
Redtown	1.5	5.6	2.5	2.8	1.5
Greytown	3.1	3.7	1.9	1.8	—
Bluetown	3.0	4.0	2.0	2.5	—
Total	2.4	4.0	2.4	2.1	2.1

are expected to have particular regard for the welfare of minors, the relationship is strongest in juvenile court, where the score for the definite custody cases was higher than that for the non-custody group. This was not, however, the case in adult court where the results were virtually 'flat'. The threshold groups present a thoroughly confusing picture: threshold custody produced the *highest* score in adult court and the *lowest* score for the juveniles.

The seriousness of the current offences corresponds most closely with custody potential in Greytown and Bluetown; in Yellowtown and Redtown, however, the results look deeply paradoxical. Redtown's 'definite custody' group had the lowest score for any of the custody potential groups, its score being less than one-third of that for 'threshold custody'. In Yellowtown the highest score was attained by 'threshold not custody' in both tribunals.

In short there is little evidence here of the 'progression' anticipated at the beginning of the section, for there is no straightforward relationship between the seriousness of the offences and custody potential. The results in Yellowtown and Redtown are particularly 'shapeless', the seriousness of offending seemed to have an almost random effect on the way the magistrates regarded the cases in relation to custody.

Table 6.5

Seriousness of previous offence score by custody potential

	Juveniles (14–16)				
	Definite custody	*Threshold custody*	*Threshold not custody*	*Not custody*	*Not known*
Yellowtown	3.7	1.5	3.5	2.3	—
Redtown	2.7	1.0	2.6	2.9	—
Greytown	4.6	2.0	3.7	2.2	—
Bluetown	1.8	—	1.8	1.4	—
Total	3.2	1.1	2.9	2.2	—

	Adults (17–20)				
	Definite custody	*Threshold custody*	*Threshold not custody*	*Not custody*	*Not known*
Yellowtown	3.2	4.5	3.2	2.8	9.0
Redtown	1.8	1.3	3.3	2.0	1.3
Greytown	4.7	5.3	3.6	3.7	—
Bluetown	2.4	2.0	1.9	1.9	—
Total	3.0	3.3	3.0	2.0	—

The seriousness of previous offending

The seriousness of previous offending was calculated as in Note 1 in Chapter 3 (see Table 6.5) and here again an average score was calculated for each of the custody potential groups.

A similar pattern of results emerges to that for current offending: previous offending appears to be only very loosely related to custody potential. Provided one looks at the overall results for the four PSDs, previous offending does seem to function as a reference point for the identification of the 'clear-cut' cases (i.e. the 'definite custody' and 'not custody' groups) although not uniformly across the four courts. The picture is most confused in the threshold cases, and it was here that the differences between the courts were most pronounced.

The relationship between past offending and custody potential is clearest in the two Greytown tribunals and in Bluetown's adult court. Yellowtown and Redtown again produced 'negative' results. In Redtown adult court the two custody groups scored much lower than 'threshold not custody': in juvenile court the 'not custody' group had the highest score.

Table 6.6

Tariff position by custody potential

	Juveniles (14–16)					
	Definite custody	Threshold custody	Threshold not custody	Not custody	Not known	Total
No previous convictions	3 (9%)	1 (3%)	5 (16%)	10 (31%)	—	19 (59%)
Low-tariff climbing	11 (11%)	3 (3%)	21 (20%)	25 (24%)	—	60 (58%)
Middle-tariff climbing	4 (11%)	2 (6%)	5 (14%)	4 (11%)	—	15 (42%)
Previous tariff jump	2 (15%)	—	2 (15%)	3 (23%)	—	7 (53%)
Post-custody/care plateau	7 (30%)	—	2 (9%)	—	—	9 (39%)
High-tariff climbing	3 (9%)	—	3 (9%)	4 (12%)	—	10 (30%)
Total	30 (13%)	6 (3%)	38 (16%)	46 (19%)	—	120 (51%)

	Adults (17–20)					
	Definite custody	Threshold custody	Threshold not custody	Not custody	Not known	Total
No previous convictions	4 (13%)	—	—	7 (22%)	2 (6%)	13 (41%)
Low-tariff climbing	7 (7%)	4 (4%)	14 (13%)	16 (15%)	3 (3%)	44 (42%)
Middle-tariff climbing	5 (14%)	2 (6%)	8 (23%)	4 (11%)	1 (3%)	20 (57%)
Previous tariff jump	2 (15%)	1 (8%)	—	3 (23%)	—	6 (46%)
Post-custody/care plateau	4 (17%)	1 (4%)	3 (13%)	5 (22%)	1 (4%)	14 (60%)
High-tariff climbing	7 (21%)	1 (3%)	10 (30%)	5 (15%)	—	19 (69%)
Total	29 (12%)	9 (4%)	35 (15%)	40 (17%)	7 (3%)	120 (41%)

Combining the seriousness of past and current offences does not change the overall picture in any meaningful way and the overall pattern of results noted in the previous sections is retained.

Tariff position

In practice magistrates probably take greater heed of previous disposals than of past offences. Generally speaking the antecedent record presented to the court does not give details of the offences beyond a generic heading, for example 'burglary' or 'theft'. In the absence of more precise information, magistrates probably judge the gravity of past offending by reference to the disposals handed out. As suggested earlier, the Benches probably looked at previous disposals in order to decide if an offender was unable or unwilling to respond to non-custodial penalties. With this in mind 'tariff position' was cross-tabulated with custody potential as in Note 2 in Chapter 3 (see Table 6.6) in order to evaluate what part previous disposals play in the eventual choice of sentence.

Though the nature of our analysis does not make it possible to draw direct comparisons, the fit between tariff position and custody potential does seem to be closer than was the case for either past or present offending. The match between tariff position and custody is clearest if one looks at the broad outline of the whole sample. The 'definite custody' cases were relatively highly convicted, 42 per cent being either high tariff, tariff jump or post-custody. The 'non custody' cases had shorter records, 62 per cent had either no previous convictions or were low tariff. 'Threshold not custody' cases were drawn from defendants with middle-range antecedent convictions, 66 per cent being either low or middle-tariff offenders.

Once again this comparatively clear-cut outline profile collapses if the PSDs are examined individually. Perhaps as a reflection of severe sentencing in the past, 33 per cent of Yellowtown's 'not custody' cases were high tariff. Yellowtown has continued to escalate cases 'up tariff', two 'definite custody' cases had no previous convictions, and a further 28 per cent were low tariff. The 'definite custody' cases in Greytown were a disparate group: at one end of the spectrum 29 per cent were low tariff and at the other end of the scale 36 per cent had previously experienced custody. Bluetown juveniles were comparatively lightly convicted: this was true even for the 'definite custody' group, all of whom had either no previous convictions or were low tariff. A characteristically paradoxical picture emerges from Redtown PSD, where 46 per cent of 'definite custody' cases were low tariff, while 47 per cent of 'threshold not custody' cases were either high tariff or had previously served a custodial sentence.

Protecting the public

Protecting the public is a significant factor in custodial sentencing. Chapter 5 notes that 80 per cent of the cases where the protection of the public was given as a reason for sentence resulted in a custodial penalty, and it was mentioned by

33 per cent of all Benches that imposed custodial sentences. Protecting the public is also one of the formal criteria for custody laid down by current legislation and should not, therefore, be ignored in an analysis of this kind.

As stated at the beginning of the chapter the need to protect the public is a difficult matter to quantify. Chapters 4 and 5 illustrate the subjective nature of the sentencers' judgements in this area: the meaning of the protection of the public depends upon the view taken of crime in general as well as the threat to the community posed by some offenders.

Despite differences in views of local crime, magistrates in all the PSDs expressed concern about burglary. We have, therefore, used this offence as a vehicle for looking at the magistrates' application of the principle of protecting the public. The sharp increase in the incidence of burglary had aroused alarm amongst some magistrates. It is one offence which is highly likely to elicit the response that the public need to be protected. Some burglaries are, of course, more serious than others: burglary of commercial premises is usually thought to be less grave than household burglary, which places the public most directly at risk. Indeed some clerks and justices have suggested that domestic burglary is too serious to be dealt with by magistrates and should, in principle at least, be committed to the Crown Court. It would, therefore, seem quite rational to expect a 'hierarchy of burglary' to correlate with the magistrates' custody potential rating. We cross-tabulated the hierarchy of the different kinds of burglary with custody potential in order to see if the magistrates actually thought in this way about the burglars they sentenced (see Chapter 3, Note 3, and Table 6.7).

There is little evidence here that offences which place the public at greatest risk are associated with a high likelihood of custody. The magistrates were unequivocal about the use of custody in only 8 per cent of cases of domestic burglary; indeed there was no apparent risk of custody for 44 per cent of defendants who committed offences of this type. Contrary to the principle of

Table 6.7

Custody potential in cases of burglary

	Definite custody	Threshold custody	Threshold not custody	Not custody	Not known	Total
Domestic burglary	3	5	12	16	—	36
Burglary of commercial premises	5	2	14	7	3	31
Burglary of schools	1	—	2	1	—	4
Unspecified burglary	—	—	1	1	—	2
Attempted burglary	—	—	—	1	—	1
Total	9	7	29	26	3	74

using custody to protect the public, burglars of commercial premises were more likely to be defined as definite custody than dwelling-house burglars. The magistrates gave some consideration to the use of custody in 68 per cent of cases involving commercial burglary, suggesting that the value of the property at stake is in reality perhaps more influential in magistrates' sentencing than the abhorrence aroused by intrusion into private homes.

Custody potential and sentence passed

Although the basis of magistrates' thinking about cases in relation to custody remains partially obscure, it is clear that determining the custody potential of a case is an important part of the sentencing process and it is, therefore, important to ascertain if these judgements are carried through in the decision about the nature and severity of the sentence imposed. Having decided whether or not they are dealing with a custody case, the Bench have then to move on to a more detailed discussion about the choice and terms of sentence. Despite the fact that many magistrates feel their options are restricted, and crave yet more powers (see Chapter 4), the magistracy actually enjoy a good deal of latitude in sentencing. English law lays down only what sentence may be imposed; it is left to the wide discretionary powers of the magistrates to determine exactly what sentence is to be activated (Ashworth 1983).

Custody potential was cross-tabulated with the type of sentence in order to gauge the effect that the magistrates' estimation of the seriousness of the case has upon the actual choice of penalty (Table 6.8). For this analysis sentences were split into three groups. 'Custody' includes all youth custody, detention centre orders and Section 38 committals to Crown Court for sentence. 'Alternatives to custody' refers to those sentences introduced or re-articulated by the 1982 CJA (supervision orders with intermediate treatment or specified activities order, probation orders with 4(a) or 4(b) requirements, community service for 16-year-olds and adults and care orders, including charge and control orders). 'Other' is made up of the remaining low- and middle-tariff sentences (conditional discharges, fines, attendance centre orders, straight supervision and probation orders).

Here again one might expect to find a progression whereby the definite custody group was dealt with by youth custody or detention centre orders, threshold cases by either detention centre orders or alternatives to custody and not-custody cases by 'other' sentences. The findings laid out in Table 6.8 are far less clear cut, particularly for the non-custodial groups. As one might expect, the most severe penalties were handed out to 'definite custody' cases, 46 per cent of this group received youth custody sentences, 93 per cent of all youth custody orders being imposed on definite custody cases. There were, however, significant differences between the sample courts. Once again the Yellowtown court was the most punitive: 67 per cent of definite custody cases received youth custody or were committed to Crown Court. Comparable figures for the other courts were Bluetown 46 per cent, Greytown 37 per cent and Redtown 23 per

Table 6.8

Types of sentences imposed on the different custody potential groups

	All cases					
	Definite custody	*Threshold custody*	*Threshold not custody*	*Not custody*	*Not known*	
Custody	59	15	—	—	1	75
Alternatives to custody	—	—	43	26	5	74
Other	—	—	30	60	1	91
Total	59	15	73	86	7	240

cent. Furthermore almost half (48 per cent) of all the youth custody sentences in excess of six months were imposed by Yellowtown magistrates.

Not surprisingly the threshold cases tended to receive lighter custodial sentences; twelve of the fifteen orders in this group were for detention centre. These borderline custody cases were fairly evenly divided between very short sentences of one month or less and more substantial sentences of three months and over. There was a noticeable absence of detention centre sentences of intermediate length in this group. One possible explanation for this may be that the threshold group comprises two kinds of defendants: first, offenders who do not have a history of offending and who received a short, sharp shock because the magistrates wished to 'nip their offending in the bud', and second more serious and persistent offenders who were poised on the brink of custody but were reprieved by the use of a community alternative.

The 'threshold not custody' offenders were a mixed bag who received not only community alternatives but also a range of lower tariff options. Undoubtedly this reflects the absence of any consensus view about the tariff of non-custodial sentences. The distribution was different in juvenile court where the majority of 'threshold custody' cases received one of the 'alternative' sentences (24: 63 per cent). This difference between the age groups is probably due to the fact that 'package' requirements were more readily available for the younger age range, in respect of whom supervision with requirements (intermediate treatment and specified activities) constituted 42 per cent of disposals in this custody potential group. In contrast there was a dearth of Schedule 11 packages for 17–20-year-old offenders: only four (11 per cent) of threshold cases were dealt with in this way. Community service order predominated for the older age group (15: 43 per cent).

Again the courts demonstrated individual preferences: 62 per cent of Redtown's adult 'threshold not custody' cases received community service compared with 33 per cent in Yellowtown. In Redtown 67 per cent of juveniles in this group received supervision with intermediate treatment, compared with 48 per cent in Bluetown.

In terms of the sentences they received the two non-custodial groups were not at all clearly differentiated: the 'not custody' cases received a similar mix of sentences to the 'threshold not custody' group. Of the 'non custody' cases 30 per cent received alternatives to custody: the tendency to use diversionary sentences, in circumstances where the defendant was at no real risk of custody, was even more prevalent in the adult sample. Of the adult 'not custody' group 48 per cent received alternative sentences, compared with 28 per cent of the lower age range. This apparent mistargeting of community alternatives is probably attributable to the catholic use of community service: twelve (30 per cent) of the adult sample received orders of this type.

Conclusion

The analysis undertaken in this chapter suggests that the magistrates' assessment of custody potential does not accurately or consistently tally between the courts or with our interpretation of seriousness. We suspect that many magistrates would say 'So what?' in reply to this finding. Why should the judgements of another court or a research team about what constitutes seriousness be preferred to their own? The point is not that our scale of seriousness is right in any absolute sense, for there can be no objective rank-ordering of seriousness that does not involve making subjective judgements about the relative gravity of different individual or categories of offences. Rather our intention has been to produce an analysis by applying a number of fixed criteria across the whole sample. Similarly it is not possible to draw up universally acceptable notions about the need to protect the public or the failure to respond to non-custodial penalties, since these too are, at present, subjective issues and not matters of empirical fact, despite Court of Appeal decisions (Ashworth 1983). Certainly our grounds for assessing 'seriousness' will not win universal approval, but had we adopted different criteria it seems unlikely that the results of a similar analysis would reveal a greater degree of consistency in sentencing practice between our courts.

From the account of sentencing practice in Chapters 4 and 5 it is evident that magistrates do not just judge seriousness by what is on the charge sheets or conveyed by the prosecutor. Their practice revolves around weighing up the evidence 'on the day', to use their own terminology they 'judge every case on its merits'. The magistrates support their claim to be uniquely equipped to make judgements of this kind with the dual assertion that they know the 'local scene' and that they are the only impartial group in the court. It is a moot point whether these claims could ever be justified, for complete impartiality may be an unobtainable goal. Furthermore the Bluetown and Yellowtown clerks gave clear accounts of the difficulties they had in recruiting working-class magistrates in sufficient numbers to achieve a socially balanced Bench.

The professionals and middle classes dominated both these Benches, which belies their claims to reflect the community accurately.

To a large extent the planks upon which the magistrates constructed their view of 'seriousness' remain elusive, at least as far as this particular kind of analysis is concerned. The magistrates' moral assessment of defendants, given as a reason for sentence in seventy-four cases, may well be the joker in the pack. The actual strength of this factor in any given case is unknown, but it was clear from our interviews with the Benches that one of the prized attributes of an experienced magistrate was the ability to make snap judgements about defendants' personalities and their propensity for future offending. A negative moral assessment of the defendant was said to be influential in 32 per cent of all custody cases, and may well have been a subliminal element on many more occasions.

The magistrates' over-concentration on what they perceive to be the unique qualities of individual defendants, to the detriment of the formal factors in sentencing, partly accounts for what we have called the 'sentencing mystery'. Most magistrates clearly regarded sentencing as an art not a science. The magistrates' approach to sentencing witnessed in Chapters 4 and 5 betrays an attitude of mind that denies the relevance of comparisons between cases. The magistrates' professional ideology includes an inbuilt abhorrence to the notion of sentencing guidelines along the lines of those introduced in some US states (Von Hirsch 1976). The magistrates have accepted guidelines in connection with road traffic offences, but even here they are insistent that the penalties suggested are not binding and should be regarded only as starting-points. Some magistrates actually claimed to feel hamstrung even by present legislation, despite its essentially permissive nature and wide element of discretion.

It is this extraordinary situation which is at the heart of the prison crisis. In the absence of any official restriction on the supply of prison places the whole system is demand led. This demand is defined by the sentencers. If they wish to use custody they do so and the prison system, funded by the taxpayers via government, must respond with more prisons, more places and in practice more overcrowding. The consequences of this are discussed in Chapter 9. First we must look at school reports and examine their contents and style in order to discover why they are such influential documents in affecting magistrates' decisions.

7 Objective or objectionable?
School reports for the juvenile court

Introduction

It should be very clear, given the results reported in Chapter 5, that school reports are extremely influential in shaping sentencers' decisions. School reports were referred to by the magistrates as important in forty-five (76 per cent) of the fifty-nine cases where they were available and as a 'major influence' in sentencing in 63 per cent. In percentage terms they carried more weight than any other single factor including SERs, which were of major influence in 61 per cent of cases where they were available. However, school reports, unlike SERs, tended to push cases towards rather than away from custody, a process which increased in proportion to the amount of negative comment teachers included (see also McLaughlin 1988).

Magistrates awarded school reports this high status because they believed them to be objective and reliable assessments of defendants' characters. This contrasted with their suspicions that SERs were often biased and 'unrealistic' documents.

While 59 of the 120 juveniles in our sample had school reports prepared about them, the availability of reports varied enormously between the four courts. Yellowtown received nineteen reports on sample cases and Redtown fourteen. Yet in Bluetown twenty-two reports were available and here magistrates would readily adjourn a case if they felt a school report was required. This contrasted with Greytown magistrates who accepted, without question, the fact that school reports were rarely available. Only four of our sample subjects had such reports prepared on them. Greytown social workers and probation officers, not at all unhappy with this 'drought', routinely included a section on schooling in their SERs: a strategy clearly aimed at maintaining this situation.

Disclosure of contents

In 1987 the government announced its intention to revise the Magistrates' Courts Rules whereby the contents of school reports, traditionally 'secret' in many juvenile courts (see Parker *et al.* 1981; Ball 1983), would be made available to the 'defence', this in practice meaning the solicitor or parents of a juvenile. Such a change, to bring school reports in line with other expert reports, was long overdue, and indeed pressure from various quarters including NACRO (1984) had been building for some time.

At the time of our fieldwork only one court, Bluetown, had a clear policy of providing parents with a copy of the report and of asking, during the course of the hearing, if they had any comments to make. While the atmosphere of the courtroom may make it very difficult for parents to voice any disagreement; those who did so had their views taken seriously. In some instances, however, this resulted in further adjourments for investigations to be made. This had its own consequences, not only in terms of delay before a final adjudication was made but also in that some juveniles had actually left school before the case was finally dealt with. This was so in nearly a third of the school reports presented in this Midlands court. There is an issue here about the extent to which greater justice in respect of disclosure may lead to other difficulties. The potential problems were well illustrated in the case of a 16-year-old girl in court on a charge of occasioning actual bodily harm during the course of what the prosecution described as a 'schoolgirl fight'. The case was treated as a minor matter, with no SER presented or requested, until the girl's mother disputed the truancy alleged in the school report. This was taken up by the Bench, who adjourned the case, asking for an SER concentrating on the school attendance issue. When the SER, duly focusing on the school issue, became available some weeks later, by which time the girl had already left school, the Bench on that occasion was not happy with it and adjourned the case again for a fuller report. On the basis of that SER, there was another adjournment, this time for an Intermediate Treatment assessment. When the case was finally dealt with, nearly five months after the first appearance, the girl, now pregnant and so considered not suitable for IT, was made subject to a supervision order although the magistrates on that occasion were no longer interested in the school issue but concerned about the girl's general welfare. Without wanting to suggest that instances like this were routine in Bluetown, it does illustrate how school reports can assume a more central place when parental reaction is taken seriously and how a rapid acceleration through the tariff can occur as a result. Bluetown's experiment with disclosure suggests that introducing formal rules about disclosure will not in itself necessarily improve the quality of justice.

In Redtown efforts towards a greater openness were also made, but much less systematically. Practice in the remaining two courts was rather more haphazard, although in Greytown only a very small number of school reports were presented anyway. Yellowtown gave no active encouragement to parents to comment on the contents and on the very few occasions when the report was questioned, the challenge was ill-received by magistrates.

The content of the reports

Despite these variations in local practice, the format of the reports was similar in all the courts. Information was supplied under pre-given printed headings covering topics which included attendance and punctuality, academic ability and achievement, attitudes to school work and behaviour in school in relation to both staff and other pupils, special interests, an assessment of the pupil's character and parental contact with the school. Although the focus was primarily on educational issues, report writers were clearly being asked to make some kind of moral assessment on the pupil's character which, as we shall see, they were apparently keen to provide. School reports presented in Bluetown, the court with the most progressive policy in respect of disclosure, did not differ in content from those presented in the other three courts. Across the courts there was a depressing similarity in terms of content, with a preponderance of extremely judgemental and negative observations under every heading on the school report forms, frequently without any substantiating evidence.

Educational and disciplinary problems were regularly cast as symptomatic of undesirable social attitudes in the individual pupil. Problems were very rarely presented in context or with any suggestion that they might arise from the characteristics of the school or the education system more generally. Thus, for example, attendance was often crudely stated as a fraction of actual over possible attendances, without any explanation of whether the poor attendance mentioned in two-thirds of the reports was due to truancy or to illness, and without reference to average attendance rates for that particular school. The report which made clear that the defendant's recent truancy and lateness was part of a more general pattern during a period of teachers' industrial action was a rare exception. Much more common was a statement such as

> His poor report at the end of his 3rd year showed his attendance to be poor − 126 half days out of a possible 160 − and he was often late for morning school.

The negative tone here suggests that the defendant was culpably absent and late, but this is implied rather than stated clearly. Similarly problems with levels of academic achievement were attributed to the unavailability of an appropriate educational environment in only one case and this was a child who had been assessed as having special educational needs. In the majority of cases, educational attainment was said to be below average because of 'under-achievement' which was generally implicitly attributed to the pupil's own moral failings. For example, the statement that

> He has required close individual attention to maintain in him any ability and willingness to cope with academic work at which his level of achievement is below average.

could equally well have been phrased in a more positive way, in terms of this boy's being able and willing to cope with academic work when given the close individual attention which he needs. However, educational issues often shaded into disciplinary issues within the school. Over half of the sample were said to be below average in their standards of behaviour in school and comments here ranged from the relatively mild:

> B can be very helpful and polite. However he does have a great difficulty in controlling his temper and this has led to a number of disruptive incidents in school.

to the much more damning:

> Generally his attitude to members of staff seems to be offensive and he has been rude and uncooperative on occasions and even used abusive language. He is stubborn and does not like criticism however well intentioned and constructive it is intended to be.

Indeed, who does? However in the school context a dislike of criticism is seen as symptomatic of a deeper unwillingness to conform and attitudes to school rules were treated as an important indicator of a more basic 'anti-authority' stance. A fifth of the sample were said to present major discipline problems for the school. They were described in terms such as:

> Impervious to normal school discipline.

> Attention seeking, especially if boys are present. She hates schools and people in authority. She can be polite but is often rude and aggressive and insolent. It is a constant battle to make her conform to school rules.

However, even those who presented no real problems of discipline were open to allegations of a more superficial ritualism which might disguise less acceptable attitudes, as in the case of the boy who was said to 'obey the rules but only because he fears the consequences of not doing so'. Again this is something that would probably be true of most people in some contexts. Lack of commitment to school rules was also 'read off' from appearance in descriptions of young people as 'scruffy' or as having 'skinhead' or 'punk' hair-styles. Thus a number of reports conveyed a very negative image even where no overt difficulty had been mentioned.

No fewer than thirty-six (61 per cent) of the reports contained at least some unsubstantiated negative comment of this type. In some cases it was mixed in with a more positive view in a way that suggests someone should investigate the incidence of a 'Jekyll and Hyde' syndrome in the nation's secondary schools!

> He has been remarkably polite and helpful, and during the Autumn term he helped paint the music room. The work was completed diligently and with enthusiasm. He appears to enjoy doing odd jobs around the school, but the availability of these jobs has decreased due to incidents of thieving. Yet he is a liar and will lie even to the point of stupidity.

The insinuation here is that this youngster was actually responsible for these incidents of 'thieving', but it is ambiguous: perhaps there had been a general curtailment of jobs until the culprit was identified. This report did at least have some positive aspects, but in a fifth of all cases the negative comments were totally unmitigated and these reports can only be described as full scale character assassinations. The following examples are not at all untypical:

Devious, plausible, manipulative and shallow.

A liar and a thief.

Openly defiant, aggressive and lies instinctively if forced to do something he does not want to do.

Devious and untrustworthy. Recalcitrant . . . selfish and egocentric,

Such unsubstantiated allegations, especially where they include allegations of criminal matters such as theft, would not be allowed in adult court and would probably provide some grounds for a libel suit if expressed in a different context. As comments made by adults with pastoral as well as educational responsibilities for young people going through the experience of a court appearance, such comments are surely unprofessional. Undoubtedly teachers have a very difficult task in dealing with fourth- and fifth-year pupils alienated from school and with few prospects when they leave (McRobbie 1978). But reports to the court cannot be regarded as an appropriate forum for the expression of teachers' frustration, however understandable this may be (Pask 1984). Compare for example two reports.

	Case 1	Case 2
Attendance	Suspended because of truancy.	40 out of 40 possible half-days.
Academic	Average to above average ability but . . . he will make every excuse and attempt to get away with the least possible effort.	Of above average ability . . . 'M' had a particular interest in reading and his excellent command of language skills reflected this.
Conduct and attitude	Motivated almost entirely by his desire to impress people. This has resulted in him being involved in stupid situations almost continually. He can turn on the charm when necessary but one soon gets the impression that one is being taken for a ride. He is a threat physically to his peers who fear his outburst of uncontrolled aggression.	'M' conducted himself well during attendance, he was unfailingly pleasant and helpful at all times and demonstrated his ability to respond positively to small group situations. Within this framework he was honest and reliable and could be entrusted to take responsibility for materials and equipment. He was equally able to accept discipline and would seek opportunity to make amends when such incidents occurred.
Other comments	The school has been quite unable to cope with the considerable problems posed by this boy and outside help has been requested. The utmost has been done to accommodate him without success. It is his excessive desire to dominate in a social situation which is the root of his problem.	'M' was a popular and respected member of the group and appeared to use his influence on other children in a positive and supportive manner. He related well to teaching staff and generally took active interest in all aspects of school life.

The second report emphasizes positive aspects, refers to the boy by his name and leaves the impression of a very different sort of person from the first. Yet the sting in this particular tale is that both of these reports were written, within the space of three months, on the same boy: the first from the secondary school from which he was suspended and the second from the education unit at the Observation and Assessment Centre at which he was subsequently placed. The magistrates accepted the secondary school account and largely discounted the Observation and Assessment Centre's report, believing it to be tarred with the 'social work' brush. The boy received six months in youth custody.

School reports as moral assessments

The use and misuse of school reports provides us with the clearest example of the importance magistrates attach to the moral agenda which underpins criminal proceedings. Our criticism is not so much that school reports contain moral judgements: this is inevitable given the sort of information which is asked for on the forms sent out to schools. The more pertinent criticisms centre first on the fact that school reports are regarded as objective documents and, second, that they are used to predict future delinquency.

The fact that magistrates are so articulate on the subject of bias in SERs and pleas of mitigation demonstrates that they can, and do, identify subjectivity, speculation and hearsay in expert evidence. Why do they not extend this skill to school reports? One reason, which we mentioned in an earlier chapter, may be that juvenile court panels attract a high proportion of teachers, particularly headteachers, to their membership (Ball 1988). A more important reason is that school reports feed into the magistrates' ideology. First, magistrates believe that school reports are objective and accurate because teachers really know the subjects stood before them. Second, as we have shown, they also believe that every case is different which thus requires every sentence to be tailored to the individual. Every deliberation must contain something unique and personal. The school report provides this something. When a knowing teacher says the pupil-offender is a bad lot then he or she truly is. Moreover magistrates assume that, in the end, school behaviour is a microcosm of a young person's wider social behaviour. Non-conformity within the school environment is thus seen as symptomatic of an underlying set of attitudes which will, if not checked, spread into other anti-social and anti-authority-type behaviour. Magistrates believe that school reports help them predict the likelihood and nature of future offending. So in the end it is precisely the moral context, the strong language and imagery peppered with incident and anecdote which magistrates value and which gives school reports their credibility. It is only those outside the magistrates' magic circle who will question whether these documents really are objective and wonder if they are sometimes objectionable.

Finally, before moving on to discuss SERs in detail, it is worth mentioning a likely unintended consequence of the increasing tendency for SERs not to be prepared on first- and second-time offenders. In the juvenile court this is likely to mean that the only report available on the majority of those charged will be the school report. Given what we have said about school reports and the tendency to push sentencing 'up tariff' this may become an important issue for those trying to 'manage' the sentencing profile of local courts.

8 Professional guesses: social enquiry reports and targeting 'alternatives to custody'

Introduction

The role of the SER continues to be controversial. As we have seen while magistrates agree that these documents are influential they clearly sift and sort through their contents in search of social information which fit their own agendas. For the social work profession the SER is a crucial conduit: its utility rests on its ability to link the provision of community-based supervision with 'appropriate' client offenders. 'Struggles' between report writers and sentencers over who is appropriate for what are routine.

In this chapter we will concentrate on the contents and orientations of SERs and the strategies report writers use in targeting their recommendations for 'alternatives' to custody. We also compare the objectives of report writers with the decisions of the court in order to assess the impact of SERs on the 'custody or not' decision. We are fortunate to be able to do this, for despite the ever-flowing debate about SERs (e.g. Raynor 1980; Paley and Leeves 1982; Tutt and Giller 1985; Stone 1987) hard evidence that reports' recommendations actually achieve certain outcomes is in short supply (see Curran 1983). The reasons for this centre, quite simply, on the inaccessibility of the sentencers and the secrecy governing their decision making. Despite a few noble attempts (Carter and Wilkins 1967; Mott 1977; Hine *et al*. 1978; Kapardis 1981) we have little reliable knowledge about the impact of SERs, beyond measurements of correlation between recommendation and actual disposal (e.g. Celnick 1985 and 1986; Stafford and Hill 1987). Yet ascertaining the nature of this relationship is extremely important. On it rests the *raison d'être*, 'the faith', of the alternatives to custody movement and, as we shall see in Chapter 9, the feasibility and credibility of the government's 'punishment in the community' arm of its penal policy.

For commentators whose critique of British penal policy owes much to the work of Foucault and Donzelot (e.g. Cohen 1985) the simultaneous creation of more prisons and more so-called alternatives to custody, under the law and order strategy of three successive Conservative governments, holds no surprises. The consistency of this thrust in penal policy is becoming rapidly more visible (Parker *et al*. 1987; Pitts 1988).

The SER is an important tool in this policy revision, given its role in identifying 'heavy end' offenders and providing the courts with 'intelligence' with which to assess seriousness and dangerousness and so make 'appropriate' 'custody or not' decisions. Consequently its format and contents have been subject to major revision for example in 1983 (Home Office Circular 17/83), 1986 (Home Office Circular 92/86) and 1987 (Department of Health and Social Security 1987) supported by the 1982 Act and new instructions to the probation service (Home Office 1984). Thus report writers are requested to spend less time on routine social information and more on the context of the offence and offender's attitude to it. They should spend less time writing reports on first- and second-time offenders and more on the recidivist. In short they should concentrate their minds on those at risk of custody. Moreover their recommendations and supervision programmes should be clearly set out and give sentencers a clear indication of exactly what will happen via supervision and probation orders. Estimating the degree to which report writers have accepted these new orders from above will be one of the aims of this chapter. There is good reason to believe that social work may well subvert or at least modify some of these instructions (Harris and Webb 1987; Bottoms and Stelman 1988).

Report writing in the four courts

The qualification and experience of report writers

Our questionnaire to each report writer was completed in 235 cases, although this represents only about 180 actual social workers and probation officers, reflecting some specialization particularly in Greytown and Bluetown. The stereotype of the young, inexperienced social worker has survived long beyond the temporary situation in the early 1970s from which it emerged. The social workers and probation officers working in our four courts rated themselves as court-goers of considerable experience, with only eight describing themselves as relatively new to the job. The vast majority of these report writers were qualified and had been for several years. Indeed the majority had been qualified over five years and about 20 per cent over ten years. The unqualified staff were predominantly from Yellowtown where 30 per cent of the department's staff remain unqualified. There was however no sense in which any of our courts were serviced by an inexperienced set of report writers.

Reports for the sample cases

Only 19 of the 201 report writers who answered this question suggested that they had inadequate time or resources to prepare the sample case report. These nineteen were spread across each area and agency, confirming our own impression that there were no major staffing or organizational problems in any of the areas. While 84 respondents had access to earlier reports prepared on their clients, 117 had not. Fifty authors had themselves prepared between two and five previous reports on the sample subject, including one who had prepared ten and one who had prepared twelve previous reports on her client. However, for the majority, this was the first or second report they or a colleague had prepared on the subject. This reflects the impact of an outline policy operating in each area, for reports not to be prepared on first- or second-time offenders. However, SERs were available in almost all sample cases because, by definition, the sample was made up of either recidivists or those convicted of serious offences. Consequently magistrates usually requested reports although for their 'current cases' social workers and probation officers themselves often took the lead.

There were differences between the courts in that Yellowtown magistrates requested reports less often then elsewhere. There was also a tendency for pre-trial reports (eight out of thirty cases) to be produced for Yellowtown's juvenile court – a practice which will probably have changed since the fieldwork.

The content of social enquiry reports

Introduction

The new instructions from the Centre have all attempted to get SER authors to change the emphasis of their reports. Authors are encouraged to focus less on personal circumstances and more on the offence and to consider the effectiveness of different sentences. Probation and social services are instructed to target their effects on high tariff cases at risk of custody. The 1982 Section 1(4) criteria adjusted by the 1988 Criminal Justice Act provide the 'official' instruments for calculating this risk, although as we have seen magistrates use many other bench-marks.

We assessed each sample report for discrete themes or orientations. Table 8.1 provides a ranked list of the six most prevalent themes. There are obviously strong hints from the incidence of various orientations that recent guidelines for report writing have been responded to selectively.

Focus on personal and family circumstances

As Table 8.1 indicates, SERs still give substantial attention to an offender's immediate domestic circumstances (J. Thorpe 1979). The tendency for juvenile court reports to have the stronger emphasis is not surprising although the extensive differences between social worker and probation officer reports are

Table 8.1

Main orientations of social enquiry reports prepared by social workers and probation officers

Particular theme	% of all reports with this orientation	% of social worker reports with this orientation	% of probation officer reports with this orientation
Family problems or disruption in parenting	41	74	32
Putting offence in context	27	15	31
Normal delinquency but formal interventions required	26	32	25
'Easily led' young offender	21	25	20
Problems at school or with employment	20	25	19
Complies with orders	15	8	17

Notes: N = 53 for social workers
N = 182 for probation officers
Up to three orientations per case were coded.

perhaps unexpected. This emphasis by report writers was found in all the juvenile courts but was lowest in Redtown. We also noted a greater emphasis in Bluetown adult court on personal circumstances and family dynamics. The following example, from this Midlands court summarizing a family interview, is fairly typical.

> Mr—— was the main spokesman when I visited the home. He expressed interest in 'M' and told me that he is well behaved at home, but also despaired about his behaviour outside the home. There was little interaction between 'M' and his mother and I felt there was some anger evident, although this was not expressed verbally. It was clear that 'M' was not going to share his views about his offending in front of his parents and I assume this was typical of many recent encounters between them. Mr —— mentioned they had sought the help of a Child Psychiatrist, as they thought there was something wrong with 'M'. They told me they knew this doctor in connection with their son 'J' who unfortunately is a brain-damaged child, and only then did it emerge the extent of the demands 'J' placed upon them, which inadvertently must have placed 'M' in an isolated and neglected position in the family.

Focus on the offence

Our assessment of the 235 reports concluded that the offence was focused on in a substantial way in 68 cases, was present in 82, only slight in 58 and absent in 23 cases. Greytown magistrates were most likely and Yellowtown least likely to receive reports highlighting the misdemeanour and the offender's attitude to it. This focus took a variety of forms ranging from the offender's views:

> 'G' tells me that at the time he had been drinking (cans purchased from an off-licence), the group of 'friends' he was with all started arguing, and 'G' used the knife. He now maintains that he was 'stupid'. 'G' tells me that the group have since retaliated, and he himself received a black eye, and other injuries.
>
> I fully discussed with 'G' the extreme seriousness of getting involved in these types of situations. He does now appear to be aware of the very dire consequences which could result.

or lack of them:

> Regarding the present offence of damaging a fluorescent light and the un-provoked response to another youth, he was not able to express the reason for this but one could speculate on his need to act out some of his frustrations of the home situation.

to the detailed and sometimes emotive feelings of parents:

> 'G's parents have been shocked and upset by these thefts and are at a loss as how best to deal with their daughter. Her mother tells me that they have made every attempt to make her feel loved and wanted and to provide her with discipline and guidance but she continues to steal from them and is disobedient and unco-operative. They are concerned about her association with various West-Indian youths and fear she may get on to the 'hard' drugs.

We looked at the incidence of focus on the offence by agency. Probation reports placed much greater emphasis on the offence and this remained true when social services and probation reports prepared for the juvenile court were isolated. However, this willingness to focus on the offence is in fact fairly selective and while 'contentualizing the offence' is an important objective for report writers, it usually involves their trying to show that the offence is not as serious as it sounds. Two sets of findings suggest this. First, when we grouped reports by their custody potential we found that the focus on the offence was more likely to occur in those cases where there was *no risk* of custody involved rather than in those at high risk. Obviously it is easier to recommend a probation order for someone being carried in a stolen car than someone who mugged an old lady. Focusing on the nature of the attack on a frail elderly person clutching her bag and bus pass is unlikely to sit easily with a diversionary recommendation. Second, this tendency to play down the offence when it was very serious emerged again when we asked report writers how much attention they paid to the Section 1(4) criteria first introduced by the 1982 Act. We had only eighty-eight respondents for this question, illuminating in itself. Only a third of these gave any emphasis to the 'serious offence' criterion whereas the vast majority of respondents did discuss the other two criteria — 'protection of the public' and 'failure to respond'.

Consideration given to different sentencing options

The willingness of report writers to consider different sentencing options and their likely effectiveness, in response to recent guidelines, was notable by its absence. In the juvenile sample, fewer than 10 per cent of reports paid substantial attention to this issue and half made no reference to it at all. A willingness to discuss different sentencing options was more evident in the adult court, particularly in Yellowtown where this was an agreed local policy. However even here a third of reports made no reference to this matter and a further quarter only slight reference. Only a very specific request from a court to write an 'all options' report seemed certain to produce such a focus.

Other important themes

Returning to Table 8.1, reports from both agencies, while emphasizing the normality of much delinquency, where in many of the sample cases obliged to identify situations where intervention was required to avoid further 'drift' into crime. While the identification of the 'easily led' offender occurred often enough for it to be included in the table there were also many cases where 'pathological' offending and normal offending, which required no special intervention, were identified.

As Table 8.1 shows, probation officers were particularly concerned to emphasize their client's willingness or not to comply with orders:

> I was not able to obtain a place for him at any hostel during the remand period. I am pessimistic about his ability to comply with a probation order which does not contain a condition of residence. He is not suitable for community service.
>
> (Comment on young adult, Yellowtown)

> Mr 'M' is considered suitable by the CS team but unfortunately there is no work available at the present time. I'd respectfully suggest that the court consider making a short probation order. . . . I've discussed the requirements of such an order with Mr 'M' and he has agreed to cooperate fully. I'd respectfully suggest that six months would provide sufficient scope for the work to be done.
>
> (Comment on young adult, Greytown)

We looked for recurring themes by court and by the cases' custody potential but few uneven distributions outside the clear probation–social services dichotomy were apparent. The biggest single atypical distribution was to be found in Yellowtown's juvenile court where 'character assassination' – 'revenge' reports prepared by social workers – came into the frame for cases at risk of custody. Two examples can be given to illustrate this theme:

'E' displayed an arrogant, egotistic attitude.

['D'] shows no remorse for his actions. He is adamant that his life is for him to do as he pleases, although the cost to someone else is high. I am appalled at 'D's attitude.

What is interesting about these two juveniles is that they both had badly disrupted and difficult home backgrounds and had been in care for a period. The report writers did not see their clients' attitudes to adults as in any way a consequence of earlier experience and could find nothing positive to say about them. Both received custodial sentences. These findings are very similar to those reported in Cleveland, where social workers routinely recommended custody for children in their care (Macmillan and Whitehead 1986).

References to custody in SERs

It is important to look at how report writers dealt with the issue of custody, given most of our sample were at some risk of 'going down'. Table 8.2 identifies whether the sample reports recommended custody directly or in a veiled manner, whether they accepted custody as a possibility and offered well-argued viable alternatives or instead presented an essentially 'weak' alternative to incarceration. Finally we identify reports which made no reference to the possibility of custody.

The actual recommending of custody was most prevalent in Yellowtown with overt recommendations being routine in the juvenile court and present in the

Table 8.2

Reference to custody included in SERs, by court

	Juveniles				Young adults			
	Yellow-town	Red-town	Grey-town	Blue-town	Yellow-town	Red-town	Grey-town	Blue-town
Recommended custody	5	—	1	—	3	—	—	1
Veiled custody recommended	5	1	1	2	4	1	2	1
Custody alluded to but genuine alternative offered	13	12	12	13	10	20	16	15
Weak alternative	2	3	1	—	4	—	2	—
Custody not discussed	4	13	14	15	9	8	8	11
Missing	1	1	1	—	—	1	2	2
Total	30	30	30	30	30	30	30	30

adult sample. The conclusion below is from a report on a Yellowtown juvenile who received six months' youth custody:

> In the event of him being found guilty . . . I respectfully recommend to Your Worships that a custodial sentence would appear to be the most appropriate action.

A young adult received an identical sentence which would presumably have pleased his probation officer, who wrote:

> I'd refer Your Worships to the conclusion reached in my original Social Enquiry Report, but in view of this youth's blatant contempt for law, I can only recommend a custodial sentence in the belief that he must now face the consequences of his actions. . . . I therefore respectfully suggest to the Bench that [he] be made the subject of a Youth Custody Order.

Veiled custodial recommendations tended to follow the same distribution, although all court samples contained at least one example of this practice:

> The court must recognise that CSO would be a 'risky' course of action. . . . I am inclined to think that whatever sanction is imposed today, even a custodial one, will not have the effect of either deterring this defendant or 'treating' his anti-social behaviour.
> (Comment on young adult, Yellowtown, 21 days' DC)

Having said all this, as Table 8.2 shows, the majority of report writers referred to custody not in order to encourage its use but in an attempt to block such a move. Hence they recognized that custody might be 'in Your Worships' minds' but argued against this via the provision of strongly recommended alternative strategies. All courts received a good supply of such reports. Practice in Redtown's adult court stands out with two-thirds of cases receiving such treatment and the remainder avoiding the discussion of custody altogether.

We looked at these responses to the custody question (after the event) in relation to the custody potential of each case as defined in Chapter 6. Were social work judgements consistent with the magistrates' perceptions and practice? In relation to juveniles in all the cases where custody was recommended this was the outcome. However, for veiled custodial recommendations the picture was more complex. Only one such 'recommendation' actually received a custodial sentence. Four were regarded as threshold cases where custody was in the end not used and four were not perceived by the magistrates as custody cases at all. Here then we have identified a process whereby report writers are either attempting to obtain a custodial sentence against their client when the courts themselves are not seeing this as necessary or are defining cases as more serious than are magistrates. Again Yellowtown provides the clearest example of this.

In cases where custody was alluded to but genuine alternatives were argued for, the bulk of such recommendations matched threshold cases where custody was not finally given. It is here that report writers had most influence upon discouraging custodial sentences. Bluetown's juvenile court report writers and IT staff produced the outstanding examples:

> 'G' presents as a pleasant-mannered, not academically inclined young man. He is a member of a law-abiding, hard-working family. Prior to his involvement in the present offence, it appears that he had developed a reputation as a 'fighter' with school contemporaries. A reputation he felt unable to alter without 'losing face'. He also appears to have had no realization of the potential reaction of society to his involvement in school disputes.
>
> The only explanation he was able to give for taking a knife on the day of this offence related to fear for his personal safety, but an explanation is insufficient to justify his action.
>
> It is to be expected that, because of the seriousness of his offence, the Court will be considering a custodial penalty; in these circumstances may I recommend that as a positive alternative to custody, 'G' would be a suitable subject for a specified activity order (Section 12 3(c) 1982 Criminal Justice Act). Therefore I would respectfully recommend that he be made subject to a supervision order, to include a specified activity order. A separate report relating to this will be available to the Court. Such a disposal would allow others to work with 'G' on altering his reputation, and allow him to receive the guidance he obviously requires at this time.

As already indicated some slippage was also apparent with genuine alternatives cropping up in 'not custody' cases. Weak alternatives were present in all categories except, as one would expect, in the 'threshold not custody' group. Reports which made no reference to custody were found across the custody and threshold categories but were obviously concentrated in those cases where no risk of custody was envisaged by the Bench.

In relation to adults the custodial recommendations correspond with 'definite custody' cases and the veiled custody split across the two threshold categories. The 'genuine alternative' recommendations were most prevalent in the threshold cases which didn't get custody followed by the 'definite custody' cases and threshold cases where custody was used. This fairly accurate targeting by report writers is however spoilt by a 'slippage' process. For young adults, no fewer than eighteen cases at 'no risk of custody' were given the 'alternatives' treatment in reports.

Finally, earlier criticism that SERs often lacked a cohesive argument or that recommendations did not follow on logically from the main contents led to further guidance in 1987 (Department of Health and Social Security 1987). We analysed reports on the basis of, first, whether the conclusion or recommendation followed on logically from the report's main emphases or thesis, and, second, whether recommendations were in themselves clear and unequivocal or vague and woolly.

We found, based on our own assessment, that about 70 per cent of reports did have a coherence whereby the conclusion followed on logically or reasonably from the earlier discussion. Redtown courts received the highest rate of reports where this occurred, with Yellowtown and Bluetown adult court reports having the greatest tendency to lack a logical flow. Probation reports were more likely (80 per cent) to have this coherence than social services reports (62 per cent).

The vast majority of recommendations were clearly stated (but see the next section), including those in Yellowtown juvenile court where custody was routinely recommended. The only clear tendency was for recommendations in the juvenile arena to be less equivocal than those for young adults. This was almost certainly due to the more limited range of sentencing options, including the absence of probation day centre programmes, available for young adults in these courts.

Targeting recommendations in social enquiry reports

Report writers' ability to predict sentencing

Official emphasis on providing alternatives to custody makes the accurate targeting of recommendations essential. However in order to do this report writers have to be able to predict those cases at risk of custody and, equally important, identify those at 'no risk' and so avoid inappropriate recommendations for community-based programmes designed for high tariff cases.

We asked report writers a number of questions about the 'tariff'. Did they expect their recommendation to be the same as the sentence given? Was the sentence actually made the one they anticipated and so on? Broadly speaking most report writers, at the time of preparing their report, expected their recommendation to be the same as the actual sentence given. However, in Redtown a substantial minority and in Greytown a small minority expected the outcome to be higher up the tariff than their recommendation. Their report writing was overtly 'strategic', aiming to drop the sentence down a rung or two if possible.

However, the actual sentence proved to be exactly the same or parallel to (e.g. attendance centre order instead of large fine) the report writer's prediction in only about 60 per cent of cases in all the arenas except Yellowtown juvenile court, where only 50 per cent of actual sentences correspond with the expected sentence. A very similar picture emerged when we compared probation and social services reports. Given what we have said about the sentencing decisions in the four areas we should not be surprised that *report writers were only able to predict or anticipate sentencing accurately in just over half the sample cases.*

The finding that of the 206 report writers who responded to a question about the difficulty of their intervention in the court case only fifty-five felt things had been 'difficult' is unexpected. Perhaps the sense of *déjà vu* produced by preparing large numbers of reports, and being unable to understand why sometimes they got it right and sometimes they did not, encouraged 152 report writers to think of their intervention – mistargeting and all – as straightforward.

Recommendations in relation to magistrates' assessment of custody potential

In order to check the targeting of recommendations generally and for the 'new alternatives' in particular we divided all SER conclusions into the categories shown in Table 8.3.

All nine custody recommendations correspond with definite custody cases. Eight of these were made in Yellowtown (five juveniles, three adults). There were also ten definite custody cases where no recommendation was made, six of which were in Greytown. The absence of recommendations in cases which were going down (although contrary to the line taken by NAPO – National Association of Probation Officers – that alternatives to custody should always be recommended) highlights a dilemma for report writers (see Thomas and Wilbourne 1985). Some sensed the inevitable and, while not willing to suggest the use of custody, saw recommending probation or CSO as a futile and perhaps counter-productive gesture. Their report conclusions were understandably tentative:

> 'R' and his father fully understand that the court will be considering the imposition of a custodial sentence today as he had this year received a range of sentences. He still has six hours outstanding from his Attendance Centre Order and is in the middle of paying a fine that was imposed in July. I have discussed with 'R' the possibility of a referral to a place on the CS Scheme but after discussion he found himself unable to make a commitment to the scheme and I have, therefore, not made the referral. In the light of all these factors I feel unable to offer the court a helpful, specific recommendation today.
>
> (Report on young adult, Greytown)

The recommending of 'alternatives to custody' in definite custody cases was fairly evenly distributed between courts, with this type of recommendation most often found in Yellowtown. 'Other' recommendations included several 'veiled custody' recommendations and the recommending of large fines or attendance centre, the latter being found most often in Bluetown where young people were quite likely to have further education or employment prospects. In the absence of 'packages' the attendance centre order was often set up as preferable to community service because of week-day commitments amongst young adults in this Midlands court.

> This young man has done very well academically and has the ability to pursue his chosen career in accountancy. He has acceptable outside interest in his football and Venture Scouts Club and I do not feel he has need of oversight by way of a Probation Order. . . .
>
> I have discussed a Community Service Order with him, and confirmed that work is available, but if he pursues his college course and continues to play football and referee children's games on Sundays, such an order would be difficult to implement.

Table 8.3

Social enquiry report recommendations by custody potential – four PSDs

	Juveniles (14–16)					Adults (17–20)					
	Definite custody	Threshold custody	Threshold not custody	Not custody	Not known	Definite custody	Threshold custody	Threshold not custody	Not custody	Not known	Line totals
No recommendation or no SER	3 (10)		3 (6.7)	2 (4.3)		7 (24.1)	1 (11.1)	1 (2.9)	1 (2.5)	2 (28.6)	20 (8.3)%
Custody	6 (20)					3 (10.3)					9 (3.8)%
Alternatives to custody	8 (26.7)	2 (33.3)	17 (44.7)	11 (23.9)		7 (24.1)	2 (22.2)	12 (34.3)	12 (30)	4 (57.1)	75 (31.3)%
Other	13 (43.3)	4 (57.1)	18 (48.6)	33 (71.7)		12 (41.4)	6 (66.7)	22 (62.9)	27 (67.5)	1 (14.3)	136 (56.7)%
Total	30 (100)	6 (100)	38 (100)	46 (100)		29 (100)	9 (100)	35 (100)	40 (100)	7 (100)	240 (100)%

As 'G' intends to take up full-time education he will have no regular income and given that he will be required to pay some compensation, the Court may feel that he could be dealt with for this offence by way of an order to attend the Adult Attendance Centre.

The most notable feature for those cases which were threshold and actually received custody is the much higher rate of 'other' recommendations rather than specific high tariff alternatives. This suggests report writers were not anticipating these cases would be at risk. There were no noticeable differences between the courts on this matter. For those cases which were on the threshold of custody but did not in fact go down there was a strong correlation between recommendations and outcome. In the Bluetown tribunals, Yellowtown adult court and most of all Greytown juvenile court, reports which recommended alternatives to custody routinely corresponded with outcome.

The proliferation of 'other' recommendations in these threshold cases is difficult to explain. The absence of a probation package in Redtown meant the straight probation order could sometimes be acceptable as an alternative to custody. Attendance centre orders, as we have illustrated, had the same role in Bluetown for young adults at risk of custody. The use of the deferred sentence and large fines for employed offenders also found their way into both recommendations and sentences at the threshold. However, the report writers' limited ability to identify cases at risk or custody on the day must be the main factor at work here.

For those cases at no risk of custody in the magistrates' eyes the high rate of other recommendations would seem appropriate. However, the proliferation of recommendations using the alternatives to custody disposals (24 per cent for juveniles, 30 per cent for young adults) is more problematic. In relation to a strategy which restricts the recommending and using of 'alternatives to custody' to cases at real risk of custody this mismatching is obviously unfortunate. On the one hand it means that some places on 'alternatives' type programmes are sometimes going to the wrong offenders taking up places required for the heavy end, on the other it means that report writers are precipitating 'slippage' by unintentionally indicating to magistrates that these programmes can be used freely rather than for very specific groups. This slippage was at very similar levels in three areas but much lower in the Redtown courts. It should be said however that its absence in Redtown was due more to magistrates' relative consistency and liberal sentencing than consistently excellent report writing.

We have in this section identified four important sets of findings. First, report writers have considerable difficulty in predicting the sentence which will finally be made on their client. Second, a minority of reports directly or indirectly recommend custody. There is nothing technically wrong with such reports, although this approach is at odds with the generally held beliefs and practices of social workers and probation officers who work in the courts (see Bottoms and Stelman 1988), and treason to those committed to using community-based sentences instead of custody. Third, we have identified signs of slippage whereby the alternatives to custody are being recommended for cases which magistrates do not see as at real risk of custody on the day. Fourth, we have identified a correlation, for the threshold cases, between strongly argued 'alternatives to custody' recommendations and the making of such disposals by magistrates for cases which by definition they would have otherwise considered custody for. We will develop these issues in the following sections.

Report writers' professional agendas

The predominant objectives

Report writers have been selective in accepting the new guidelines and 'encouragement' to modify their report writing because they have their own professional agendas, departmental goals and traditions. We asked them what their main objectives were in constructing their reports for our sample cases. Table 8.4 lists these in hierarchical order. Obviously some report writers had more than one objective in mind, which accounts for the 348 actual responses cited.

The top five sets of objectives obviously dominate and three of these —avoiding a custodial sentence, offering a structured (e.g. 'a package') alternative to custody and keeping the client's sentence 'down tariff' – can be seen as attempting to secure a non-custodial sentence or practising a 'diversion' approach. The other two most frequently quoted objectives are somewhat different. 'Contextualizing the offence' by discussing the circumstances surrounding its commission is a more general objective and one which report writers have been requested to include by official guidelines. The most often quoted objective – to indicate the need for social work intervention – may or may not be consistent with diversion. For example a Redtown juvenile with three previous convictions received a nine-week detention centre order for theft of a motor cycle, although the probation officer felt

> that little if any spark comes through this brief account of 'S's situation perhaps reflects accurately how life seems to him just now. There is little about which to get excited or enthusiastic about and little prospect of any improved opportunities. I respectfully suggest that a period under Supervision might be appropriate at this stage. . . . 'S' would be required to attend an activity group each week of his Order on a Monday evening. If he develops an interest in any of the activities experienced at the Outdoor Pursuits Centre next week then it might be possible to introduce him to local facilities.

The magistrates were less concerned about the lack of lawful opportunities in this boy's life than that 'he wouldn't be bothered . . . would he bother to go . . . he needs discipline . . . to learn self-discipline . . . so that he is responsible for his actions'.

A young adult in the same court, who received three months' detention centre

Table 8.4

Report writers' objectives in preparing social enquiry reports for sample cases

Objective	Frequency	% of all responses	% of sample cases involved
Client requires welfare intervention	79	18.0	39.9
Avoid a custodial sentence	58	13.2	29.3
Contextualize the offence	35	8.0	17.7
Offer a structured alternative to custody	31	7.1	15.7
Keep sentence 'down tariff'	27	6.2	13.6
Avoid use of supervision/probation order	19	4.3	9.6
Indicate offender has little previous	18	4.1	9.1
Suggest client will comply with orders	18	4.1	9.1
Wash hands of client	16	3.6	8.1
Indicate offending is part of a local problem	12	2.7	6.1
Suggest plan to 'avoid further offending'	11	2.5	5.6
Point out client is at 'crossroads'	8	1.8	4.0
Return case to sentencers/classic justice	5	1.1	2.5
Refer to intentions of a previous Bench	4	0.9	2.0
Try to avoid imposition of a fine	4	0.9	2.0
'Medicalize' the case	3	0.7	1.5
Not answered	88	20	44.4
Total	436		

Note: Valid cases 198

for burglary, was also regarded by the report writer as a victim of his circumstances and in need of welfare intervention:

> 'K' is now in work. He tells me that he is now happy and settled and both
> he and his father are confident that he will not re-offend. All his
> offences are joint charges and he tells me that he would not have
> committed these offences alone. He tells me that he is ashamed and
> frightened that he may receive a custodial penalty and that if he does so
> he will lose his place on the work scheme. In interview 'K' impressed me
> as a personable young man. He is a member of a local youth club and
> enjoys boxing, fishing and camping and it would appear that this
> appalling behaviour was totally out of character. The court may agree
> that this behaviour was a reaction during his parents' difficult divorce
> and wish to treat these in isolation rather than an indication of 'K's

future behaviour. I feel that his anxiety about his parents' divorce has not totally left him and would ask the court to place him on Probation today as I feel it is important that this young man has a third party independent of his parents to whom he can turn. If the court so wishes, 'K' could also undertake a Community Service Order whilst being on Probation.

Other important objectives

Moving down the list in Table 8.4 three other themes are evident. The first involves attempting to block certain sentences being made. Most often this involves 'guarding' the probation or supervision order and attachments from what the report writer or his or her agency regard as inappropriate or unnecessary usage.

Second, report writers also felt obliged to try and persuade magistrates to avoid the use of fines where this might aggravate a client's already difficult financial situation:

> I have considered a number of options for sentence today. Mr M's financial position wouldn't lend itself to a further financial penalty as he is already struggling to meet the present commitment.

The dilemma of course is whether to block the possibility of non-payment of a fine, which might lead to custody, with a higher tariff disposal.

> The Court will obviously wish to punish him for his offence and I would respectfully point out that it has taken him a great deal of time to pay off his current fines without adding to the misery and that a period of Community Service might be more appropriate in that he will have to repay society.

Yellowtown magistrates duly fined the latter example £100, so cancelling any possibility of tariff slippage!

A third theme concerns the client's ability or willingness to comply with court orders such as probation or community service. By implication the offender's level of respect for the court and societal rules is indicated. Most of the reports developing this theme actually threw doubt on the defendant's ability to comply with orders, although a minority did emphasize compliance:

> The reason I say this is that 'P' has no difficulty in conforming to the rules of an establishment as is shown by the attached Detention Centre report and a decision of this [custodial] nature would I feel prove to be an easy option. 'P' is willing to be considered for a Community Service Scheme and an application has been filed in order for him to be considered.

One further theme revolves around the two objectives classified as returning the case to the sentencers and washing one's hands of the client:

> During the short time I've been supervising 'J' I have found him to be an intelligent but rather feckless individual, who has still not faced up to the fact that he must make a determined effort himself if he wants to straighten himself out. He is in breach of his probation order and had in fact committed further offences within a few weeks of that order being made. In the circumstances a short custodial sentence might be thought appropriate to bring home to him the necessity of changing his life-style.
>
> (Report on young adult, Yellowtown)

> I don't think a further Probation Order is viable. 'C' did not keep the conditions of the last. Admittedly, I don't think he received a lot of encouragement to do so at home. There is an anti-authoritarian attitude there. I've been told to get out of the house on more than one occasion.
>
> (Report on young adult, Bluetown)

> 'E' has been offered much support and help from our own department but has not accepted it . . . would leave it to the court to decide what, if anything, can be done to deter this boy from further offending, but also ensure that he faces the consequences of his action.
>
> (Report on young adult, Yellowtown)

Differences between social workers and probation officers

We examined this pattern of objectives in terms of whether reports had been written by social workers or probation officers. We did not find major differences although some different emphases were apparent. As might be expected given the focus on juveniles, the 'need for social work intervention' (Curnock and Hardiker 1979) was more prevalent in social workers' reports (52 per cent compared with 36 per cent for probation officers). Social workers were nevertheless more likely to view the recommending of 'structured alternatives to custody' as essential (see also Thomas and Wilbourne 1985) and 50 per cent saw avoiding custody as a major objective compared with only 23 per cent of probation officers. Probation officers on the other hand cited 'contextualizing the offence' and generally keeping cases 'down tariff' more frequently.

Objectives by custody potential

In relation to each case's custody potential the three most quoted objectives in order of frequency are laid out below:

'Definite custody'	*'Threshold custody'*
1 Needs welfare intervention	1 Needs welfare intervention
2 Avoid use of custody	2 Contextualize offence
3 Wash hands of client	3 Avoid use of custody

'*Threshold not custody*'	'*Not custody*'
1 Needs welfare intervention	1 Needs welfare intervention
2 Avoid use of custody	2 Contextualize offence
3 Keep 'down tariff'	3 Avoid use of custody

Interestingly the need for welfare or social work intervention predominates across all the categories of custody potential, this dominance perhaps reflecting the essential professional ethos of social work with offenders (see Osborne 1984). For those cases regarded by magistrates as 'definite custody', report writers did see avoiding this outcome as a primary objective. However, almost as many respondents saw the need to distance and dissociate themselves from the offender and indeed if we regard 'returning the case to the sentencers' as similar to 'washing hands of client' this becomes the most prevalent objective. For those cases which were 'threshold' but received custody, report writers saw the avoidance of custody as primary less often than might be expected, placing more significance on the need to contextualize the offence and emphasize the efficacy of social work intervention. Their diversionary objectives figure more prominently in those threshold cases where custody was in the end not used, which again suggests these objectives may have encouraged such an outcome. In relation to cases at 'no risk of custody' the appearance of custody avoidance as a frequent goal is again evidence of report writers' difficulty in predicting sentencing outcomes.

Finally we looked specifically at where the three 'diversion from custody' objectives fell in relation to the custody potential of each case. The small numbers for some courts and categories make comparison difficult although Redtown report writers showed the greatest tenacity in the use of diversionary tactics for 'definite custody' cases in both arenas and the least tendency to allow diversionary goals to 'slip' into reports on cases at no risk of custody. In all the other courts 'slippage' was considerable, with report writers seeing their primary task to divert cases from custody when magistrates saw no case for custody in the first place.

We noted when analysing the contents of recommendations by custody potential that there were signs of a considerable amount of mistargeting or slippage. In this section we have offered further evidence of this in that attempts to divert offenders from custody or keep them down tariff were seen as important goals in cases which were in reality not at risk of custody. It was obviously not the intention of these report writers to use their agency's main 'alternatives' for low-risk cases. Indeed we established from their questionnaire responses that their perceptions of viable alternatives to custody corresponded with the 'new alternatives' and the 'local' alternatives where packages were not available.

On the other hand we have identified 'precious' social work objectives which may not support this thrust. The overriding commitment amongst report writers to identify clients who need or might benefit from social-work-type intervention is a case in point. Although making this a major theme in the court report will not automatically detract from diversionary goals there is obviously a danger of this happening. However, 'washing one's hands of the client' or returning the case to the sentencers are the two objectives most overtly concerned with inducing a custodial sentence.

All this will be perplexing for those wishing to construct some universal principles of good practice in social enquiry work (see Bottoms and Stelman 1988). It shows just how far away from consensus and clarity the social work profession remains. While much of this is the product of inconsistency and idiosyncrasy in the courts themselves there is clearly much to be done within social work itself: not least because of the challenges which lie ahead over the 'punishment in the community' debate which we will discuss in Chapter 9.

Social workers' and probation officers' role in the courtroom

There are two schools of thought in social/probation work about attending court when one's report is to be presented. One says that there are more important things to be done than hang around outside the courtroom for up to two hours just to cover the outside possibility that the Bench or judge might wish to discuss some of its content. The other says that it is worth the effort, particularly if you are recommending supervision or probation or an alternative to custody (see Eggleton 1988). Our findings lend weight to both viewpoints.

Our court observation periods indicated that there was almost always a duty social worker or probation officer present in the courtroom. Although court officers sometimes had to be called from another room, it was a rare event for a clerk or Bench to be unable to consult with them. In relation to our 240 sample cases there were only 16 occasions when there was no appropriate officer present at the time the case was dealt with and here again, even on these occasions, a duty officer could almost certainly have been called. In 138 cases the duty officer alone represented the local authority or probation service. In Yellowtown juvenile court there were two full-time court liaison officers who were not practising social workers. Indeed their lack of commitment to the goals of social/probation practice in relation to providing alternatives to custody was undoubtedly a factor in the court's punitive sentencing. Something of an ideological struggle between these court officers and the 'young turks' of the expanding IT service was apparent throughout our fieldwork period. No such dilution or undermining of diversionary strategies was observed outside Yellowtown. In the other three juvenile courts, social services and probation shared responsibility (probation normally dealing with 15- to 16-year-olds). While there was one regular court officer for social services in each area, the probation function was carried out by groups of two or three specialist 'juvenile offender' officers who acted both as court officers and field officers – preparing the bulk of SERs. In all three courts this system appeared to work well and guaranteed a 'well-informed' probation presence able to deal with any enquiries from the court. In Greytown it was common on juvenile court 'day' to find the social services officer and all three juveniles court probation officers sitting in their allotted pew.

Overall, as well as the duty officer, the report writer was present in about 40 per cent of the sample cases. IT officers would normally be present where a supervision package was being recommended.

There is obviously a multitude of reasons why a court officer might be consulted: how long will reports take to prepare, case conferences decisions, availability of places in care and so on? In relation to the sentencing decision the majority of our sample cases were dealt with without the duty officer or report writer making or being required to make any verbal contribution. However, a substantial minority of cases did involve the duty officer, report writer or IT officer making a contribution, which on occasions was crucial to the case's outcome. Bluetown juvenile court stands out in this respect. In a third of our sample, all threshold, the presence of the report writer and specified activities officer to discuss the content of the recommended package corresponded with an alternative to custody being utilized.

An even higher level of dialogue was apparent in Redtown and again where the magistrates were considering custody, although the use of custody was not invariably blocked by such consultation. Requests from court officials involving report writers or their representative were recorded in a third of the sample cases in Yellowtown and Greytown juvenile courts but no clear pattern of outcomes emerged. Verbal contributions from probation officers in the adult arena were less common, being very rare in Redtown and Bluetown and present in only about a quarter of sample cases in Yellowtown and Greytown.

The impact of reports on sentencing

Methods of evaluating impact

We have noted a correlation for threshold cases, between the recommending of alternatives to custody and a non-custodial outcome. The million dollar question, and one which most previous social enquiry research has not been able to answer fully, is whether there is a causal relationship involved. Are sentencers, pondering the use of custody, persuaded by reports which recommend well-thought-out options which keep the offender in the community? By being able to place the analysed SER, the author's objectives and the magistrates' perceptions of the report and its effect up against each other, we are able in this section to present a much more accurate evaluation of the impact of reports on sentencing. The same has been true of identifying 'slippage'. Normal 'monitoring' techniques employed by researchers, and increasingly by probation and social services departments, cannot get beyond the correlation stage. However, it is quite inadequate to announce proudly that '70 per cent of our recommendations are accepted' for all the reasons we have shown. The 'monitorist' approach needs to be used with caution. A little knowledge is a dangerous thing.

Table 8.5

Cases where SERs influenced the Bench

Influence	Definite custody	Threshold and custody	Threshold but not custody	Not custody at all	Row total
Up tariff	15	5	4	9	33
Neutral	21	1	14	15	51
Down tariff	3	5	46	49	103
Total	39	11	64	73	187

Influential reports

The Bench of the day saw the SER as having some influence on their deliberations in about 80 per cent of cases. Although this suggests reports have a central role in the sentencing process, we should recall from Chapter 5 that the influence a report has may not always be the one intended. Magistrates sift, sort and re-use information provided in reports.

Table 8.5 shows the distribution of these influential reports in relation to custody potential and effect upon the sentencing decision. Taking all those cases which received custody (i.e. 'definite' and 'threshold custody' together) it is clear that in twenty cases the sentencers were encouraged by the report to make use of custody. In twenty-two other cases, although influential, the report did not inform the actual sentencing decision. In eight cases magistrates, although making a custodial sentence, did feel the report had made them ponder this course or indeed reduce the length of sentence. Of the twenty custody cases where the report encouraged detention six were in Yellowtown juvenile court and three in the adult arena. There were four such reports in Red-town, five in Greytown and three in Bluetown.

Of the sixty-four cases where custody was a possibility but the Bench finally opted for a community-based disposal only four reports pushed the case closer to custody but no fewer than forty-six played a part in moving the Bench away from a custodial decision. The divided practice in Yellowtown social services again emerged, with five reports having this diversionary effect. There were also four such cases in the adult arena. In Redtown four juvenile and eight young adult cases were noted. In Greytown five juvenile and seven young adults were diverted and in Bluetown no fewer than nine juveniles along with four adults.

The 'not custody at all' category contained seventy-three cases where the report had some bearing. In nine cases (including three in Greytown juvenile court) the report's contents made the situation more serious in the magistrate's eyes. In fifteen the contents were influential but not in relation to the sentence and in forty-nine cases the report encouraged magistrates to make low tariff

Table 8.6

Cases where the SERs were a major influence upon sentences

Influence	Definite custody	Threshold and custody	Threshold but not custody	Not custody at all	Row total
SER crucial for whatever reason	6	3	13	18	40
SER offers variable alternative to custody	—	—	15	1	16
Total	6	3	28	19	56

disposals. Ten of these cases were in Redtown juvenile court, otherwise they were fairly evenly distributed, although Bluetown with seven in each arena again figured strongly.

Reports as 'reasons' for the sentence made

We were also able to identify those cases where the SER was even more influential in that the Bench indicated it reached its sentencing decision primarily on the basis of the report. This occurred whether by a conscious decision to follow the report's recommendations or in threshold cases by unequivocally accepting a viable 'alternative' to custody described in the report or an appendage. Table 8.6 identifies these cases. The only unexpected feature to arise by individual court was the fact that Bluetown magistrates felt they used custody on three occasions for young adults as a consequence of their interpretation of the SER.

Summary

Our social workers and probation officers are predominantly qualified and very experienced in social enquiry work. Their report writing was rarely hampered by inadequate preparation time or back-up resources. They or their 'duty officer' representatives were nearly always available in court to present reports in the sample cases. Report writers' perceptions of what were viable alternatives to custody largely corresponded with those made available or rearticulated by the 1982 Act.

A content analysis of sample reports showed that 'putting the offence in context' and discussing their client's family problems and disruption in parenting were the most common and discernible themes. The implications and guidelines for report writing which came out of the 1982 Act, 'SNOP' (Home Office

1984) and recent circulars have been responded to selectively. While the focus upon the offence is much evident in post-1983 reports, authors find discussing the nature of 'serious' offences problematic as it undermines the 'diversionary' objectives of many of their reports. The focus upon the defendant's personal and family circumstances still dominates reports, particularly in juvenile court and when written by social workers. Few reports discussed a range of sentencing options and their likely effectiveness. Most reports made a clear and unequivocal recommendation and in the majority of cases the recommendation or conclusion followed on sensibly from the main body of the report.

Despite the exhortations of their professional associations and the evangelical commitment to decarceration of the 'instead of custody movement' centred around IT officers, a significant minority of report writers recommended custody overtly or in a veiled manner. Most of these influenced the magistrates to think in this direction. Social workers in Yellowtown made such recommendations in a third of our juvenile sample!

More often however report writers recommended community-based disposals making full use of the new alternatives created by the CJA. In the majority of such cases this was purposefully done, with the report writers setting out to 'avoid custody' and keep the case 'down tariff'. Nevertheless the most commonly quoted objective of report writers was to indicate to the court their client's need for welfare or social work intervention, a goal not invariably consistent with a diversionary strategy especially in the context of an offender's overall delinquent career.

By obtaining the views of sentencers about 'live' cases and reports we have been able to show that magistrates were influenced, in some way, by SERs in no fewer than 80 per cent of cases. However, when we unpack the contents of this influence a rather diverse picture emerges. This is because magistrates re-use the information provided in reports to make moral assessments of offenders. Thus in a minority of cases the sentencers moved their decision 'up tariff' on the basis of their interpretation of something in the report. In other cases the report influenced the retiring-room discussion but not the actual sentence. Reports do not divert 'definite custody' cases. From the sentencers' point of view custody is custody is custody. However, at the threshold, where custody is a probability or possibility but not a certainty, reports which offered well-thought-out alternative sentences are very often influential and in a minority of cases a direct cause of a community-based sentence being made.

The debate about the role of social enquiry reports is clearly far from over. On the basis of our findings the 'practice theory' used for training social workers and probation officers (Curnock and Hardiker 1979; Paley and Leeves 1982; Bottoms and Stelman 1988) and the interpretation of guidelines are still very live issues. Report writing has obviously changed in recent years but the diversity of practice and purpose noted by J. Thorpe (1979) for the 1970s remains in the 1980s.

Given that definite custody cases are not open to negotiation, the biggest single difficulty for report writers is not getting their 'community option' recommendations taken up *per se*, but targeting these recommendations accurately. Because of idiosyncrasies in sentencing, which we have identified, report writers were able to predict sentences in only slightly over half the cases. Not surprisingly therefore they often misjudged which cases were at the threshold of custody and which were at no risk of custody at all. This produced several unintended consequences. First, threshold cases, which in the end received custody, rarely had reports which recommended one of the new high tariff alternatives and so the opportunity of diversion was missed. Second, an alarmingly large number of cases, at no risk of custody on the day, attracted reports offering the alternatives to custody. This widespread 'slippage' must be a major concern, for it undermines the purpose of the new supervision pro-grammes (e.g. funded by the DHSS Initiative) and probation packages and creates the possibility of requirements and attachments to supervision and pro-bation orders becoming routine for low- and middle-tariff cases.

More fundamentally these findings expose the faulty logic in government plans for 'punishment in the community', which assume that social work agencies can target their efforts on offenders at risk of custody. We will address this issue in the next chapter.

9 Bolstering the penal crisis

Pragmatism and the prison

During 1988 nearly a quarter of a million citizens of the United Kingdom, a disproportionate number of whom will be black, spent some time locked up in their own country's penal institutions. All the statistical indications are that the steep rise in imprisonment which has taken place during the 1980s will continue well into the next decade.

In September 1986 the United Kingdom's prison population stood at just under 54,000. This is the highest prison population both in absolute numbers and as a proportion of inhabitants of any EEC country (Counseil de l'Europe 1987). Over 46,000 of this daily population were incarcerated by a court in England (and less often in Wales). While West Germany (down 18 per cent), Sweden (down 12 per cent) and Italy (down 11 per cent) all managed to reduce their prison populations per 100,000 inhabitants between 1983 and 1987, England and Wales produced an 8 per cent increase; with Scotland and Northern Ireland performing similarly (Counseil de l'Europe 1987).

This punitive pattern of sentencing is feeding a growing penal crisis in the United Kingdom. Manifestations of this are numerous. Insanitary and overcrowded conditions in penal establishments (see McDermott and King 1988) reach the national news as do regular outbreaks of inmate unrest and protest, some causing hundreds of thousands of pounds worth of damage. Simultaneously prison officers attempt, through their trade union, to use the crisis to their own financial and organizational advantage, whereby their industrial action leads to prisoners being held inappropriately in local police station cells.

The political fallout of all this is clearly seen in the timetables of government ministers. They, too, routinely find themselves obliged to step within the prison, whether it be to open new establishments, visit army camps which are being converted into temporary centres, survey the consequences of riots at first hand or be seen at a remand centre where the rate of suicide has become a public scandal. In between such visits, they must explain away their inaction on the spread of AIDS in prison despite the exhortations of their own expert advisors (Advisory Council on the Misuse of Drugs 1988) and, if all this were not enough, undertake political speeches calling upon magistrates to be more circumspect in their use of custody.

In this chapter we will outline the reasons why a prison population, which would be inconceivable or unacceptable in many other western European countries, is so clearly tolerated and condoned in the United Kingdom and why things will get considerably worse before a concerted effort to deal with the crisis is mounted. We will not be attempting to develop a blueprint for change: they are already available (see e.g. PAPPAG 1986; NACRO 1988d). It is an essential part of our thesis that such exhortations will anyway be ignored for some time yet.

In Chapter 1 we placed the 1982 Criminal Justice Act in an historical and socio-legal context. Given that the 1988 Criminal Justice Act is designed, principally, to tune the 1982 Act finely, and given that its drafting began in 1985, it is probably safe to regard these two statutes, along with the Police and Criminal Evidence Act 1984, as the legislative manifestation of the 'new right's' law and order 'strategy' which was originally designed for the 1979 General Election. The 1988 Act, with its concerns about correcting 'lenient' sentencing, checking on school attendance amongst juveniles, pursuing the drug traffickers and re-punishing offenders who breach the conditions of community-based sentences, keeps faith with the 'get tough' harsher sentencing pronouncements of the 'law and order' lobby, which start with custody as *the* punishment and judge all other measures through comparison. There are hints, but no more, that political doubts about this strategy are emerging, for instance in the tightening of criteria defining the use of custody. These '1980s' acts are the pillars of an ideological and strategic approach which has, because of an exceptional period of political dominance via the three Thatcher administrations, been fully operationalized.

Because this has been the case, because no political excuses about a lack of time or resources for the strategy can be made, the failure of the whole approach is becoming more and more apparent. The constantly spiralling costs of an expanding police force, a billion pound prison building programme and overflowing gaols, do not sit well with a government committed to the goals of 'value for money' and 'accountability' to the tax payer. When the financial costs of the law and order programme are set against the crime picture, the results are plain. The last few years have seen both the crime rate and public concern about its increasingly violent nature rise sharply. For a government which came to power in 1979 with promises about dealing firmly and effectively with crime and disorder, the return on a 25 per cent increase in public expenditure on law and order has been disastrous.

Thus penal policy is at a critical point. The 'far right' may, in due course, reluctantly accept that the medicine hasn't worked. It will, of course, call for a bigger dose of the same. The intellectuals and realists in both government and the civil service will find it difficult to resist this. They may occasionally be found fantasizing at 'progressive' conferences about the possibility of a revision of penal policy whereby the fulcrum of change would be an officially set limit on the size of the prison population. As yet, to advocate this in public would be unthinkable and such a statement will not be made by a minister in, or intending to remain in, an administration headed by Margaret Thatcher.

'Real' short-term political goals are patently more modest and highly pragmatic. They are operationalized in the usual mode of low-key discussions, private words and public warnings. These goals include attempting to dampen the worst effects of the penal crisis until the 1990s, after the next General Election, and beginning to moderate and modify the 'law and order' approach to the use of the prison. It is important to note that the opening shots in this minor revision stem not from any new ideological perspectives but from feedback through 'normal channels' insisting that the penal system is over-heating and dysfunctioning.

Thus, while a decade ago it was the sentencers who were calling for change, the 'intelligence' and criticism are now flowing in from prison governors and boards of visitors, the prison inspectorate and civil servants. The locus of concern has changed. Judges and magistrates will soon be on the defensive, trying to protect their present powers and independence. They will not like the new agendas which their own remand and sentencing practices are actually stimulating.

The first signs of real concern in the Home Office about the pressure on the prison system are already showing. New messages are emerging in the official discourse of political speeches and discussion documents. The most extraordinary speech had to be delivered some considerable distance from the Home Counties, in Sydney, Australia, where Sir Brian Cubbon, Permanent Under-Secretary at the Home Office, noted:

> In the 1970s and 80s, most economically developed countries have . . . seen increases in demand for punishment, stemming from increased offending rates or tougher sentencing policies. The obvious solution is to extend capacity and build more prisons; and my country's government has embarked on a building programme which should yield an additional 21,000 places by 1995. But we all know that extending prison capacity is the necessary solution which never quite solves the problem. Will we never find a point of intervention in sentencing decisions themselves; can we never contemplate inserting mechanisms of 'demand management' into the sentencing process, so that the volume of demand for imprisonment can be more closely tied to the available supply [?]
>
> (Speech to Australian Bicentennial Internation Congress on Corrective Services,
> Sydney, January 1988)

The official answer to this question is 'No'. On the domestic front, while speeches are now being made around the country aimed at 'educating' the

magistrates and encouraging them to use community disposals wherever possible, they remain indirect or 'inoffensive'.

> But custody is a last resort. The Court of Appeal has now made it clear
> that courts should not sentence on a purely punitive or deterrent basis
> without regard to the costs of the disposals or the individual charac-
> teristics of the offender. . . . We must try to ensure that custody is used
> only when the offence is so serious that a sentence outside prison would
> bring the system into disrepute. . . . Despite the statutory restrictions of
> the use of custody for those under 21, over 20% of the young men
> sentenced are given a custodial sentence. This is too high.
>
> (The Home Secretary to South East London Magistrates' Association, January
> 1988)

A number of circulars and discussion documents are also signalling the need for
change. Although they may well be ignored at a local court level, the Judicial
Studies Board issued, in 1987, *Notes for the Guidance of Magistrates*. These
get very close to telling clerks and magistrates (but not judges!) how to go about
reaching a sentencing decision. More important was the Green Paper,
Punishment, Custody and the Community (Home Office 1988a) and instructions connected with it such as those for the probation service, *Tackling
Offending: An Action Plan* (Home Office 1988b).

The Green Paper, while being unnecessarily complacent about the
proportionate custody rates for juveniles, focuses once again on the fact that
young adults are being locked up at the rate of one per hundred of the overall
17–21-year-old population in any one year. This is inappropriate because

> Most young offenders grow out of crime as they become more mature
> and responsible. They need encouragement and help to become law
> abiding. Even a short period in custody is quite likely to confirm them as
> criminals, particularly if they acquire new criminal skills from more
> sophisticated offenders.
>
> (Home Office 1988a: para. 2.15)

The Green Paper does, of course, avoid laying the blame for all this either at the
feet of the judiciary or its own penal policy. Instead, it blames the probation
service for not providing alternatives to custody – punishments in the community – which are tough and demanding enough to command the respect of
the magistrates and judges.

While we would not doubt that the probation service needs to get its own
divided house in order and become more decisive about its role in the criminal
justice system, it is hard not to conclude that *Punishment, Custody and the
Community* (Home Office 1988a) is scapegoating the service in order to make
the point about the unnecessary use of custody without upsetting either arm of
the judiciary. By insisting that custody can be reduced through change in the
probation service, the Home Office is either misunderstanding or fudging the
issue. We have demonstrated that social enquiry report writers, as potential

community-based programme providers, *cannot* target accurately those at risk of custody because of the idiosyncratic and inconsistent nature of local sentencing practices and complete lack of agreement amongst sentencers about which cases are 'serious' enough to deserve custody. In demanding that the service gear itself to such targeting (Home Office 1988b), the government is missing the point. Probation's mistargeting and the accompanying slippage of community service and probation and supervision with requirements into use with cases at no risk of custody is, as we showed in Chapter 8, a product of the sentencer's power, not probation influence. The real issues are the number and length of custodial sentences, the misuse of the fine and the use of custodial remands before convictions.

That a Green Paper, carefully worded so as not to offend the judiciary, brought immediate condemnation from the Magistrates' Association is obviously consistent with our argument. According to its chairman, the association has 'very strong reservations' about the proposed alternatives to custody outlined. Magistrates, he said, should not be asked to adopt 'horizontal' rather than 'vertical' sentencing policies whereby

> no matter how often people reoffend, provided they do not reoffend in those categories that we feel should warrant a prison sentence, they should go on and on at the same level, sending someone back to community service.

> (quoted in *The Times*, August 1988)

That Mr Hosking, their chairman, went on to say that magistrates 'all try incredibly hard to avoid sending people to prison' and 'try to do an honest job for the nation' will be unsurprising to readers of this book. The impasse is total. The more overt the messages from government about curbing punitive sentencing, the more antagonistic will be the judiciary. The political permission to engage in a full-blown and 'damaging' debate will thus not be given at this stage. Political and class allegiances must not be threatened. And so the pressure will have to build. There is plenty of time for it so to do. No further major piece of 'sentencing' legislation is likely to emerge before 1992. The present administration will try, through tinkering, to get by, perhaps by using the forthright report on parole by the Carlisle Committee as the necessary political excuse to increase early release. Furthermore, even in the unlikely event that a Labour administration is formed in the early 1990s, the Labour party will not go into the next General Election with any kind of innovatory law and order strategy which could be labelled as 'going soft on offenders'. Consequently Labour's first main Criminal Justice Act would either be more of the same, or, if more radical, then badly delayed as the political consequences of taking on the judiciary would be weighed and reweighed many times over by a nervous, new administration.

Beyond the call of duty

Let us summarize and recall why the magistrates do not see the penal crisis, which they are inadvertently helping to create, as any of their business. Magistrates are lay people, predominantly middle-aged, middle class and highly 'respectable'. They are, in the main, intelligent and sensible people who, in their own domestic, professional or business lives, would insist on applying rules like consistency, accountability and financial management. Yet, as magistrates, they collectively become something else. They put on the mask and play in role and become highly selective in which parts of their life-experienced 'selves' they employ when acting as magistrates. Their socialization, their training and the absorption of the magistrates' ideology defines where and how the selection is made.

This training, through the local clerks, is sufficient to give them an outline of their functions, the objectives of sentencing and the role of law for use in their local court but it does not involve substantial relearning nor does it look beyond the parochial, beyond local traditions and handed-down ways of doing justice. Instead, their training, stiffened by advice from local cadres of senior colleagues, provides magistrates with a framework in which to be themselves. English criminal law, as we have noted, emphasizes 'flexibility' and discretion and so creates plenty of space for this collective self-expression by the Justices.

One of the most remarkable features of each court we investigated was the all-embracing nature of the local version of the magistrates' ideology. Wherever we went, Benches emphasized the importance of their *rite de passage* to becoming a real magistrate through watching and sitting with more experienced colleagues. Newcomers are proud to learn that they are special people who have a unique position in both the local community and local court. Magistrates must believe that they are impartial. They point to the deviousness of the defence lawyer's rhetoric and the defendant-centredness of most social workers and probation officers and perhaps even the over-enthusiasm of police evidence, to demonstrate why they must be so. They guard the truth and thus hold the key to the 'right' sentence. They believe that without their ability to sit, think and rise above the false trails laid by other court actors, justice would not be done and public opinion would not be served (but see Walker and Hough 1988). This, they say, is their special art, the essence of the mystery. It is hard to describe to the outsider. Many explained it something like this hypothetical Bench:

> It's so complicated; there's public opinion, the need to protect the community, the seriousness of the offence, the criminal record, what our colleagues did last time, the person's home background . . . every case is different. You just get to know what's right, sometimes you find yourself using quite small cues which just come to you when you look the offender in the eye or read her school report. It's very hard to explain, really each case has to be judged on its merits. We usually get it right, you know. We're pretty experienced, sensible people. We're from

the local community and so we know what's what and who's who . . .
not easily fooled.

Well, no, we don't know about how other courts around the country
sentence. That's none of our business but surely those magistrates know
what they're doing in their neck of the woods, just as we do here. Yes,
suppose we should know a bit more about what our own colleagues do
on other weeks or with similar cases. But it's very hard to get to know.
We seem to get by OK, that's the main thing.

We feel we made the right decisions today, three of those cases were
very complicated, we're very tired now, it's been a long day but you feel
you've done a good job, done what's expected. We really don't like
using custody, none of us do, but sometimes you really have no alternative, as today, you have to do what you think is right.

Yes, things have generally improved with the new legislation; there's
more choice, more powers, we can tailor the sentence better particularly
now with custody. It's a shame the judges aren't a bit more realistic.
They're in another world some of them, they should come and sit with
us, not the other way round! Penal crisis? Well there was a bit of a crisis
in the 1970s when there weren't enough detention centre places available
for juveniles but that seems to have passed now. It's quite right too. You
shouldn't have to think about whether there are places in the local prison
when you're deciding on the right sentence. That would be terrible. No,
on balance, things are better, we've got a few problems about court
security and replacing our junior clerks when they move on but things
aren't too bad!

This isn't chance you know. We've tried to make sure, through the
Association, that the government, and those cosseted civil servants in
Whitehall, get to know what it's like out here in the real world. They
should come and sit in our court for a couple of weeks and see what
we've got to contend with. That would tone down their speeches a bit!

This is not to parody the magistrates. We have gone to considerable lengths in
earlier chapters to demonstrate that they can, and often do, produce justice
with considerable skill. No one reading this book could doubt that the
magistrates apply the criteria and accepted wisdom they inherit with great
vigour and dedication. However, as we have shown, the overall impact is highly
punitive. Be it giving a fine where it will not easily be paid and so lead to prison
for default (see Moxon 1983), or using community service because 'disciplined'
employment is in short supply or slipping requirements on to probation orders
because they're a 'good thing', the collective result is to push towards the
prison. Be it committing to Crown Court for sentence or using custody unspar-
ingly, the pressure builds. While magistrates' justice is arguably cheap to
administer, the end result is expensive. Nor is the price inflation-proofed. It is
rising continuously and, in our opinion, unnecessarily. Each stage of the
making and maintaining of the local magistracy has been amenable to the

creation of this state of affairs by providing for official discretion. The essential thesis of this chapter is that this official discretion is, on balance, used in a punitive way. The repetition of punitive decisions cannot, in the end, be disguised by the exceptions, even contradictions, like Redtown. The end product of local discretion, when all the secure vans have delivered all the local custody decisions to the prison gates, is a penal crisis.

Magistrates are recruited in a partial and unreliable way (see Burney 1979; King and May 1985). Clerks in two of the courts we studied complained that they could do nothing about this because the whole process of selection – the emphasis on the suitability to 'fit in', the need to find people who could take time off work, even the willingness to be associated with the magistracy – is so elaborately tailored to attract a section of middle-class life and rule out the rest. Yellowtown's magistrates were clearly the least acceptable face of nepotism. That the process of becoming and being a magistrate remains almost a secret further protects the whole enterprise from scrutiny. There is no sign that all this will change on its own.

That we uncovered major differences in sentencing practices between our four courts is unsurprising given the results of earlier studies (Anderson 1978; Parker *et al.* 1981; Moxon *et al.* 1985; Burney 1985a). What we have discovered, which is more original, is how and why these differences, which are not the result of dealing with cases of differing seriousness, occur and are sustained. We have shown how local training and the apprenticeship model further builds on the partial selection process to consolidate and maintain local sentencing traditions.

Magistrates, like the judges (see Ashworth *et al.* 1984), see no need for sentencing guidelines. More worryingly they perceive any discussion with outside bodies about their role as 'political interference' rather than participation or consultation as it would be defined in other European countries (e.g. Von Hirsch 1987). They pay scant attention to decisions of the Court of Appeal (see Henham 1986) and are openly partial in their intake of law. Instructions from the Centre are 'accommodated' at the local level in fascinatingly idiosyncratic ways. Not surprisingly, therefore, sentencers make the critical 'custody or not' decisions in a manner far removed from official guidelines. For many, custody has no alternatives. They judge the seriousness of an offender's criminal record more on the basis of what their colleagues did last time than on what the offender did. They regard moral assessments of the defendant as a crucial part of their craft. The amalgam of cues and views which produces a sentencing decision is then justified with the magic words 'we judge each case on its merits'. To do otherwise is to go beyond the call of duty and to destroy the perfect antidote to suggestions that the sentence is inappropriate or should be comprehensible to those outside the magic circle. There is no way through such ideological defences. This ideology is almost perfect in its functionality. This is why we believe the impasse in penal policy will continue.

The magistrates, like the judges, are deeply resistant to discussing regulation. Furthermore, they can resist outside scrutiny with great skill and determination and because of who they are have much political power to call upon. While we believe they will, in due course, be drawn into dispute with government, it will not be with an administration which has so deliberately created a retributive atmosphere and provided sentencers with so much power and freedom to use the prison. The full consequences of law and order in the 1980s will be realized during the 1990s.

Bibliography

Advisory Council on the Misuse of Drugs (1988) *A.I.D.S. and Drug Misuse, Part I*, London, HMSO.

Anderson, R. (1978) *Representation in Juvenile Court*, London, Routledge & Kegan Paul.

Ashworth, A. (1983) *Sentencing and Penal Policy*, London, Weidenfeld & Nicolson.

Ashworth, A., Genders, E., Mansfield, E., Peay, J., and Player, E. (1984) *Sentencing in the Crown Court: Report of an Exploratory Study*, Occasional Papers 10, Oxford, Centre for Criminological Research, University of Oxford.

Baldwin, J. (1976) 'The social composition of the magistracy', *British Journal of Criminology*, 16: 171–4.

Ball, C. (1983) 'Secret justice: the use made of school reports in the juvenile court', *British Journal of Social Work*, 13: 197–205.

—— (1988) 'Reports for the juvenile court', in NACRO *School Reports in Juvenile Court: A Second Look*, London, NACRO.

Bartle, R. (1985) *Crime and the New Magistrate*, Chichester, Barry Rose.

Bittner, E. (1967) 'Police on skid row: a study of peace keeping', *American Sociological Review*, 32: 699–715.

Bottomley, K. (1973) *Decisions in the Penal Process*, London, Martin Robertson.

Bottoms, A. E. (1981) 'The suspended sentence in England and Wales 1967–78', *British Journal of Criminology*, 21, 1: 1–26.

Bottoms, A. E. and Stelman, A. (1988) *Social Inquiry Reports*, Aldershot, Gower.

Bowden, J. and Stevens, M. (1986) 'A corporate strategy in Northampton', *Justice of the Peace*, 150: 345–7.

Brody, S. (1976) *The Effectiveness Of Sentencing – A Review of the Literature'*, Home Office Research Study 35, London, HMSO.

Burgin, Y. (1988) 'Information received by the court – school reports and social inquiry reports', in NACRO *School Reports in Juvenile Court: A Second Look*, London, NACRO.

Burney, E. (1979) *J.P.: Magistrate, Court and Community*, London, Hutchinson.

—— (1985a) *Sentencing Young People*, Aldershot, Gower.

—— (1985b) 'All things to all men: justifying custody under the 1982 Act', *Criminal Law Review*, May, 285–93.

Carlen, P. (1976) *Magistrates' Justice*, London, Martin Robertson.

Carter, R. and Wilkins, L. (1967) 'Some factors in sentencing policy', *Journal of Criminology, Criminal Law and Political Science*, 58.

Cawson, P. (1976) *Young Offenders in Care*, London, DHSS.

Celnick, A. (1985) 'From paradigm to practice in a special probation project', *British Journal of Social Work*, 15: 223–41.

—— (1986) 'Negotiating alternatives to custody: a quantitative study of an experiment in social enquiry practice', *British Journal of Social Work*, 16: 353–74.

Chambers, G. A. (1982) 'The Sheriff's perspective', in J. H. Curran and J. A. Chambers, *Social Enquiry Reports in Scotland*, Scottish Office Central Research Unit, Edinburgh, HMSO.

Cohen, S. (1985) *Visions of Social Control*, Cambridge, Polity Press.

Collison, M. (1980) 'Questions of juvenile justice', in P. Carlen and M. Collison (eds) *Radical Issues in Criminology*, Oxford, Martin Robertson.

Conseil de l'Europe (1987) *Rubrique Statistique du Bulletin d'Information Penitentiaire, No. 8*. Strasbourg, Council of Europe.

Corbett, C. (1987) 'Magistrates' and court clerks' sentencing behaviour: an experimental study', in D. C. Pennington and S. Lloyd-Bostock (eds) *The Psychology of Sentencing*, Oxford. Centre for Socio-Legal Studies, University of Oxford.

Cross, R. (1981) *The English Sentencing System*, 3rd edn, London, Butterworth.

Crow, I. and Simon, F. (1987) *Unemployment and Magistrates' Courts*, London, NACRO.

Cullen v. *Rogers* (1982) *Weekly Law Reports*, 1: 729–45.

Curnock, K. and Hardiker, P. (1979) *Towards Practice Theory*, London, Routledge & Kegan Paul.

Curran, J. (1983) 'Social enquiry reports: a selective commentary on the literature', in J. Lishman (ed.) *Social Work with Adult Offenders*, Research Highlights, University of Aberdeen.

Darbyshire, P. (1984) *The Magistrates' Clerk*, Chichester, Barry Rose.

Department of Health and Social Security (1987) *Reports to Courts: Practice Guidance for Social Workers*, London, HMSO.

Devlin, K. (1970) *Sentencing Offenders in Magistrates' Courts*, London, Sweet & Maxwell.

Ditchfield, J. (1976) *Police Cautioning in England and Wales*, Home Office Research Study 37, London, HMSO.

Donzelot, J. (1979) *The Policing of Families*, London, Hutchinson.

Edwards, S. (1984) *Women on Trial*, Manchester, Manchester University Press.

Eggleton, D. T. (1988) *The Presentation Style of Probation Officers in Courtroom Dramas*, Leicester, unpublished M.Phil. thesis, University of Leicester.

Fitzmaurice, C. and Pease, K. (1986) *The Psychology of Judicial Sentencing*, Manchester, Manchester University Press.

Ford, P. (1972) *Advising Sentencers*, Oxford, Basil Blackwell.

Foucault, M. (1977) *Discipline and Punish*, London, Allen Lane.

Gaudet, F. (1949) 'The sentencing behaviour of the judge', in V. Branham and S. Kutash (eds) *Encyclopaedia of Criminology*, New York, Philosophical Library.

Green, E. (1961) *Judicial Attitudes in Sentencing*, London, Macmillan.

Gross, H. and Von Hirsch, A. (eds) (1981) *Sentencing*, New York, Oxford University Press.

Grunhut, M. (1956) *Juvenile Offenders Before the Courts*, Oxford, Clarendon Press.

Hardiker, P. (1977) 'Social work ideologies in the probation service', *British Journal of Social Work*, 7, 2: 131–54.

Harris, R. and Webb, D. (1987) *Welfare, Power and Juvenile Justice*, London, Tavistock.

Hedderman, C. (1988) *The Treatment of Male and Female Defendants in Magistrates' Court*, Cambridge, unpublished Ph.D. thesis, University of Cambridge.

Henham, R. (1986) 'The influence of sentencing principles on magistrates' sentencing practice', *Howard Journal*, 25, 3: 190–8.

Hine, J., McWilliams, W., and Pease, K. (1978) 'Recommendations, social information and sentencing', *Howard Journal*, 17, 2: 91–100.

Hogarth, J. (1971) *Sentencing as a Human Process*, Toronto, University of Toronto Press.

Home Office (1965) *The Child, the Family and the Young Offender*, Cmnd 2742, London, HMSO.

—— (1968) *Children in Trouble*, Cmnd 3601, London, HMSO.

—— (1974) *Young Adult Offenders: Report of the Advisory Council on the Penal System*, London, HMSO.

—— (1976) *Observations on the Eleventh Report of the Expenditure Committee*, Welsh Office, Department of Health and Social Security, Department of Education and Science, Cmnd 6491, London, HMSO.

—— (1978) *Youth Custody and Supervision: A New Sentence*, Cmnd 7406, London, HMSO.

—— (1980) *Young Offenders*, Cmnd 8045, London, HMSO.

—— (1982) *Criminal Statistics for England and Wales*, London, HMSO.

—— (1983) *Circular 17/1983: Social Inquiry Reports*, Home Office, Probation Service Division. London, HMSO.

—— (1984) *Probation Service in England and Wales: Statement of National Objectives and Priorities*, London, HMSO.

—— (1986) *Circular 92/1986: Social Inquiry Reports*, Home Ofice, Probation Service Division. London, HMSO.

—— (1988a) *Punishment, Custody and the Community*, Cm 424, London, HMSO.

—— (1988b) *Tackling Offending: An Action Plan*, London, HMSO.

Hood, R. (1962) *Sentencing in Magistrates' Courts*, London, Stevens.

Horsley, G. (1984) *The Language of Social Enquiry Reports*, Norwich, Social Work Monographs, University of East Anglia.

Hough, M. and Lewis, H. (1986) 'Penal hawks and penal doves: attitudes to punishment in the British Crime Survey', *Home Office Research Bulletin* 21, London, HMSO.

Hough, M. and Mayhew, P. (1983) *The British Crime Survey – First Report*, Home Office Research Study 76, London, HMSO.

Hough, M. and Moxon, D. (1988) 'Dealing with offenders: popular opinion and the views of victims in England and Wales', in N. Walker and M. Hough (eds) *Public Attitudes to Sentencing*, Aldershot, Gower: 134–48.

House of Commons Expenditure Committee (1975) Eleventh Report, *Children and Young Persons Act 1969*, vols I and II, HC534–1, London, HMSO.

Jones, R. (1983) 'Justice, social work and statutory supervision', in A. Morris and H. Giller (eds), *Justice for Children*, London, Macmillan.

Judicial Studies Board (1987) *Notes for the Guidance of Magistrates*, London, Judicial Studies Board.

Justices' Clerks' Society (1980) *Sentencing in the 1980s*, Coventry, Justices' Clerks' Society.

Kapardis, A. (1981) 'Magistrates' opinions, characteristics and sentencing', *Justice of the Peace*, 145: 289–91.

Kapardis, A. and Farrington, D. (1981) 'An experimental study of sentencing by magistrates', *Law and Human Behaviour*, 5: 107–21.

King, M. and May, C. (1985) *Black Magistrates*, London, Cobden Trust.

Kress, J. (1980) *Prescription for Justice: The Theory and Practice of Sentencing Guidelines*, Cambridge, Mass., Ballinger.

McDermott, K. and King, R. (1988) 'Mind games', *British Journal of Criminology*, 28, 3: 357–77.

McLaughlin, H. (1988) *Professional Ideologies in Juvenile Justice*, Lancaster, unpublished M.Phil. thesis, University of Lancaster.

Macmillan, J. and Whitehead, P. (1984) 'Juvenile in Cleveland', Middlesbrough, unpublished paper, Teesside Polytechnic.

—— (1986) 'Checks or blank cheque', *Probation Journal*, 32

McRobbie, A. (1978) 'Working-class girls and the culture of femininity', in Centre for Contemporary Cultural Studies (eds) *Women Take Issue*, London, Hutchinson.

McWilliams, W. (1968) 'Pre-sentence study of offenders', *Case Conference*, 15: 136–8.

Morris, A. and Giller, H. (1979) 'Juvenile justice and social work in Britain', in H. Parker (ed.) *Social Work and the Courts*, London, Edward Arnold.

—— (ed.) (1983) *Providing Criminal Justice for Children*, London, Edward Arnold.

Morris, A., Giller, H., Szwed, E., and Geach, H. (1980) *Justice for Children*, London, Macmillan.

Mott, J. (1977) 'Decision making and social enquiry reports in one juvenile court', *British Journal of Social Work*, 7, 4: 421–32.

Moxon, D. (1983) 'Fine default, unemployment and the use of imprisonment', *Research Bulletin*, 16, London, Home Office Research and Planning Unit.

Moxon, D. Jones, P., and Tarling, R. (1985) *Is There a Tariff?*, Home Office Research and Planning Unit Paper 32, London, HMSO.

NACRO (1984) *School Reports in Juvenile Court*, London, NACRO.

NACRO (1987a) *Diverting Juveniles from Custody: Findings from the Fourth Census of Projects Funded under the DHSS IT Initiative*, London, NACRO.

NACRO (1987b) *Imprisonment in Western Europe: Some Facts and Figures*, London, NACRO.

NACRO (1988a) *The Criminal Justice Bill 1987*, London, NACRO.

NACRO (1988b) *Criteria for Custody*, London, NACRO.

NACRO (1988c) *School Reports in Juvenile Court: A Second Look*, London, NACRO.

NACRO (1988d) *Punishment Custody and Community: A Response by the National Association for the Care and Resettlement of Offenders*, London, NACRO.

Osborne, S. (1984) 'Social enquiry reports in one juvenile court: an examination', *British Journal of Social Work*, 14: 43–9.

Packer, H. (1969) *The Limits of the Criminal Sanction*, Stanford, Calif., Stanford University Press.

Packman, J. (1975) *The Child's Generation*, Oxford, Basil Blackwell and Martin Robertson.

Paley, J. and Leeves, R. (1982) 'Some questions about the reverse tariff', *British Journal of Social Work*, 12: 363–80.

PAPPAG (Parliamentary All Party Penal Affairs Group) (1986) *The Rising Prison Population – A Ten Point Programme to Reduce the Use of Custody*, London, PAPPAG.

Parker, H., Casburn, M., and Turnbull, D. (1981) *Receiving Juvenile Justice*, London, Basil Blackwell.

Parker, H., Jarvis, G. and Sumner, M. (1987) 'Under new orders: the redefinition of social work with young offenders', *British Journal of Social Work*, 17: 21–43.

Parker, H., Bakx, K. and Newcombe, R. (1988) *Living With Heroin*, Milton Keynes, Open University Press.

Pask, R. (1984) 'Production of court reports', in NACRO *School Reports in Juvenile Court*, London, NACRO.

Patchett, K. and McLean, D. (1965) 'Decision making in juvenile cases', *Criminal Law Review*, 699–710.

Perry, F. (1979) *Reports for Criminal Courts*, London, Owen Wells.

Pitts, J. (1988) *The Politics of Juvenile Crime*, London, Sage.

Prison Department (1984) *Tougher Regimes in Detention Centres*, Young Offenders Psychology Unit, London, HMSO.

Rawson, S. (1982) *Sentencing Theory, Social Enquiry and Probation Practice*, Norwich, Social Work Monographs, University of East Anglia.

Raynor, P. (1980) 'Is there any sense in social enquiry reports?', *Probation Journal*, 27: 78–84.

Reynolds, F. (1985) *A Lack of Principles: Implications for the Juvenile Justice System of a Three Year Study of Juvenile Offenders in Northamptonshire*, Oxford, Barnett House.

Rutherford, A. (1986) *Growing Out of Crime: Society and Young People in Trouble*, Harmondsworth, Penguin.

R. v. Bradbourn (1985) 7, Criminal Appeal Reports (S.), p. 180.

R. v. East Kerrier Justices ex parte Mundy (1952), 2QB 719 and 2AER 144.

R. v. Gillam (1980) 2, Criminal Appeal Reports (S.), p. 267.

Shapland, J. (1981) *Between Conviction and Sentence: The Process of Mitigation*, London, Routledge & Kegan Paul.

Stafford, E. and Hill, J. (1987) 'The tariff, social inquiry reports and the sentencing of juveniles', *British Journal of Criminology*, 27, 4,411–20.

Stanley, C. (1988) 'Making statutory guidelines work', *Justice of the Peace*, 8 October: 684.

Stern, V. (1987) *Bricks of Shame*, Harmondsworth, Penguin.

Stewart, J. E. (1980) 'Defendants' attractiveness as a factor in the outcome of criminal trials', *Journal of Applied Psychology*, 10: 348–61.

Stone, N. (1987) 'Must I see the probation officer?', *Justice of the Peace*, 29 August: 552–5.

Streatfeild (1961) *Report of the Interdepartmental Committee on the Business of the Criminal Courts*, Cmnd 1289, London, HMSO.

Sumner, M., Jarvis, G., and Parker, H. (1988) 'Objective or objectionable? School reports in the juvenile court', *Youth and Policy*, 23: 14–18.

Tarling, R. (1979) *Sentencing Practice in Magistrates' Courts*, Home Office Research Unit Study 56, London, HMSO.

Thomas, D. (1979) *Principles of Sentencing*, London, Heinemann.

—— (1987) 'Sentencing: some current questions', in D. C. Pennington and S. Lloyd-Bostock (eds) *The Psychology of Sentencing*, Oxford, Centre for Socio-Legal Studies, University of Oxford.

Thomas, H. and Wilbourne, R. (1985) 'A view from the bridge', *Probation Journal*, 32, 4: 131−4.

Thorpe, D., Smith, D., Green, C., and Paley, J. (1980) *Out of Care: The Community Support of Juvenile Offenders*, London, Allen & Unwin.

Thorpe, D. (1983) 'Deinstitutionalization and justice', in A. Morris and H. Giller (eds) *Justice for Children*, London, Macmillan.

Thorpe, J. (1979) *Social Enquiry Reports: A Survey*, Home Office Research Study 48, London, HMSO.

Thorpe, J. and Pease, K. (1976) 'The relationship between recommendations made in court and sentence passed', *British Journal of Criminology*, 16, 14.

Tutt, N. (1981) 'A decade of policy', *British Journal of Criminology*, 21, 3: 246−57.

Tutt, N. and Giller, H. (1984) *Social Inquiry Reports*, Manchester, Social Information Systems (audio tape).

Von Hirsch, A. (1976) *Doing Justice*, New York, Hill & Wang.

—— (1987) 'Guiding principles for sentencing: the proposed Swedish law', *Criminal Law Review*, November: 746−55.

Walker, D. (1987) 'Are day centres alternative probation?', *Social Work Today*, 26 January: 12−13.

Walker, N. (1972) *Sentencing in a Rational Society*, Harmondsworth, Penguin.

Walker, N. and Hough, M. (eds) (1988) *Public Attitudes to Sentencing*, Aldershot, Gower.

Watson, J. (1942) *The Child and the Magistrate*, London, Shaw and Sons.

Wilkins, L. (1980) *The Principles of Guidelines For Sentencing*, Washington DC, United States Deparment of Justice.

Zander, M. (1975) 'What happens to young offenders in care?', *New Society*, 33, 668: 185−8.

Index